MODERN SOUTH KOREAN AIR POWER, Republic

Robin Polderman

MODERN SOUTH KOREAN AIR POWER

Republic of Korea Air Force Today

Robin Polderman

HARPIA
PUBLISHING+

Consulting and inspiration by Kerstin Berger

Front cover artwork by Ugo Crisponi, AviationGraphic shows a ROKAF F-15K Slam Eagle carrying a TAURUS KEPD 350K cruise missile under the wing, together with GBU-38 Joint Direct Attack Munitions, and AIM-9X Sidewinder and AIM-120C AMRAAM air-to-air missiles.

Rear cover artworks by Ugo Crispoini, Aviation Graphic show from top to bottom: FA-50 of the 16th Fighter Wing carrying AIM-9L Sidewinder air-to-air and AGM-65 Maverick air-to-ground missiles, RC-800B Baekdu signals intelligence aircraft of the 296th Reconnaissance Squadron, An-2 of the 208th Squadron wearing a North Korean-style colour scheme.

Editorial by Thomas Newdick

Layout by Norbert Novak

Maps by James Lawrence

Printed at finidr, Czech Republic

Harpia Publishing is a member of

ISBN 978-1-950394-07-4

Republic of Korea Air Force

Contents

Republic of Korea Air Force

Introduction

East-Asia is home to some of the world's most influential powers, a complex web of flourishing economies and historical conflicts, where honour, nationalism and the need for self defence strongly reign.

The region is also home to some of the world's strongest militaries, making the area a hotspot with ample potential for future armed conflict.

South Korea finds itself in the middle of this all, and was forced to build up a credible defence to deter its neighbours, especially the one to the immediate north, from making any opportunistic move.

Despite tensions around the 38th parallel north often reaching boiling point, the majority of both North and South Koreans believe a unification is just a matter of time, although the number is dwindling. Yet the Koreas are very much apart when ideology and economy are concerned, making a unification presently an unrealistic dream and further away than ever.

In August 2017 the then US President Donald Trump threatened that *'North Korea will be met by fire and fury, like the world has never seen'* following revelations Pyongyang had created a miniaturised nuclear weapon to fit inside its ballistic missiles.

Despite the rhetoric exercised by the USA, North Korea sent a delegation to the Winter Olympics held in the South in the beginning of 2018, a first sign of a slight thaw in the ongoing cold war.

When South Korean President Moon Jae-In and North Korean leader Kim Jong-Un shook hands in the Joint Security Area in April 2018, the eyes of the world were upon them, with Kim Jong-Un becoming the first North Korean leader since 1953 to enter the South when he stepped over the border in the Joint Security Area (JSA) at Panmunjeom.

Despite a Joint Declaration issued in September 2018 in which some minor agreements were detailed, North Korea's ballistic-missile activities and its associated nuclear-weapons programme continue at an unabated pace and are a major worry to the government in Seoul.

Taking into account the violations of its airspace by nuclear-capable states China and Russia, as well as standing disputes with neighbouring Japan, it comes as no surprise more than 2.7 per cent of South Korea's GDP is allocated to the defence of its territorial integrity.

Countries throughout the world have reduced the size of their standing armies to compensate for the expanded roles of airpower, and South Korea is no different.

The Republic of Korea Air Force (ROKAF, 대한민국 공군) has served as a core power of the national defence since 1949, and its importance has grown even more as the development of technology has taken a leap.

Making effective use of this technology, South Korea continuously strives to stay one step ahead of its unpredictable northern neighbour. As part of the drive to maintain this edge, the ROKAF has the responsibility to feed accurate intelligence information to the decision makers in Seoul.

But it can not rely on its intelligence, surveillance and reconnaissance (ISR) capacity alone. The ROKAF needs to be ready to strike at any given moment, since the geography of the Korean peninsula makes reaction time short and extremely critical.

Republic of Korea Air Force

With the North Korean People's Army Air and Anti-Air Force continuously suffering under decades of economic stagnation, the ROKAF has meanwhile flourished, blooming into a modern air arm that is well equipped for its duties. The path of modernisation it has taken in the past two decades has led it to become one of the most capable, well trained and technologically advanced air arms on the globe.

Should a second chapter of the Korean War begin, the ROKAF is ready to perform the full spectrum of tasks bestowed upon it. Whether it be intelligence gathering, surpression of enemy air defences, the extraction of a downed pilot, or decapitation strikes against North Korean leadership, the ROKAF has the capability to do all.

The present day Republic of Korea Air Force is a modern air arm and a credible conventional deterrent to war, doing justice to its motto 'The Highest Power Defending Korea'.

Robin Polderman, September 2021

Acknowledgements

Many thanks to Heinz Berger for his confidence in the timely completion of my research as well as Albert Grandolini for the historical pictures from his archive.

A word of thanks to Jamie Chang for his knowledge and graciously allowing me the use of his excellent photos and Fyodor Borisov, Mark Codeno, Hywell Evans, Barry Griffiths, Hwangbo Joonwoo, SangYeon Kim, YoungKyun Shin, Katsuhiko Tokunaga, ChunYang as well as Wim Verkerk for providing additional pictures.

My gratitude to Arno Kok for allowing me the use of his extensive ROKAF photo collection and for his camaradarie during the journeys that formed the nucleus of this book. Also many thanks to the people that helped out by providing information and unit patches but declined to be named.

Last but not least I am eternally indebted to my family; Esther, Luca and Mila, for putting up with my constant travels in order to document yet another air force.

Abbreviations

ADD	Korean Agency for Defense Development
AEW&C	airborne early warning and control
AESA	active electronically scanned array (radar)
AFB	Air Force Base
AMARG	USAF Aircraft Maintenance And Regeneration Group
AMRAAM	Advanced Medium-Range Air-to-Air Missile
ASCC	Air Standardization Coordinating Committee
ASPJ	Airborne Self Protection Jammer
ASW	anti-submarine warfare
BRU	Bomb Rack Unit
BVR	beyond visual range
BVRAAM	beyond visual range air-to-air missile
C²	command and control
CBU	Cluster Bomb Unit
CCD	charge coupled device
CCIP	Common Configuration Improvement Program
CEP	circular error probability
CMA	Inter-Korean Comprehensive Military Agreement
CMDS	countermeasures dispensing system
COIN	counter-insurgency
CSAR	combat search and rescue
DAAFAR	Defensa Anti-Aérea y Fuerza Aérea Revolucionaria (Cuban Revolutionary Air and Air Defence Force)
DAPA	Korean Defense Acquisition Program Administration
DIRCM	directional infared countermeasures
DMZ	De-Militarized Zone
DoD	US Department of Defense
DPRK	Democratic People's Republic of Korea (North Korea)
DSCA	US Defense Security Cooperation Agency
ECM	electronic countermeasures
ELINT	electronic intelligence
EO/IR	electro-optical/infrared
FAC	forward air control/controller
FFAR	folding fin aerial rocket
FIS	Fighter Interceptor Squadron
FISINT	Foreign Instrumentation Signals Intelligence
FIW	Fighter Interceptor Wing
FLIR	forward looking infrared
FMS	Foreign Military Sales
FW	Fighter Wing
FWS	Fighter Weapons Squadron
FWW	Fighter Weapons Wing
FY	Fiscal Year
GBU	Guided Bomb Unit
GPS	Global Positioning System
G-LOC	g-induced loss of consciousness

HALE	high-altitude long-endurance
HF/DF	high frequency direction finder
HOTAS	hands on throttle and stick
HUD	head-up display
IAEA	International Atomic Energy Agency
ICBM	intercontinental ballistic missile
IFF	identification friend or foe
IIR	imaging infrared
IMINT	imagery intelligence
INS	inertial navigation system
IOC	initial operating capability
IR	infrared
ISR	intelligence, surveillance, reconnaissance
JASDF	Japan Air Self-Defense Force
JDAM	Joint Direct Attack Munition
JHMCS	Joint Helmet Mounted Cueing System
JSA	Joint Security Area
KADIZ	Korean Air Defense Identification Zone
KAL-ASD	Korean Air Aerospace Division
KOMPSAT	Korea Multi Purpose Satellite
KPA	Korean People's Army (North Korean Army)
KPAAF	Korean People's Army Air and Anti-Air Force
KTX	Korean Trainer Experimental
LDGP	low-drag general-purpose
LEX	leading-edge extensions
LIFT	lead-in fighter training
LOROP	long-range oblique photography
MALE	medium-altitude long-endurance
MDL	Military Demarcation Line (middle of the DMZ)
Medevac	medical evacuation
MESA	Multi-role Electronically Scanned Array surveillance radar
MFD	multifunction display
MIMEX	Major Item Material Excess
MND	Ministry of National Defence
MoU	memorandum of understanding
MRL	multiple rocket launcher
MRTT	Multi-Role Tanker Transport (KC-330 Cygnus)
MTCR	Missile Technology Control Regime
MUM-T	manned unmanned teaming
NBVR	near beyond visual range
NCO	non-commissioned officer
NPT	Treaty on the Non-Proliferation of Nuclear Weapons
NVG	night-vision goggles
OPCON	wartime Operational Control
OPFOR	opposing forces (aggressor units used during training)
PACAF	US Pacific Air Forces
PBU	Peace Bridge Upgrade (F-16C/D Block 32)

PGM	precision-guided munition
PLAAF	China People's Liberation Army Air Force
PPL	private pilot licence
QRA	quick reaction alert
RFP	request for proposals
RF	radio frequency
RF-A	Red Flag – Alaska
ROKA	Republic of Korea Army
ROKN	Republic of Korea Navy
RPV	remotely piloted vehicle
RS	Reconnaissance Squadron
RWR	radar warning receiver
SAR	synthetic aperture radar
SATCOM	satellite communications
SEAD	surpression of enemy air defences
SHP	shaft horsepower
SIGINT	signals intelligence
SRBM	short-range ballistic missile
SLBM	submarine-launced ballistic missile
TEL	transporter erector launcher
TER	triple ejector rack
TFS	Tactical Fighter Squadron
TFW	Tactical Fighter Wing
TFWG	Tactical Fighter Weapons Group (29th TDTFG)
TSP	Theater Security Package
TISEO	Target Identification System Electro Optical
TRG	Tactical Reconnaissance Group
TRS	Tactical Reconnaissance Squadron
TRW	Tactical Reconnaissance Wing
UAV	unmanned aerial vehicle
UFCP	up-front control panel
USD	US Dollars
US DSCA	United States Defense Security Cooperation Agency
USFK	United States Forces in Korea
VKS	Vozdushno Kosmicheskiye Sily (Russian Federation Aerospace Forces)
VNAF	Republic of Vietnam Air Force
WCMD	Wind Corrected Munitions Dispenser
WMD	weapons of mass destruction
WSO	weapon system officer

HISTORY OF THE REPUBLIC OF KOREA AIR FORCE

The modern day Republic of Korea Air Force finds its roots in the establishment of a Korean Flying School in Willows, California, during the early 1920s. The occupation by Japan had prompted Korean aviation pioneers to look elsewhere to fulfil their dreams. Some Korean pilots were trained in Chinese aviation schools and ended up with Chinese squadrons during the Sino-Japanese War of the 1930s.

Following the capitulation of Japan in August of 1945, Korea was divided in two seperate occupation zones with the Soviets administering the northern zone and the United States the southern. The establishment of seperate governments eventually created two seperate states: the Democratic People's Republic of Korea in the north and the Republic of Korea in the south.

On 1 October 1949 the Republic of Korea Air Force came to life by Presidential Decree No. 254, which stipulated the establishment of an Air Force Headquarters. Planning for a future air force had already began during 1944, when the Korean Provisional Government situated in Shanghai had established an air force planning committee.

The nucleus of the ROKAF was formed by the air unit of the Department of Internal Security, which had received 10 Piper L-4 Grashoppers on 4 September 1948, straight from the US and assembled by Korean technicians.

An initial group of ROKAF pilots pose in front of a Standard Aircraft Corporation J-1 biplane in the early 1920s.
(ROK MND)

Unprepared for war

Peace on the Korean peninsula was shortlived however, as another war broke out a mere five years after cessation of World War II hostilities. In a reckless move, the Soviet Union declared it viewed North Korean leader Kim Il-sung's government sovereign over both Koreas and had hastily reinforced the North's armed forces. Backed by its communist big brother, the North Korean armed forces crossed the 38th parallel on 25 June 1950 and steamrolled further south in what came to be known as the Korean War.

The ROKAF could field no more than a fleet of 22 aircraft, consisting of the earlier mentioned L-4s, some Stinson L-5 Sentinel light observation aircraft and 10 AT-6 Texan trainers imported from Canada. The Texans were bought after the Korean people donated 350 million Won (USD 62 million) following a public campaign to boost the fledgling ROKAF. The Texans were used as makeshift fighter-bombers until the Korean air force was able to field the F-51D Mustang.

Pilot training for the F-51D took place at Itazuke Air Base in Japan and the first ROKAF Mustangs were deployed to Daegu Air Base on 2 July 1951. Eventually a

Following initial deliveries of observation aircraft and trainers, the outbreak of the Korean War saw the fledgling ROKAF acquire its first fighters in the shape of the F-51D Mustang.
(Archive Albert Grandolini)

total of 130 F-51D Mustangs would be received, and deliveries included some rare TF-51D-25-NTs, the dualseat version of the standard F-51D. The last examples of the Mustang faded into retirement on 27 June 1957, four years after the signing of the Armistice agreement with the North.

In the years after the Korean War, the ROKAF tried to build up a credible defence, heavily assisted by the United States. Between 1951 and 1970 the Mutual Aid Program (later: Military Aid Program) provided Korea with equipment (either new or second-hand) and training free of charge. Infrastructure was repaired and new aircraft introduced. Maintenance depots for aircraft overhaul and modification were set up and an Air Force Academy was established in 1956. The 1950s also saw the influx of more Texans in the shape of former USAF T-6Ds and T-6Fs.

The first transport squadron came to life at Daegu Air Base on 15 October 1955, operating the Curtis C-46 Commando. The ROKAF received its first helicopters on 1 August 1958. On this date, the 33rd Rescue Squadron at Osan was established with a pair of Sikorsky H-19D Chikasaw and seven pilots.

First jets

In order to be more autonomous in the defence of its own airspace the USAF supplied Korea with its first jet fighter, the F-86 Sabre. Five examples were received on 20 June 1955. The ROKAF received more than 122 F-86F-25s and F-86F-30s, the dedicated fighter-bomber variants of the Sabre, between 1955 and 1962. Most of these had received the F-40 wing, which featured leading-edge slats and increased wingspan by 24in (60cm). The Aero-3B Sidewinder rails were retrofitted making these aircraft capable of using the AIM-9B air-to-air missile. The inner-most pylon below each wing could hold a 1,000lb (454kg) bomb.

The ROKAF also operated 10 examples of the RF-86F reconnaissance Sabre. These were standard F-86F aircraft changed into a reconnaissance version by means of a conversion kit.

In November 1960 the ROKAF received 42 F-86D Sabre Dogs, the radar-equipped, all-weather version of the Sabre. These aircraft only carried the AIM-9B Sidewinder and did not have an onboard gun. The last F-86Ds were withdrawn in 1979, while some of the F-86Fs soldiered on until finally retired on 30 June 1993, making the ROKAF the last air force in the world which operated the Sabre.

To effectively train its pilots in operating the F-86, Korea also took delivery of the ubiquitous Lockheed T-33 jet trainer. For training, FAC and light ground attack duties 26 T-28 Trojans were introduced between 1961 and 1963. The last of the T-28s would be phased out on 25 April 1989.

The supersonic era

In the late 1950s the Korean People's Army Air and Anti-Air Force (KPAAF) took delivery of the MiG-17, an aircraft that was thought to outclass the Sabre. The introduction of the F-86D Dog Sabre in 1960 had not changed the balance in favour of the ROKAF. After the first supersonic MiG-21F-13 (ASCC Fishbed C) appeared in the skies over

Different variants of the F-86 Sabre family served with the ROKAF between 1955 and 1993, although the radar-equipped F-86D only flew in Korean service for 19 years. (Archive Albert Grandolini)

North Korea, the ROKAF appealled to the US government to supply it with Lockheed's F-104G Starfighter. A change in US military aid policy however, meant Korea was offered the nimble Northrop F-5A Freedom Fighter instead.

On 5 April 1965 a cargo ship carrying 16 Northrop F-5A and five F-5B Freedom Fighters arrived in the port of Jinhae, in the southeast of Korea. After unloading and test flights, they were officially inducted in ROKAF service on 30 April of the same year, during a ceremony at Suwon Air Base in the presence of then president Park Chung Hee. Before the arrival of the aircraft, four ROKAF instructor pilots had been trained in the United States.

Barely operational, the F-5As were used to intercept a Soviet An-8 (ASCC Camp) transport aircraft off Korea's East Coast on 11 May 1966.

During the late 1960s the F-5s were called upon several times to attack DPRK spy boats operating in the South's territorial waters.

Starting in 1967 the F-5 Freedom Fighters took up residence at the newly constructed air base near Gwangju.

Eventually South Korea received 88 F-5As and 20 F-5Bs under MAP. To make up for attrition and to establish a lead-in fighter training (LIFT) programme the ROKAF decided to buy 16 additional F-5B two-seaters under a Foreign Mlilitary Sales-contract named Peace Needle in 1974.

Between 1965 and 1973 the Curtis C-46 Commando aircraft of the 55th Air Force Support Group provided airlift for Korea's Armed Forces during the conflict in Vietnam. A total of 48 Commandos flew in ROKAF markings before the type was completely replaced by second-hand Fairchild C-123 Providers at the end of the 1970s. The first C-123 for the ROKAF was delivered during 1973.

A Fairchild C-123 Provider participating in a road landing exercise.
(Archive Albert Grandolini)

ROKAF forward air control

In the opening stages of the Korean War, the forces under United Nations Command, including the fledgling ROKAF, did not have assets available for forward air control (FAC) nor was it trained to take on this mission. Air arms involved in the conflict had to quickly adapt, and makeshift FAC aircraft were soon in the skies over the battlefield.

Different variants of the L-19 Bird Dog (redesignated O-1 in 1962), served with the ROKAF as late as 1991.
(Archive Albert Grandolini)

While deployed to Korea, this F-111A of the 391st FS (normally based at Mountain Home, Idaho) was photographed flying in formation with a pair of ROKAF F-4Ds.
(Archive Albert Grandolini)

The ROKAF established its first FAC unit, the 31st Tactical Control Squadron, at Sacheon Air Base on 20 October 1958.

In order to be closer to the DMZ, the unit and its 24 Cessna O-1G (L-19 Bird Dog) and 14 Cessna O-2A Skymaster aircraft moved to Hoengseong Air Base on 13 October 1975. The unit not only provided FAC for other ROKAF assets but also for the ROK Army.

The unit was divided into the 236th and 237th Squadrons under the 8th Tactical Air Control Wing on 1 August 1979 as the FAC mission became more important, and the T-28A Trojan was added to the fleet at Hoengseong Air Base. The Trojans had been replaced in the training role but were believed to still be of value as an FAC aircraft. The last T-28s were withdrawn from service on 25 April 1989 followed by the remaining O-1Gs in 1991. During the 1980s the ROKAF pushed for replacing the low performance O-2A with the OV-10 Bronco, but the ROK Army just received a large number of MD500MD helicopters to perform the same role.

Following the loss of two O-2s, the 237th Squadron managed to fly 112,800 accident-free flight hours until 27 December 2006, when a retirement ceremony for the Skymasters was held at Seongnam Air Base.

Phantom introduction

During the 1960s the KPAAF had received the Ilyushin Il-28 bomber (ASCC Beagle) which was able to reach the South from bases in the northern part of its territory. Due to the short range of the F-5A the ROKAF identified a pressing need to obtain a fighter-bomber with longer range to be able to attack those KPAAF air bases in case of conflict.

In stark contrast with a few years before, the USAF now strongly recommended the F-104G Starfighter. This jet would enable the ROKAF to deal with incoming threats from the North. The Koreans, however, insisted on the McDonnell Douglas F-4D Phantom II as it wanted a longer-range multi-role aircraft instead of another short-legged interceptor, albeit one that was much faster than the F-5A.

At the request of the United States, South Korea started dispatching troops to partake in the Vietnam War from April 1964 to March 1973. A total of 340,000 Korean personnel participated in the bloody conflict for over eight years, at a toll of 5,066 deaths, and the Korean government used their involvement as a trump card to negotiate the introduction of F-4 fighters. Eventually its needs were met and Korea became the third country to operate the Phantom after the United States and the United Kingdom.

On 29 August 1969 six F-4Ds arrived, the first of 18 to be given to the ROKAF under the USD 100 million 1968 MAP. On 23 September of the same year, President Park Chung-Hee activated the first ROKAF F-4D squadron, the 151st TFS, during a ceremony at Daegu Air Base. The unit is nicknamed 'the fighter squadron of the people' and has played the role of an elite unit of the ROKAF for more than 50 years. In line with their elite status, the 151st FS became the first ROKAF F-35 squadron during 2019.

In December 1969 a total of 13 Helio U-10B Courier aircraft arrived. This single-engine propeller aircraft equipped with communications, search light and loud speakers is intended for counter-intelligence work.

In the following year the ROKAF introduced the Douglas C-54 Skymaster cargo aircraft to augment the fleet of Curtis C-46 Commandos. At least 15 examples of the venerable C-54D/E/G, a military variant of the DC-4, served in ROKAF service until 31 March 1992. They were used to shuttle personnel and cargo between the various ROKAF air bases and were replaced by the C-130 Hercules.

For initial training at the Air Force Academy the Cessna T-41B (the military version of the Cessna 172E Skyhawk) was introduced on 27 March 1972. A total of 30 examples of the T-41B would be in use for 34 years before being retired.

For advanced training the ROKAF introduced the Cessna T-37C Tweet, with the first of 25 examples received on 7 June 1973, as part of the US MAP. A further 42 T-37s were acquired second-hand from the Brazilian Air Force, the first of which arrived during 1981. Following Brazil's start-up of a nuclear programme and its subsequent refusal to sign the Treaty on the Non-Proliferation of Nuclear Weapons, its relationship with the United States detoriated. The country withdrew from the US Military Assistance Program during 1977 and soon received notice from Cessna it would receive no further support for its fleet of T-37C aircraft, forcing a sale. The Tweet provided the ROKAF with stellar service until retirement on 29 February 2004.

Helping South Vietnam

In the early 1970s South Vietnam's Air Force (VNAF) had suffered heavy losses as it battled the communist North. The VNAF badly needed a cease fire to be able to survive much longer but fears arose the cease-fire agreement conditions might curtail replacement aircraft deliveries. Swift action was needed and the US government decided to replenish the VNAF almost overnight with MAP delivered F-5 aircraft taken from the inventory of the ROKAF (along with Iranian and Taiwanese aircraft). A total of 36 F-5A and eight RF-5A aircraft were hastily disassembled, loaded onto USAF transports and flown out to Bien Hoa Air Base in South Vietnam. The whole operation was codenamed Enhanced Plus.

To make up for the F-5 aircraft transferred to the VNAF, the USAF had offered an equal number of improved Northrop F-5E fighters. The ROKAF however, insisted on

A camouflaged F-4D carrying the badge of the 151st FS on the intake and four AIM-9 Sidewinders under the wings. The text on the nose indicates this aircraft was purchased using capital donated to the National Defense Fund. (Archive Albert Grandolini)

The initial batch of ROKAF F-5E Tiger IIs, built in the United States, was delivered in the South East Asia colour scheme. (Archive Albert Grandolini)

receiving additional F-4D aircraft so a compromise was reached. In November 1972 the Koreans received around 20 F-4D aircraft on loan, transferred from the 3rd TFW at Kunsan, to bolster the squadron of F-4Ds already in its possession.

With South Vietnam surrendering to Communist Forces in 1975, the people of Korea realised a strong military was needed to deter North Korea from invading. Following a request by the United States to return the F-4Ds that were supplied in 1972, the 'Donation for National Defense' movement managed to raise 16.3 billion Won (USD 41.5 million) in gifts. After this sum was handed over to the Korean government, five of the loaned F-4D aircraft were purchased from the USAF and became Korean property on 12 December 1975. In a ceremony at Suwon Air Base, each of the aircraft was adorned with the name 'Pilseung flight' in Hangeul script on the forward fuselage. After further negotiations, a total of 18 F-4D aircraft loaned in 1972 were transferred to ROKAF ownership permanently, increasing the total to 36.

In August 1974, the 105th TFS converted to the F-5E following the delivery of the first aircraft, which arrived by C-5A Galaxy straight from McClellan AFB in the US.

A total of 20 former South Vietnamese Air Force A-37Bs were received during 1976, with the last examples soldiering on with the Black Eagles aerial demonstration team until 2007.

To house its incoming order of F-4E Phantom II aircraft, the ROKAF built Cheongju Air Base, and opened the facility on 1 September 1978, housing the newly established 17th Tactical Fighter Wing. During 1984 the construction of a civil airport terminal began, and the base currently doubles as Cheongju's international airport.

Troublesome 1980s

On 18 May 1980 riots broke out in the southern city of Gwangju after student protests were met with unproportional violence by government forces. The situation quickly escalated and in only a few days more cities in the south were the scene of the people rising up to the regime.

In response, the aircraft of the newly established 17FW at Cheongju Air Base were evacuated and took up residence at the air bases of Daegu, Suwon and Yecheon.

years that followed a total of 15 T-41B aircraft were handed over to the Philippines Air Force where they continue to fly today. The T-103 fleet made its last flight on 17 April 2018, logging a total of 58,000 flight hours in 14 years, and was retired in favour of the KAI KT-100 of indigenous design.

The 31 August 2004 saw the founding of the 58th Air Transport Group, nicknamed Dayman Wing, for the deployment of a pair of C-130 Hercules aircraft to Kuwait. The unit flew almost 6,000 hours supporting coaltion troops in Iraq and was disbanded on 19 December 2008.

The F-5A and F-5B Freedom Fighters of the 1st Fighter Wing were withdrawn from use on 3 August 2005. The final two squadrons operating the type, the 102nd and 122nd, moved to Daegu Air Base to prepare for their F-15K conversion. The 110th FS, flying F-4Ds from Daegu, gave up its Phantoms in September 2007 and became the third squadron to receive the F-15K.

On 16 June 2010 a retirement ceremony for the F-4D of the 151st FS, the last squadron operating this version of the Phantom, was held at Daegu Air Base. The unit flew the F-4D for 41 years and had flown it accident free for 24 years and seven months, during which it racked up 88,000 flight hours.

Following the participation of North Korea in the XXIII Winter Olympics in Pyeong Chang, South Korea, plans were made for a reciprocal visit. On 3 July 2018 a ROKAF C-130H-30 flew the national basketball team to Pyongyang airport, to participate in the Unification Basketball Match on the following day. In doing so, it became the first ROKAF C-130 – and the second ROKAF aircraft, after the Boeing 737 – to fly in airspace over North Korea since the division of the two countries.

The Korean Air Force Academy started accepting woman for all branches of the air force in 1997, with the first female pilots graduating during 2002. In November 2007, Captain Ha Jung-mi, achieved a piece of South Korean history by becoming the first female ROKAF pilot to fly the F-16. After transitioning to the F-16 from the A-37B, Jung-mi became part of the 157th FS at Haemi Air Base.

In 2006, the Cessna Citation 500 in use with the 256th Squadron as a calibration- and liaison aircraft, was sold on the civil market.

The Russian-built Ilyushin Il-103, dubbed T-103 in ROKAF service, was used for basic training at the Air Force Academy. In total, fewer than 70 were built by the manufacturer, of which 23 were received by Korea.
(Robin Polderman)

Structural and cultural changes

To enhance efficiency during both war- and peacetime operations, and better incorporate newly acquired weapon systems, the ROKAF decided to adopt a new command structure.

Starting on 1 January 2016, the traditional geographically-divided structure was abolished in favour of one defining functions, namely an Air Combat Command (ACC) and an Air Mobility and Reconnaissance Command (AMRC).

In the previous situation, if a fighter unit from the Northern Combat Command was tasked to fly a mission together with a unit from the Southern Combat Command, the lines of communication would be unnecessary long. This has been alleviated by gathering all fighter units under the same command, the ACC.

The headquarters of the ACC was established at Osan Air Base, while that of the AMRC resides at Daegu.

The ROKAF had never assigned a female as squadron commander until December 2019, when not one but three women assumed command over a squadron. Lt Col Jang Se-jin took command of the 261st ARS, followed by Lt Col Park Yi-jeon who was assigned to lead the FA-50 equipped 202st FS. Finally, Lt Col Pyeon Bo-ra became the commander of an undisclosed KT-1 squadron of the 3rd FTW.

Black Eagles: pride of the ROKAF

In 1953 the ROKAF formed its first aerobatic team, flying four North American F-51D Mustangs until 1958. A team consisting of four North American T-33s took over. During 1962, the honour of having an aerobatic demonstration team was bestowed upon the 10th TFW when a new team, appropriately named Blue Sabres, was established, flying four specially painted North American F-86F Sabre fighters. The team received Northrop F-5A Freedom Fighters in 1967 and was renamed as 'Black Eagles'. It only performed at the annual Air Force Day on 1 October, until the show was suspended in

The curtain fell for the A–37Bs of the Black Eagles in October 2007, when the Seoul Air Show became the last opportunity for the public to see the type in action.
(Robin Polderman)

A T-50B of the Black Eagles display team being put through its paces. Due to the COVID-19 pandemic, the number of public displays during 2020 and 2021 was severely curtailed. (AV Kok)

1969. The team was active again between 1973 and 1978, with the RF-5A being absorbed in the team starting in 1974. Following disbandement the F-5 squadrons were called upon for flyovers during certain events until the reestablishment of the team with the A-37B Dragonfly on 1 December 1994. The team formed part of the 238th FS at Hoengsoeng Air Base and their first display with six A-37Bs was flown in September of 1995.

The team split from the 238th FS and became the 239th Special Flight Squadron on 1 April 1999.

During the Seoul airshow on 21 October 2007 the Black Eagles peformed a last demonstration flight with the A-37B. The team was temporarily disbanded awaiting the introduction of the KAI T-50B Golden Eagle. The team moved to Gwangju and started flying the T-50 trainer during 2009, loaned from the 1st FW. After arrival of the dedicated aerobatic T-50Bs, the first one which arrived on 27 May 2010, the Black Eagles moved back to Hoengseong on 1 December 2010. It was here where the first full display with the T-50Bs took place on 1 April 2011.

The transition from the A-37B to T-50B was quite a large step for the Black Eagles and not just a simple change of aircraft. The T-50B is a much more manoeuvrable aircraft and it allowed the team to fundamentally change its repertoire. Additionally, the higher thrust-to-weight ratio of the T-50B allows for different manoeuvres to be flown. The Hands-On-Throttle-And-Stick (HOTAS) design of the Golden Eagle as well as the availabilty of a HUD enables pilots to more easily process all flight-related information during the display, without the need to glance down into the cockpit like on the A-37B Dragonfly.

These improvements in display flying also allowed the team to add two aircraft to the show and become an eight-aircraft display team.

Black Eagles selection

Before becoming a member of the Black Eagles, pilots go through a rigorous selection process. They must have more than 800 flight hours on fast jets or, if they have flown the F-16 previously, 650 hours. The difference lies in the fact the F-16 and T-50B have similar flight characteristics. Prospective Black Eagles pilots must have graduated in the top third of their class during flight training, while candidates for team leader must have finished in the top five. They must be flight lead qualified, meaning able to lead a four-ship flight and have experience in doing so. The candidates are subject to multiple interviews by a selection board comprising of current Black Eagle pilots and will only be admitted if a unanimous decision is reached. Most pilots in the Black Eagles hold the rank of major; only one currently ranks as captain.

Once selected, new Black Eagle pilots will relocate to Gwangju Air Base for two months in order to follow a T-50 transition course, which includes theory and 10 actual sorties. After new pilots have joined the team, training to display-ready status requires up to 50 sorties within a six-month period. All training for new Black Eagles members is conducted by current demonstration pilots. The training sessions begin with two-ship formations and proceed through eight-ship formations at low altitudes.

The Black Eagles T-50Bs carry a unique paint scheme which features a golden eagle design on the wings (yellow on the bottomside and white on top). The artwork was selected in a two-month contest that attracted a total of 260 entries. The competing designs were published on the ROKAF intranet pages to allow all air force personnel to vote. Private Jung-Gwan Hwang, an architecture major from the ROKAF Training and Doctrine Command, is credited with the design.

The Black Eagles team is composed of eight pilots which perform the show. The squadron commander, a lieutenant-colonel and usually a former team member, does not fly in the shows. Additionally, the team has more than 50 people involved in maintenance, logistics, security and public affairs. The latter crew members provide narration, produce video footage and set up sound equipment.

The 53rd Air Demonstration Group was established on 1 April 2013 to allow for smoother operation of the Black Eagles squadron. The unit, commanded by a colonel, is no longer with the 8th FW but reports directly to the ROKAF HQ.

Besides displaying in their home country Korea, the Black Eagles have performed in Malaysia, Singapore and the United Kingdom. To participate in airshows in Malaysia and Singapore the T-50Bs of the Black Eagles departed Hoengseong and flew 5,390km (3,350 mile) one-way, making scheduled stops in Sacheon, the island of Jeju, Kaohsiung (Taiwan), Cebu (Philippines) and Brunei, before reaching their destination.

In order to be able to fly demonstrations in the United Kingdom during summer 2012, the T-50Bs were dismantled, loaded onto Korean Air Boeing 747 freighters and flown to Manchester Airport. From there the 10 jets were taken by road to RAF Leeming for reassembly and subsequent test flights. The team's pilots moved to Gwangju, to prepare for their European adventure using the T-50s of the 1st FW.

The Black Eagles successfully participated in the Waddington Airshow as well as the Royal International Air Tattoo at RAF Fairford, and managed to win awards at both venues.

For the 2021 season, the team received an invitation to perform at the Russian MAKS International Aviation and Space Salon at Zhukovsky air base near Moscow, but the Korean participation was cancelled due to the global COVID-19 pandemic.

Defectors from the North

Since the Korean War, a number of both Chinese and North Korean pilots have flown their aircraft to South Korea. The majority of the Chinese pilots did so not because they wanted to live in South Korea or supported the South Korean regime, but because they aspired to join the Republic of China, otherwise known as Taiwan.

During the 1980s, in the timespan of less than four years, the ROKAF became the owner of five Chinese-built fighter aircraft (four J-6/MiG-19 [ASCC Farmer] and a single J-7 I/MiG-21F-13 [ASCC Fishbed]) after their KPAAF and PLAAF pilots decided to defect. Among them was a rare Shenyang JZ-6, the reconnaissance variant of the J-6, carrying a camera pack in a fairing under the forward fuselage. Its Chinese pilot, Chen Baozhong, had taken off from an air base near the city of Dalian in Liaoning province, and flew straight to Suwon Air Base.

On 7 August 1983, Chinese testpilot Sun Tianqin defected to South Korea in a Chengdu J-7I aircraft and landed at Seongnam Air Base.

Instead of relegating them to museum objects, the ROKAF decided it could benefit considerably if it were to fly those aircraft, in order to learn their strong points and weaknesses. Aiming to develop tactics to deal with them effectively in case of war, the MiGs were pitted against ROKAF aircraft during simulated engagements.

Reportedly these flights originated from Cheongju and continued into the late 1990s, with at least two F-6/J-6 (MiG-19) and the J-7 (MiG-21) taking part. While undertaking these flights, the aircraft were devoid of any markings. However, a photo taken of two of these aircraft on the ground in 1983 show ROKAF roundels and a ROKAF serial number applied. When the ROKAF ran out of spare parts, and newer aircraft appeared in the inventory of their rivals, the aircraft were grounded and relegated to ground instructional airframes. Eventually all ended up as display items on ROKAF bases and in aviation museums on the Korean mainland or on Jeju island.

Details surrounding the use of the aircraft remain sketchy and it is currently unknown if the 29th undertook these flights on its own or if they received help from other countries. Given the close ties that exist between South Korea and the US, it is not unthinkable either the USAF 6513th Flight Test Squadron 'Red Hats', a MiG test

This Shenyang J-6C is preserved at the aviation museum in Seongmu, on the grounds of the Air Force Academy. It landed at Cheongju Air Base on 24 October 1986, flown there by a Chinese defector.
(Robin Polderman)

and evaluation squadron, or the 4477th Test and Evaluation Squadron 'Red Eagles', a MiG aggressor squadron, was involved.

Some Korean aviation magazines even reported the ROKAF having tested the MiG-29, but this seems unlikely.

Table 1: List of known defectors

Date	Type	Air Force	Pilot Name	Landed at
28 April 1950	Il-10	KPAAF	Lee Kun Soon	Busan
21 September 1953	MiG-15	KPAAF	No Kum-sok	Gimpo
21 June 1955	Yak-18	KPAAF	Un-yong and Eun-song	Seoul
3 December 1970	MiG-15	KPAAF	Pak Sun-kok	Daegang-ri beach
16 October 1982	J-6C	PLAAF	Wu Jung-ken	Seongnam
25 February 1983	F-6	KPAAF	Lee Ung-pyong	Suwon
7 August 1983	J-7I	PLAAF	Sun Tianqin	Seongnam
25 August 1985	Il-28	PLAAF	Xiao Tianrun	Iksan (off airport)
21 February 1986	JZ-6	PLAAF	Chen Baozhong	Suwon
24 October 1986	J-6C	PLAAF	Zheng Caitian	Cheongju
23 May 1996	F-6C	KPAAF	Lee Chul-su	Suwon

AIRCRAFT MARKINGS, SERIAL NUMBER SYSTEM AND UNIT DESIGNATIONS

Aircraft markings

The gaudy squadron markings that appeared on ROKAF F-86 and F-5A aircraft during the 1950s and 1960s respectively, did not have eternal life. As the cold war with North Korea intensified, stricter security measures imposed effectively meant the end of these markings. On top of that, camouflage colours were applied over the bare aluminium exterior of many of the combat aircraft in use. However, as time passed, the application of squadron markings on ROKAF aircraft seems to have been reinstated, albeit slowly.

In the late 1970s, the F-4D aircraft flying out of Daegu had a squadron badge applied on the intakes. Still, many F-4E and F-5E/F aircraft were devoid of unit markings well into the 1980s. Following an apparent ease in regulations, the Phantom II and Tiger II aircraft were decorated with a squadron badge, wing badge, or both. Additionally, the F-4 Phantoms (F-4D, F-4E and RF-4C), received a lion head painted on both intakes, while the (K)F-5E/F fleet gained artwork in the form of a double tiger head (originating from the nickname Tiger II) on the forward fuselage below the canopy. Curiously, the fleet of (R)F-5A and F-5B Freedom Fighters also received the tigerheads.

When the ROKAF received surplus American F-4Es at the end of the 1980s, at least one, serial number 70-369, retained the sharkmouth it had received during service with the 497th TFS of the USAF Pacific Air Forces at Daegu Air Base.

There appears to be no uniform rule on which emblem needs to be applied on the aircraft, and the application of badges seems to differ between units. For example, each of the fighter wings currently operating the F-5 has its own way of applying markings. The F-5s from the Suwon based 10th FW carry the wing badge prominently on the tail, with a small squadron badge painted on the double tigerhead artwork on the forward fuselage. The F-5 aircraft of the 18th FW do not carry a wing badge but only a squadron badge on the vertical tail, whereas the Tigers of the 206th FS likewise do not carry markings denoting the 1st FW but have the squadron badge applied below the cockpit.

Most of the Korean-built KF-5E/F aircraft have the legend 제공 (Je-gong, which loosely translates as Skymaster), painted on both sides of the nose.

The ROKAF fleet of F-16s were totally devoid of any markings that could lead to the identification of their squadron, wing or home base until recently. Identification markings were applied on the F-16s of the 20th FW out of Haemi Air Base during 2017, proudly displaying the toned-down wing badge on a prominent place on the Fighting Falcon's vertical tail.

대한민국공군
REPUBLIC OF KOREA AIR FORCE

Old roundel

Current roundel

Current low-visibility roundel

The 201th FS was established in 1976 to operate the F-5E/F. Currently based at Suwon, the unit now flies the indigenously produced KF-5E/F. All aircraft carry artwork on the forward fuselage in the
shape of a double tiger head with the squadron emblem superimposed.
(Robin Polderman)

The 38th Fighter Group from Gunsan, parent unit to a Tiger squadron, the 111th FS, followed suit and started painting the tip of the vertical tail of their KF-16C/Ds in tiger stripes. Additionally, during 2020, one KF-16C was observed flying around with a tiger head on the tail. In early 2021, a KF-16C of the unit was photographed carrying an eagle's head on the tail, along with the code 'EG', which stands for 'Eagle Group', the name given to the 38th FG, while a KF-16D was coded 'TS', ('Tiger Squadron').

The two squadrons of the 16th FW, consisting of the TA-50s of the 115th FS and the FA-50s of the 202nd FS, adorned their aircraft with a low visibility squadron badge during 2020. The markings were applied in front of the air intake on the starboard side of the fuselage, with the toned down wing badge in a similar location but on the port side.

Application of the 11th FW badge on the fleet of F-15K Slam Eagles is rather inconsistent; some carry the badge on the forward section of the Conformal Fuel Tanks (CFT), while others do not. A few have been noted carrying a squadron badge on the starboard side CFT, but sightings of those are few and far between.

The CN235 squadron at Gimhae and the C-130 squadrons based at both Gimhae and Seongnam are unique, as the artwork applied to the nose of these aircraft does not resemble the actual squadron patch as worn on the flight suit of the aircrew. In fact, the artwork on the nose of the CN235s of the 258th AS was almost identical to the squadron patch, but the emblem was revised somewhere in the second half of the 2010s, and now bears little to no resemblance.

The trainer aircraft of the ROKAF are a mixed bag when it comes to the application of squadron- or wing markings. The KT-100 fleet is devoid of the 212th FTS badge, whereas the KT-1s do wear the squadron patch. The T-50s carry no markings to identify the squadron they belong too.

Aircraft newly introduced into ROKAF service or with a sensitive role seem obliged to fly the skies over Korea unidentified.

In April 2005 the ROKAF decided to adopt a new roundel. In order to more closely reflect the national flag of Korea, three black bars were placed on either side of the circular Taegeuk symbol, taking the place of the red and blue USAF style bars. A low visibility variant in a single grey colour was introduced in the same time. It took some time to replace the old roundel with the new one. In early 2006 some ROKAF aircraft were observed still wearing the old variant.

The application of special colour schemes associated with a certain event, like the colourful anniversary schemes applied to Japanese Air-Self Defense Force and USAF aircraft, is unheard of within the ROKAF. The units do celebrate unit anniversaries as well as the achievement of a certain number of accident-free flight hours, but this is in no way reflected in the colour scheme on their aircraft. Notable exception was the application of 'Spooky' artwork to the air intakes of several RF-4C aircraft upon their retirement in 2014.

Wing and squadron badges

Within the ROKAF, the figures, shapes and patterns on most wing badges have been designed to depict the wing's number. It appears some of the squadron patches have been created along the same lines. Although a few badges have stood the test of time and remain unchanged since leaving the drawing board in the early 1950s, it seems altering the squadron- and or wing badge is a normal occurence within ROKAF units. In some cases this meant a slight redesign while other units sometimes introduced a completely different badge. The reason for the redesign is not always clear; occasionally this seems to be done out of dissatisfaction with the current design and more frequently when a new aircraft type, and sometimes a new mission, is introduced.

The fact is that a considerable number of helicopter, transport, as well as fighter squadrons, groups and wings, have changed the design of their badge in the past decade. The 11th FW flying out of Daegu revamped the design of their badge around 2014. The Korean national Taegeuk symbol got a more prominent place on the badge and the background colour was changed from blue to black as a signal of the wing's ability to strike at night. The final change was made to the bird; it now holds an AMRAAM missile in one of its claws.

Another example is the 206th FS at Gwangju Air Base. They introduced a completely new design in 2015, coincidentally also the year in which the squadron took over the training role from the disbanded 205th FS at Gangneung.

Following the introduction of the F-35A, the 152nd FS refreshed its squadron patch during 2020. The figure, a warrior from the Joseon Dynasty, was reworked and a more detailed missile, resembling the AIM-120C carried by the F-35A, was added to replace the stylised AIM-9 Sidewinder on the previous iteration of the squadron badge.

With the ROKAF's mission being primarily in the sky, it comes as no surprise images of birds, stars and lightning feature prominently on the various badges worn by the aircrew.

A number of fighter wings have both an official as well as an unofficial badge. More often than not, the unofficial badge seems to be preferred by the aircrew and proudly worn of the flightsuit.

The 1st FW became the first to introduce an unofficial wing badge carrying the motto 'First and Best', during 1968. It was instigated by the 1st FW commander at the time, General Yoon Ja-joo, who later moved on to become Chief of Staff of the ROKAF. The exact design is still worn as a morale patch today. As is the case in the USAF, the closest ally of the ROKAF, Friday patches have started to appear. As their name implies, they are usually only worn on a Friday or during special occassions. The squadrons of the 11th FW at Daegu in particular have frequently issued these patches for its aircrew.

When looking at the patches worn by some of the aircrew onboard a ROKAF transport aircraft, one could be in for a surprise. Maintenance aircrew (loadmasters/board-mechanics) on these aircraft, as well as on the helicopters of the 6th SRG, wear the patch of the maintenance unit instead of that of the flying unit.

Since 1996, patches are only worn by aircrew. Following the Gangneung submarine incident, when a number of North Korean infiltrators were caught wearing copies of ROKA patches, restrictions were put in place for South Korean military personnel regarding unit patches attached to uniforms.

The command of the 8th FW at Hoengseong Air Base, located fairly close to the DMZ, introduced a low visibility variant of their wing patch to be worn on the flightsuit. The emblem however, was very shortlived and the full colour version was soon reintroduced.

In 2015 new rules were enforced regarding patches. Aircrew were obliged to wear the Korean flag on the right shoulder, a wing/group patch or aircraft-type patch on the left shoulder and the squadron patch featuring prominently on the left chest. A name tag displaying the pilot's name as well as a wing is worn on the right chest. Prior to 2015, this was not standardised nor enforced, and the Korean flag was not always worn on the flight suit but a wing or group patch was placed in that position instead.

Aircraft camouflage

The trend of using any colour on an aircraft as long as it is grey has reached the ROKAF too, although fortunately a few colourful exceptions remain, at least for the time being.

With close ties to the USAF and many aircraft supplied by manufacturers from the US, it comes as no surprise the United States Federal Standard 595 colourchart has been in long time use. However, with local Korean companies producing paint, variations are likely to occur and the FS numbers quoted below could well deviate from the official FS colour chart. During 2014, the FS-595 colour chart was superseded by the AMS-STD (Aerospace Material Specification – Standard) 595A, detailing standard colours used in US Government procurement and basically using the earlier FS numbers. Although ROKAF aircraft are usually kept in pristine condition, being exposed to the fickle Korean weather usually means paint fades fast, especially on aircraft that are continously parked out in the open.

Fighter aircraft
When the ROKAF took delivery of the F-4D/E aircraft in the mid to late 1970s, these aircraft were sprayed in the South East Asia scheme of Forest Green (FS 34079), Light Green (FS 34102) and Tan (FS 30219) , with the underside in Gray (FS 36622). To make them less visible high in the sky over Korea, they received a colour scheme comprising of Light Compass Ghost Gray (FS 36375) and Dark Compass Ghost Gray (FS 36320) as they went through overhaul.

The initial batch of 40 F-5E aircraft built by Northrop were also delivered in the South East Asia colour scheme. The requirements were amended and further deliveries of the F-5E/F as well as the locally produced KF-5E/F aircraft sported the Compass Ghost colours. The initial batch of F-5Es were painted in the same grey colour scheme at a later point in their career.

When the ROKAF purchased the F-16 in the early 1980s, it ordered the aircraft to be painted in the same Ghost Gray colours too. For the sake of standardisation, the fleet of TA-50 and FA-50 aircraft were painted in similar fashion.

The second-hand former USAF F-4E Phantom II aircraft received in the late 1980s carried the Hill One scheme, consisting of Medium Gray (FS 36270) and Medium Gunship Gray (FS 36118). Apparently this colour scheme proved effective, as both the F-4Ds and new-built F-4Es received earlier, lost their Ghost Gray colours and were repainted in the Hill One scheme following overhaul.

The Lockheed Martin F-35 Freedom Knight aircraft delivered to the ROKAF sport the standard scheme of overall Camouflage Gray (AMS-STD 36170).

The fleet of F-15K aircraft were painted according to USAF specifications and received an overall scheme of Dark Gunship Gray (FS 36118). When it comes to the ROKAF's newest aircraft, the KF-21, KAI initially stated it would paint these aircraft in the same colour as that used on the Slam Eagles. At the roll-out of the first prototype

A formation of ROKAF fighter aircraft (F-4E, KF-5, F-15K and KF-16) demonstrating the effectiveness of their camouflage over a winter landscape.
(ROK MND)

For the 70th anniversary of the ROKAF, the T-50B aircraft of the Black Eagles received special markings on the tail in gold. (USAF/SSG Greg Nash)

however, the colour sprayed on the jet seemed to be considerably lighter than the dark grey used on the F-15K.

The small fleet of KA-1 light attack aircraft are painted in colours used in the Europe One scheme, consisting of Forest Green (FS 34079), Light Green (FS 34102) and Dark Gunship Gray (FS 36081). Given the fact that most, if not all, of the green on helicopters and transport aircraft is in the process of disappearing, it would come as no surprise if the KA-1s would soon appear in an overall dark grey colour.

Helicopters

The past decade has seen the HH-32A, CH-47/HH-47 and HH-60P shed their multi-colour camouflage jacket and reappear in a uniform grey. This colour was said to be Medium Gunship Gray (FS 36118) overall, but looks to be considerably lighter.

The former US Army CH-47s were handed over to the ROKAF wearing a wraparound scheme of very faded Olive Drab, and became one of the first types to be repainted. Before donning their grey jacket, the Kamovs and HH-47s wore a scheme consisting of Light Green (FS 34102), Black (FS 37038) and an unidentified dark brown colour.

The VIP helicopters use dark blue, most likely FS15052, as their primary colour, along with white accents. These helicopters do not carry the ROKAF roundel, but have the Korean flag painted on the engine cowling. Before the HH-60P Black Hawks in use for SAR were resprayed in overall grey, they flew around in the same dark blue colour as the VIP helicopters.

Transports and special mission aircraft

The CN235 and C-130 aircraft were delivered to the ROKAF carrying the earlier mentioned Europe One colour scheme. Only the C-130H-30 aircraft carried a scheme in which the grey had been replaced by Tan (FS 30219) but, following overhaul, these aircraft recieved the Europe One colours.

Change is again forthcoming as in early February 2021 the first transport aircraft appeared in a grey colour scheme, with the topside painted Medium Gunship Gray (FS 36118) and the undersides a lighter grey, possibly Medium Gray (FS 36270). Home based at Seongnam, MC-130K serial number 95-180 was the first aircraft to be repainted in this way, also carrying 'R.O.K Air Force' titles in both English and Korean. In April 2021, CN235M-220 serial number 10-045 emerged from overhaul in an overall medium grey colour scheme, carrying a full-colour roundel and black titles. The ROKAF will repaint its fleet of CN235 and C-130 aircraft one by one as they pass through depot overhaul.

The VIP aircraft in use are overall white with red and blue accents. Instead of a roundel, these aircraft carry the Korean flag on the tail. All VIP aircraft used to have a light blue cheatline, but were repainted during the late 2000s.

The secretive fleet of RC-800 and RC-2000 aircraft are painted in the same blend of greys as the older fighters in use; Dark Compass Ghost Gray (FS 36320) on top and Light Compass Ghost Gray (FS 36375) on the bottom.

When it comes to the colour scheme of the secretive An-2 (ASCC Colt), the ROKAF keeps a keen eye on its northern neighbour. In use to develop tactics to counter the North's vast fleet of An-2 aircraft, it comes as no surprise the ROKAF An-2s mimic the KPAAF examples as closely as possible when it comes to colour. As North Korea

started applying a camouflage scheme to its Antonovs during the past decade, the ROKAF followed suit. They now wear a colour scheme of light green, dark green and tan, with the undersides painted blue-grey. The biplane fleet carry their registration and ROKAF roundel not only on the side, but also on top of the upper wing as well as on the underside of the lower wing.

Standing out among the assets of the ROKAF when it comes to colour, are the aircraft of the Black Eagles. In the era of the A-37B, the Black Eagles used white as primary colour applied to the aircraft, along with red and blue accents. This changed with the introduction of the KAI T-50B, which were painted overall black, with white accents on the upper fuselage and a yellow bird superimposed on the bottom. To commemorate the 70th anniversary of the ROKAF in 2019, all Black Eagles aircraft received a '70' in gold on both sides of the vertical tail.

Serial number system

Within the ROKAF, there is no uniform system when it comes to allocating a serial number to an aircraft.

On its fighter aircraft inducted during the 1970s and 1980s the US-assigned Foreign Military Sales (FMS) number is used, with a minor change. The first digit of the Fiscal Year (FY) was deleted, and the hyphen moved one position to the right to create the ROKAF serial. This system was used on the F-4 and most of the F-5E/F aircraft delivered to Korea. As an example, the F-4E carrying FMS serial number 76-0498 became 60-498 upon entering Korean service, whereas F-5E 75-0590 became 50-590.

The exception to the rule is the first batch of F-5E aircraft delivered. The last four digits of the FMS serial number were used for identification, preceded by a '0', making FMS F-5E 74-1471 show up as 01-471 in ROKAF service. This system seems subject of a revision however, as KF-5E 10-622 was painted up as 81-622 in early 2021, and has flown as such ever since.

The latter method is more in line with the system used to identify the Korean F-16 Fighting Falcons. Taking the FMS serial number, the first digit following the hyphen was deleted, and the last two digits of the FY were used, instead of only one. For KF-16D serial number 01-529, the last delivered F-16 to the ROKAF, the FMS identity is 01-0529.

Fast forward to the F-35A and the system is totally different. The first Freedom Knight for the ROKAF carries serial number 18-001, but its FMS identity is 15-5221. Here, to form the aircraft's serial number, the ROKAF chose to combine the last two digits of the year in which the aircraft was produced (2018) with a sequential number starting at 001. The same style of numbering was applied to the F-15K, KC-330, KA/KT-1 and KT-100.

Of note is the numbering system on the T-50 aircraft. The ROKAF views the T-50, T-50B and TA-50 as the same family of aircraft hence the sequential numbering. The T-50s are numbered 001–050; T-50Bs 051–060; TA-50s 061–082 and two attrition replacement T-50Bs were numbered 083 and 084. This sequential number is preceded by the year of manufacture. The FA-50, which externally much resembles the TA-50 but is viewed as a different class of aircraft, starts at 001 again in combination with the year it was produced.

The 111th FS was established on 13 January 1958 flying the F-86, before receiving the F–5E/F in 1985. The unit converted to the KF-16 in 2006, and began applying tail codes (EG for 'Eagle Group' and TS for 'Tiger Squadron') and tail art (an eagle or tiger head) on its KF-16s during 2020 (Jamie Chang)

The serial number system on the ROKAF F-35A fleet is straightforward, with this aircraft being the 18th Lightning II built for the ROKAF and 2020 being the year it rolled off the Fort Worth production line.
(via ROKAF)

The numbering of these indigenous aircraft leads to interesting situations: serial number 10-060 is a T-50B assigned to the Black Eagles, while 16-060 is an FA-50 and 11-061 a TA-50. This could be confusing which, knowing the ROKAF's obsession with security, might well be intentional.

There is at least one aircraft in ROKAF service where a different serial number was applied specifically to avoid confusion. When the five former US Army CH-47s were handed over to the ROKAF during 2014, four of these received serial numbers very close to their former identity. US Army serial numbers 88-00093 through 88-00096 became ROKAF serial numbers 88-093 through 88-096 respectively, upon entering service with the 231st SRS at Cheongju. The US Army serial number of the remaining Chinook, 88-00081, provided a challenge as the squadron already had a HH-47D with a number ending in 081. It was decided to allocate serial number 88-092 to the helicopter, in line with the other second-hand examples.

The C-130 fleet carries the last digit of the production year coupled to the Manufacturer Serial Number (MSN) as their identification. For example, C-130H serial number 05-182 was built during 1990 and has MSN 5182. Initially though, only the MSN was carried on the tail as a serial number, until the system was changed in the early 2000s.

Currently only two aircraft types do not carry a serial number consisting of five digits. The An-2 fleet uses civil registrations in the HL-1082 to HL-1091 range, while both veteran HS748 aircraft of the 256th Airlift Squadron still carry a four-digit number on the tail.

Table 2: ROKAF's serial number systems

Serial number breakdown	Aircraft type
Year of production (2 digits) plus sequential number	F-15K, F-35A, KC-330, KA/KT-1, KT-100, T/TA/FA-50
Year of delivery (2 digits) plus sequential number	HH-32A
Derived from FMS	F-4E, (K)F-5E/F, (K)F-16C/D, CH-47NE*
Year of production (2 digits) + MSN	RC-2000
Last digit of year of production + MSN	C-130 (all variants), CN235 (all variants)
Last digit of year of contract + part of MSN	E-737
(Part of) MSN	Bell 412, HH/VH-60P, HS748**, RC-800
Civil registration	An-2
Unknown system	AS332L1, HH-47D, VH-92***
Other systems	Boeing 737, Boeing 747

* with one notable exception
** carries a four-digit serial number
*** only first aircraft can be explained

A few unknowns remain. The HH-47Ds received sequential serial numbers that cannot be explained, whereas the AS332L1 Super Puma fleet most likely received serial numbers derived from their MSN. But as the MSNs of these helicopters remain in the dark, it is impossible to say if said number was used to produce the serial number applied to the tail.

The first VH-92 delivered, carrying 05035, most likely has the last two digits of the contract year (2005) and the last three of the MSN (920035) glued together to form the serial number. But the other pair of helicopters delivered do not seem to follow the same system, as their MSN does not match up with the serial number carried on the tails.

The E-737 AEW&C aircraft seem to have the last digit of the contract year (2006) coupled to the last four of their MSN. As an example, ROKAF serial number 64-700 rolled off the Boeing production line with MSN 34700.

The Boeing 737 uses the delivery year (85) followed by a random '101' making 85101. The Boeing 747-4B5 leased from Korean Air follows the same pattern, with 2010 being the year the aircraft was aquired followed by '001', making the serial number 100001.

Unit designations

The Korean alphabet is named Hangeul and consists of 19 consonants and 21 vowels that can be used to 'construct' letters, basically by writing vowels under consonants. Modern Hangeul is read from top to bottom, left to right, and a total of 11,172 letter combinations are possible to form syllables.

The Ministry of Culture and Tourism adopted a new system for the romanisation of the Korean language during 2000, superseding the McCune-Reischauer system that had been in use since World War II. This explains the discrepancies found in, for example, the names of air bases when comparing old publications with recent ones. Under the new system, Taegu became Daegu and Kunsan became Gunsan, to name but a few. The revised romanisation has not seen widespread adoption, hence the USAF still using the name Kunsan to denote the air base that houses the Wolf Pack.

As the Koreans have always been very concerned with military security, a similar system to that used in the former Warsaw Pact was adopted, where each unit would receive a Military Unit number. For example, Military Unit 1234 could either be an artillery batallion, navy catering unit or air force fighter squadron. Luckily this practice has almost disappeared over time and nowadays the vast majority of units, aircraft types and unit patches are shown openly in various publications and by different news outlets, including the ROKAF Public Relations department. Exceptions remain though, with a ROKAF press release issued in August 2021 still referring to the 255th SOS as the '2348 Squadron', and the unit emblem blurred out in the accompanying photograph.

In the Hangeul alphabet, 비행대대, which loosely translates as 'flight battalion' are the letters used to denote a squadron, with 비행 translating as 'flight' or 'flying' and 대대 as 'battalion'. A 'flight group' is written as 비행전대 , while a 'wing' is 비행단 in the Korean language.

Within the ROKAF structure, wings and groups are designated by a number containing either one or two digits. Squadrons have three digits, with the first one always either a '1' or a '2'.

A group always consists of at least one squadron, along with maintenance- and support units. There is no clear rule when a group becomes a wing. There are wings which consist of only two flying squadrons while the 6th Search and Rescue Group, for example, controls three helicopter squadrons. Wings are often commanded by a general, while the head of a flight group is usually a colonel. Again, exceptions seem to be the rule here.

Some unit names are translated with western squadron designations in mind, which sometimes leads to confusion. In western publications, being in print or online, the 281st squadron flying out of Sacheon has been called either the 281st Test & Evaluation Squadron, 281st Flight Test Squadron or 281st Test Flight Squadron. If the name in Hangeul, 제281시험비행대대, is translated literally than 시험 means 'test' while 비행대대 would translate as 'flight batallion' (which is a squadron), making it the 281st Test Squadron. The sign outside the squadron building at Sacheon however, reads '281st Test Flight Squadron' in English, and this is what has been used in the Order of Battle in this publication.

At the centrally located air base of Cheongju, the 제29전술개발훈련비행전대 (29th TDTFG) is the ROKAF unit responsible for tactics development and providing tactical training to frontline units. Although the text on the patch could be translated literally as 29th Tactical Development Training Flight Group, the unit itself uses '29th Tactical Fighter Weapons Group' on unit coins and other memorabilia. The correct name in the English language is therefore open to debate.

Changing names
Transport squadrons were named 'tactical airlift squadron' (전술공수비행대대) until 2019. The ROKAF acknowledged the fact that the scope of these squadrons was much wider than just providing tactical airlift, hence the name was changed and use of the word 'tactical' was dropped. The 251st, 256th and 258th Squadrons, flying the C-130, CN235 and HS.748, now use 'airlift squadron' (공수비행대대) and their flight suit patches have been altered to reflect the name change.

On 3 November 2020 the ROKAF established a new unit, the 39th Reconnaissance Wing (제39정찰비행단), which basically elevated the 39th Reconnaissance Group, established on 1 January 1989, to independent wing status.

The 39th RW, headquartered at Jungwon Air Base near Chungju, is in charge of the ROKAF's key strategic and tactical reconnaissance assets, which are used to keep tabs on developments over the border in North Korea. The establishment of the 39th RW makes Jungwon the only air base within the current ROKAF structure to house two seperate wings.

Squadrons subordinate to the 39th RW are either reconnaissance squadrons (정찰비행대대), flying the RQ-4, RC-800 or RC-2000, and a tactical reconnaissance squadron (전술정찰비행대대) operating the RF-16s.

The 237th Fighter Squadron (전투비행대대), operating the KAI KA-1 FAC and light attack aircraft, used to be named the 237th Tactical Control Squadron, but underwent a name change in December 2012, shortly after it had moved from Seongnam to its new home base at Hoengseong Air Base near Wonju.

Table 3: Most used unit designations in Hangeul

Korean	English	Korean	English
비행대대	squadron	전투	fighter
비행전대	(flying) group	공수	airlift
비행단	wing	정찰	reconnaissance
전술	tactical	비행	flight training

ORBAT of the Republic of Korea Air Force

Air Combat Command (ACC, HQ at Daegu)

Unit (Wing/Squadron)	Location (Base)	Aircraft type	Remarks
1st Fighter Wing			HQ Gwangju Air Base, Gwangju
189th Flight Training Sqn 'Charging Archer'	Gwangju	T-50	
206th Fighter Sqn	Gwangju	F-5E/F	
216th Flight Training Sqn	Gwangju	T-50	
8th Fighter Wing			HQ Hoengseong Air Base, Wonju
103rd Fighter Sqn	Hoengseong	FA-50	
203rd Fighter Sqn	Hoengseong	FA-50	
237th Fighter Sqn	Hoengseong	KA-1	
288th Electronic Warfare Sqn	Hoengseong	Harpy	
10th Fighter Wing			HQ Suwon Air Base, Suwon
101st Fighter Sqn	Suwon	KF-5E, KF-5F	
153rd Fighter Sqn	Suwon	F-4E	
201st Fighter Sqn	Suwon	KF-5E, KF-5F	
11th Fighter Wing			HQ Daegu Air Base, Daegu
102nd Fighter Sqn 'Blue Dragon'	Daegu	F-15K	
110th Fighter Sqn	Daegu	F-15K	
122nd Fighter Sqn 'Roaring Jaguars'	Daegu	F-15K	
16th Fighter Wing			HQ Yecheon Air Base, Yecheon
115th Fighter Sqn	Yecheon	TA-50	
202nd Fighter Sqn	Yecheon	FA-50	
17th Fighter Wing			HQ Cheongju Air Base, Cheongju
151st Fighter Sqn	Cheongju	F-35A	
152nd Fighter Sqn	Cheongju	F-35A	
18th Fighter Wing			HQ Gangneung Air Base, Gangneung
105th Fighter Sqn	Gangneung	(K)F-5E, (K)F-5F	
112th Fighter Sqn	Gangneung	(K)F-5E, (K)F-5F	

19th Fighter Wing			HQ Jungwon Air Base, Chungju
155th Fighter Sqn 'Rhino'	Jungwon	KF-16C Block 52, KF-16D Block 52	
161st Fighter Sqn 'Boramae'	Jungwon	F-16C Block 32, F-16D Block 32	
162nd Fighter Sqn 'Black Eagle'	Jungwon	F-16C Block 32, F-16D Block 32	
20th Fighter Wing			HQ Haemi Air Base, Seosan
120th Fighter Sqn	Haemi	KF-16C Block 52, KF-16D Block 52	
121st Fighter Sqn	Haemi	KF-16C Block 52, KF-16D Block 52	
123rd Fighter Sqn	Haemi	KF-16C Block 52, KF-16D Block 52	
157th Fighter Sqn	Haemi	KF-16C Block 52, KF-16D Block 52	
29th Tactical Fighter Weapons Group	Cheongju		
191st Tactics Training Sqn	Cheongju		Aircraft as and when required
192nd Tactics Development Sqn	Cheongju		Aircraft as and when required
Adversary Flight	Cheongju	KF-16C Block 52	As and when required
38th Fighter Group 'Eagle Group'			HQ Gunsan Air Base, Gunsan
111th Fighter Sqn	Gunsan	KF-16C Block 52, KF-16D Block 52	

Air Mobility & Reconnaissance Command (HQ at Gimhae)

Unit (Wing/Squadron)	Location (Base)	Aircraft type	Remarks
3rd Flying Training Wing			HQ Sacheon Air Base, Sacheon
213th Flight Training Squadron 'Dragon Flight'	Sacheon	KT-1	
215th Flight Training Squadron	Sacheon	KT-1	
217th Flight Training Squadron 'White Eagle'	Sacheon	KT-1	
236th Flight Training Squadron	Sacheon	KT-1	
5th Air Mobility Wing			HQ Gimhae Air Base, Busan
251st Airlift Sqn	Gimhae	C-130H, C-130H-30, C-130J-30	
258th Airlift Sqn	Gimhae	CN235M-100, CN235M-220	
261st Air Refuelling Sqn	Gimhae	KC-330 (A330 MRTT)	
15th Special Mission Wing			HQ Seongnam Air Base, Seoul
255th Special Operations Sqn	Seongnam	C-130H, C-130H-30, MC-130K	
256th Airlift Sqn	Seongnam	CN235M-100, HS.748	
39th Reconnaissance Wing			HQ Jungwon Air Base, Chungju
131st Reconnaissance Sqn	Sacheon	RQ-4B Block 30	
159th Tactical Reconnaissance Sqn	Jungwon	KF-16D Block 52, RF-16C Block 52	
296th Reconnaissance Sqn 'Black Bat'	Seongnam	RC-800B, RC-800G, RC-2000	
6th Search and Rescue Group			HQ Cheongju Air Base, Cheongju
231st Search and Rescue Sqn	Cheongju	CH-47NE, HH-47D	
233rd Search and Rescue Sqn	Cheongju	HH-60P, VH-60P	Plus a HH-60P detachment at Haemi
235th Search and Rescue Sqn	Cheongju	AS332L1, Bell 412, HH-32A	Plus a HH-32A detachment at Pilseung
28th Flight Group			HQ Seongmu Air Base, Cheongju
208th Sqn	Seongmu	An-2	Located at north side of Seongmu AB
51st Air Control Group			HQ Gimhae Air Base, Gimhae
271st Air Control Sqn	Gimhae	E-737	

Direct Reporting units

Unit (Wing/Squadron)	Location (Base)	Aircraft type	Remarks
35th Flight Group	Seongnam		
257th Airlift Sqn	Seongnam	Boeing 737-300, Boeing 747-8i, VCN235M-220, VH-60P, VH-92	
52nd Test and Evaluation Group			HQ Sacheon Air Base, Sacheon
281st Test Flight Sqn	Sacheon	FA-50, T-50	
53rd Special Flight Group (53rd Air Demonstration Group)			HQ Hoengseong Air Base, Wonju
239th Special Sqn 'Black Eagles'	Hoengseong	T-50B	Black Eagles aerobatic team
Air Force Academy			HQ Seongmu Air Base, Cheongju
55th Flight Training Group	Seongmu		
212th Flight Training Sqn	Seongmu	KT-100	

PACAF Air Bases
1   Gunsan
2   Osan

ROKAF Air Bases
1   Cheongju
2   Daegu
3   Gangneung
4   Gimhae (Busan)
5   Gunsan
6   Gwangju
7   Haemi (Seosan)
8   Hoengseong (Wonju)
9   Jungwon (Chungju)
10 Pilseung range (heliport)
11 Sacheon
12 Seongmu
13 Seongnam
14 Suwon
15 Yecheon

KPAAF Air Bases
1   Ayang-ni (abandoned)
2   Banghyeon (Panghyon)
3   Bukchang (Pukchang)
4   Deoksan (Toksan)
5   Gaechon (Kaechon)
6   Gang Da-ri (Kang Da-ri)
7   Gangdong (Kangdong)
8   Geukdong (Kuktong)
9   Gilju-Kilju (Chaegung-Dong)
10 Goksan (Koksan)
11 Gueum-ni (Kuum-ni)
12 Gwail (Kwail)
13 Gwaksan (Kwaksan)
14 Hwangju
15 Hwangsuwon
16 Hyeon-ri (Hyon-ni)
17 Iwon (Riwon)
18 Jangjin (Changjin)

19 Manpo
20 Nuchon-ni
21 Oncheon (Onchon)
22 Onjeong (Onjong)
23 Orang
24 Pyongyang Heliport Facility
25 Pyongyang-Mirim
26 Pyongyang-Sunan
27 Samjiyeon (Samjiyon)
28 Seoncheon (Sonchon)
29 Seondeok (Sondok)
30 Seungam-ni (Sungam-ni)
31 Suncheon (Sunchon)
32 Taecheon (Taechon)
33 Taetan
34 Uiju
35 Wonsan-Galma (Wonsan-Kalma)
36 Yongpo-ri (Yonpo)

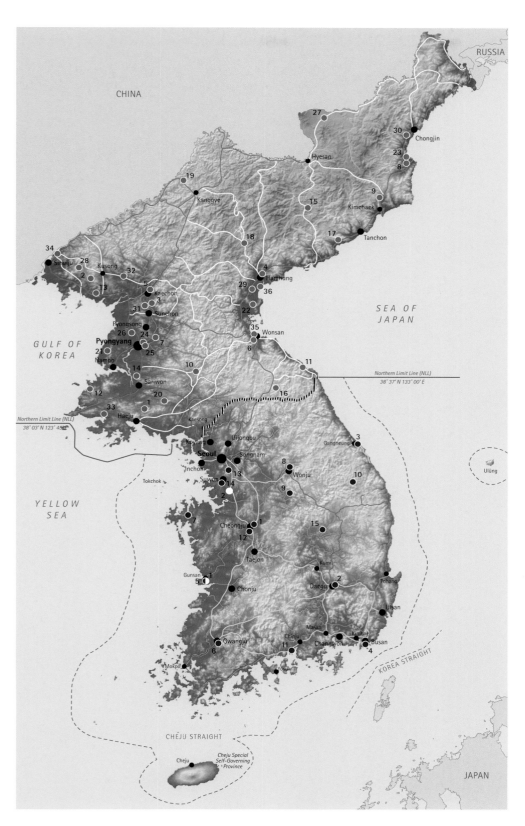

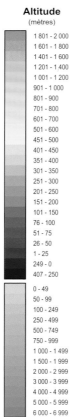

A physical map of Korea showing the air bases of the ROKAF, PACAF and KPAAF. (Map by James Lawrence)

ROKAF AIRCRAFT IN SERVICE

Both the ROKAF Super Pumas are often erroneously described as AS332L2 versions, although the five-bladed tail rotor and the shape of the aft fuselage easily identifies them as members of the AS332L/L1 family.
(Robin Polderman)

Aérospatiale AS332L1 Super Puma

To replace the Bell 412 in the presidential helicopter role the ROKAF ordered three Aérospatiale (now Airbus Helicopters) AS332L1 Super Puma helicopters for delivery in 1988. They served in this role until 1999, when the Super Pumas were completely replaced by the VH-60P. Allegedly the ROKAF deemed the entrance of the Super Puma located too high for use in the presidential transport role.

The AS332L1 is a civil version of the Super Puma with room for 19 seats. Currently the type still serves with the 235th SRS at Cheongju Air Base and is used to transport the defence minister and other high-ranking military officials.

One AS332L1 was written off on 14 March 2002 when it flew into a mountain in bad weather near Goesan, not far from home base Cheongju.

Airbus KC-330 Cygnus (A330-200 MRTT)

South Korea selected the A330 MRTT on 30 June 2015 as part of a deal with Airbus worth USD 1.3 billion. The other contenders for the bid were Boeing's KC-46A and a Boeing 767 conversion offered by Israel Aerospace Industries.

The first KC-330 Cygnus
produced for the ROKAF, serial
number 18-001, showing off its
refuelling boom during flight.
(ROK MND)

According to DAPA, the MRTT beat its rivals due to it being a proven aircraft that
is competitively priced, along with having superior performance regarding endurance,
fuel capacity and personnel- and cargo capacity.

With the acquisition of the A330 a long existing gap in strategic airlift capacity was
filled. The MRTT extends the operational radius of the ROKAF's fighter and surveillance aircraft to remote areas such as the Dokdo disputed islands, and above the North
Pyongyang-Wonsan line should the need arise. Additionally, having a strategic airlifter
available will increase South Korea's ability to deploy personnel overseas for peacekeeping operations and take part in other international support missions.

The first MRTT was delivered to Busan's Gimhae Air Base (which doubles as the
city's international airport) on 12 November 2018. After acceptance testing by a joint
ROKAF/Airbus team the aircraft was officially handed over on 30 January 2019.

A second A330 was received in March of the same year, with a third delivered during September, and the fourth and last following that December. The fleet of MRTT,
dubbed KC-330 Cygnus in ROKAF service, is a true European affair with the airframes
being built at Toulouse in France, modified to MRTT in Getafe, Spain and painted at
Manchester airport in the United Kingdom.

Shortly after achieving Initial Operating Capability (IOC) the Cygnus fleet was heavily utilised for overseas missions. In June 2020 a number of KC-330 flights were carried
out to the United Arab Emirates to support the rotation of the ROKA Akh unit, a special forces unit tasked with training elements of the UAE military since 2011.

During July 2020 a Cygnus flew to Hawaii to pick up the remains of 120 unidentified
Korean War veterans, while two KC-330s were dispatched to Iraq the same month to
evacuate South Korean citizens in the midst of the COVID-19 pandemic.

For self protection the fleet of KC-330 aircraft is equipped with the Northrop Grumman AN/AAQ-24(V) Nemesis Large Aircraft Infrared Countermeasures (LAIRCM) system using the AN/AA-54 warning system for infrared missiles as well as small turrets firing laser beams to confuse the incoming missile seeker head.

The ROKAF keeps the An-2 out of the limelight, although it has used the type since at least 1968. The small fleet currently flies in a scheme similar to that applied to the An-2 fleet of the northern neighbour.
(AV Kok)

Antonov/PZL-Mielec An-2

One of the most secretive aircraft within the ranks of the ROKAF, despite its age, is the venerable An-2 (ASCC Colt). The type has been in ROKAF use since 1968 with at least two in service during 1983.

At the end of the 1980s a Polish-built WSK PZL-Mielec An-2TD that had been used by Northrop for evaluation purposes vanished from the US civil register and apparently found its way to South Korea.

At least two additional An-2P aircraft, both former Polish Air Force and built in 1974, where exported to South Korea in late 2012.

Operating from the northern part of Seongmu Air Base the type entered the limelight when a widely reported crash occured on 4 May 2009. The aircraft came down in a vineyard near its home base and was destroyed by a post-crash fire after the crew had escaped safely. Another example was lost when it had to ditch in a river following failure of the Shvetsov ASh-62 radial engine on 25 June 2015. Again the crew managed to escape unscathed.

A third example was put down in a shallow river on 4 February 2016 after another suspected engine failure, but this aircraft appeared to have received minimal damage and is likely to have been salvaged and put back in service.

Within the ROKAF the An-2 is used as an OPFOR aircraft. Not just to train ROKAF fighter units, but also to harass ground based air defence units and even ROKA and/or ROKN units. During base exercises the An-2s were used to insert OPFOR paratroopers at low level and play the role of defecting North Korean aircraft. Additionally, the fleet is used to develop tactics to counter the KPA's large fleet of An-2 aircraft. The location of the An-2 squadron at Seongmu, a mere 11km (7 miles) away from the Cheongju-based aggressor and tactical development units, might not be entirely coincidental after all.

The type is also rumoured to be used for the clandestine insertion of ROK Special Forces into North Korea. Since the DPRK's air force has the An-2 in widespread use, its appearance in the skies over North Korea might not look or sound suspicious. However, the distance from the An-2 home base to the DMZ seems to be quite far making this scenario less likely.

Noteworthy is the fact that ROKAF An-2s were operating in a dark green colour with duck egg blue undersides, identical to the scheme used by the DPRK on its An-2 fleet. After the first pictures emerged in the early 2010s of DPRK An-2s carrying a new colour scheme consisting of dark green, medium green, and brown, it appears all ROKAF examples were resprayed in the exact same colours.

Ten different An-2s were noted in ROKAF service, while a recent Google Earth picture of Seongmu Air Base revealed seven of them lined up on the tarmac outside of their hangars.

Coincidentally the registrations used on the An-2 fleet, in the range of HL1082 through HL1090, are also used on Cessna 172S Skyhawk aircraft entered in South Korea's civil aviation register.

Within the ROKAF, the aircraft is designated both L-2 and T-11 and is flown by pilots who are Non-Commissioned Officers (NCO).

Initially the squadron operating the fleet of An-2 aircraft was simply dubbed 'Colt squadron' and was part of the 25th Flying Group. Since 2010, the squadron is known as

All three Bell 412 helicopters delivered to the ROKAF are still in use today. Two of them are seen parked inside one of the open hangars at Cheongju Air Base.
(ROK MND)

The sole Boeing 737 in use with the ROKAF was delivered during 1985 and continues to provide sterling service from its home base of Seongnam.
(Jamie Chang)

208th Squadron and forms part of the 28th Flight Group. Reportedly, the unit takes its orders from the Republic of Korea Defense Intelligence Command (KDIC).

Bell 412

The Republic of Korea has been an avid user of the Bell Huey family since 1968, when it received six UH-1D helicopters under the Military Assistance Program. Additional second-hand Bell 204B helicopters from the United States were received during 1976. These were followed by examples from the Bell 205 and Bell 212 family, with the Bell 212 having two engines as opposed to the single engine earlier variants. Development of an upgraded version featuring a four-bladed main rotor started in the late 1970s, and this variant was dubbed the Bell 412. Three examples of this helicopter were acquired during 1982, shortly after the type had received its certification and Bell Helicopter started mass production of this variant.

Between 1982 and 1988, the Bell 412s were in use to provide local transportation for Korea's President until replaced by the AS332L1 Super Puma helicopter. For their VIP role the helicopters were painted in a blue and white colour scheme which they still wear today.

The type currently forms part of the 235th SRS at Cheongju Air Base and is mainly in use as a training helicopter.

Boeing 737-300

In order not to be dependent on the Korean civil airlines network to transport the president overseas, the ROKAF decided to purchase a Boeing 737-300.

The aircraft was built at Boeing's Renton factory in Washington state and fitted out with a VIP interior. It was delivered on 15 August 1985 and continues to serve the South Korean president today, although long haul flights have now been taken over by a leased Boeing 747.

On 13 June 2000, the Boeing 737 made history when it became the first ROKAF aircraft to land in North Korea after it touched down at Pyongyang's Sunan International Airport with then President Kim Dae-jung onboard.

The aircraft forms part of the 257th Airlift Squadron and is based at Seoul's Seongnam Air Base.

Boeing 747

The Boeing 737 in use as Presidential aircraft since 1985 lacked in range when overseas trips are concerned. Since 1980, the Korean President has relied on Korean Air Lines to carry himself and his entourage on medium to long-range trips, using a wide variety of aircraft including the Airbus 300, Boeing 707/747/777 and McDonnell Douglas DC-10.

After the ROKAF issued a request for proposals during 2010, both Boeing and EADS made an offer, with the latter company withdrawing from the competition shortly thereafter. Eventually Boeing's offer for an executive 747-8 airliner costing over USD 300 million was not taken up, and the ROKAF started looking elsewhere for a cheaper alternative.

In March 2015 the ROKAF signed a five-year, 141 billion Won (USD 114 million) deal with Korean Air to lease one of their Boeing 747-400 aircraft for use as Air Force One (dubbed Code-One in ROKAF parlance). The Boeing 747-4B5 which was chosen, flew with civil registration HL7465 before joining the ranks of the ROKAF. The lease period has been extended until October 2021 as the government failed to find a new contractor in time.

On 29 May 2020 South Korea signed a five-year contract with Korean Air Lines to lease a Boeing 747-8i jet as the next presidential plane.

Under the 300 billion won (USD 242 million) deal, the airline will provide pilots, cabin crew and maintenance staff. The contract, starting in November 2021, also stipulates the availability of a back-up plane of the same type for the president's overseas trips.

The selected aircraft, registered HL7643 in Korean Air service, has undergone conversion to presidential transport by the VIP & Special Mission Aircraft Division of Lufthansa Technik at Hamburg Airport, where it arrived on 1 March 2021.

The Boeing 747-8i will be equipped with various security and communication devices, as well as a missile detection and countermeasures system, before joining the 257th Squadron.

Boeing E-737 Peace Eye

South Korea had long recognised the need to improve its surveillance capability, not only for monitoring a possible move from its northern neighbour, but also for keeping tabs on the KADIZ. An advance in Command and Control capability increases the ROKAF's self-reliance and eases the burden on the USAF E-3 Sentry fleet based at Kadena Air Base in Okinawa, Japan, normally used to assist Korea in monitoring its airspace.

Formerly registered HL7465 with Korean Air, the current livery worn by the largest aircraft in use with the ROKAF clearly identifies its role as VIP transport.
(Jamie Chang)

Back in 1996 the country launched the E-X programme to evaluate and eventually acquire the best possible AEW&C solution for South Korea.

It would take until 7 November 2006 before South Korea signed a USD 1.6 billion contract with Boeing for the delivery of four E-737 aircraft by 2012. Boeing's competitor for the contract, Israeli company IAI Elta offering an AEW&C aircraft based on the Gulfstream G550, was eliminated from the competition during August 2006.

Included with the contract was a full complement of flight and mission training systems, as well as mission support.

Boeing's E-737 is based on a 737-700 Increased Gross Weight (IGW) airframe equipped with Northrop Grumman's MESA (Multi-Role Electronically Scanned Array) 360-degree surveillance radar and its associated systems. The MESA radar, mounted in a dorsal fin on top of the aircraft, can be operated as the aircraft reaches an altitude of 5,000ft (1,524m) right up to a service ceiling of 41,000ft (12,497m). Compared to older AEW&C aircraft, which normally operate around 25,000ft (7,620m), the higher ceiling provides a 20 to 50 per cent increase in range and line-of-sight advantage against low-flying missiles and aircraft in various terrains. This significantly enhances early warning and reaction times. An added advantage of this type of radar is its capability to detect and track maritime targets.

Maximum range of the radar is quoted as being in excess of 200nm (370km) and it is able to track 1,000 airborne and/or surface targets simultaneously. Alledgedly, even North Korea's An-2 fleet with its wooden propellers and canvas-covered wings can not hide from the MESA radar.

For the ROKAF, operating its own fleet of AEW&C aircraft had been a long-standing ambition. The four E-737s were received in 2011 and 2012, with the aircraft pictured being the last example to be delivered. (Jamie Chang)

Additionally, the E-737 functions as a back-up radar system in case ground-based control radars are incapacitated.

Following a naming contest held in 2008, the ROKAF decided to name its E-737 aircraft as Peace Eye, reflecting the aircraft's role in keeping watch over the Korean peninsula.

As part of both the transfer of technology agreement and the offset programme, engineers from KAI worked on the project in Boeing's Seattle facility from 2009 onwards.

The first aircraft was delivered to Gimhae Air Base, which doubles as Busan's international airport, for acceptance tests on 1 August 2011.

On 13 December 2011 the second aircraft was handed over to the ROKAF, after modification into an AEW&C configuration by KAI at Sacheon. The third aircraft followed suit on 17 May 2012 with the fourth and final E-737 arriving in Busan on 24 October 2012.

To operate the fleet of Peace Eye aircraft, the 51st Air Control Group was established on 28 October 2010.

Following an evaluation, the ROKAF concluded its current fleet of four Peace Eye aircraft is inadequate for the missions it needs to perform. When maintenance is figured in, an average of two aircraft could be available at any time. With Korea being surrounded by sea on three sides and an unpredictable neighbour to the north, choices need to be made where exactly the aircraft will patrol.

Two General Electric-powered F-15Ks, carrying Sniper targeting pods, photographed low over the Korean coast. (ROKAF)

The E-737 Peace Eye is capable of flying 11-hour missions and has two pilots and six to ten crew members on board. Korea has the desire to expand its AEW&C coverage, and therefore purchase more aircraft.

A decision on a possible acquisition is not expected before 2022.

Boeing F-15K Slam Eagle

In the mid-1990s Korea initiated its F-X Next Fighter programme to evaluate and acquire 120 modern fighter aircraft to ensure the ROKAF's viability into the coming decades. The programme was divided into multiple phases, and all new aircraft had to be in service by 2020 to replace variants of the outdated F-4 Phantom. Phase I of the programme would see the purchase of 40 aircraft with initial deliveries set for 2002.

During 1996 the Russian firm KnAAPO offered the Su-35 (ASCC Flanker-E) to the ROKAF. The aircraft would be equipped with the AL-31FP thrust vectoring engines and the Russians would commit to a full transfer of technology with assembly of the aircraft to take place in South Korea. The USD 5 billion contract would be partially written off against Russia's outstanding debts with South Korea.

The two seat Su-30MK (ASCC Flanker-C) prototype, along with a single-seat Su-27, made the journey to South Korea and was put through its paces at the October 1996 Seoul airshow by a KnAAPO demonstration pilot. After the airshow the Su-30MK relocated to Cheongju Air Base where four different ROKAF pilots flew backseat during a 10-day evaluation period. The Russians even proposed to pit the aircraft against the F-5 and F-16 in mock dogfights, but this was kindly refused by the Korean side.

The ROKAF F-X Evaluation Group, consisiting of 12 pilots and engineers, visited Warton (UK), Turin (Italy) and Getafe (Spain) to evaluate the Eurofighter Typhoon. Their December 2000 visit saw the commander of the FX Evaluation Group, Brig Gen Shin Bo Hyun, take to the air in the Getafe-based two seat Eurofighter prototype for an evaluation flight. In doing so he became the first non-European pilot to fly the Eurofighter Typhoon.

Dassault Aviation pitched its Rafale fighter for the F-X programme. The portfolio of industrial cooperation and technology transfer proposed to Korea by Dassault, was one of the largest and most comprehensive packages ever proposed in this field, reaching 70 per cent of the total cost of the F-X programme. The Rafale was demonstrated to the ROKAF during three consecutive editions of the Seoul airshow, the last evaluation taking place during 2001.

The ROKAF started the evaluation of the F-15E during 14 flights from Elmendorf Air Force Base, Alaska, using a fleet of three Strike Eagles which manufacturer Boeing had leased from the USAF. Flown by USAF pilots of the 90th Fighter Squadron with their Korean counterparts in the backseat, the flights took place in October 2000.

In the end, the Boeing F-15 Eagle beat off challenges from the other three contenders and the ROKAF announced in 2002 it had ordered 40 examples of the F-15K, dubbed Slam Eagle, in a contract worth USD 3.6 billion.

The Slam Eagle is equipped with the Raytheon AN/APG-63(V)1, a reliable combat radar with new search and target detection capabilities and 10 times more computing power than earlier versions used in the F-15. The Honeywell Advanced Display Core Processor of the F-15K enables the aircraft's computer system to process target data faster, display better information to the crew, and control more advanced weaponry. It uses less power than the central computer in the USAF's F-15E Strike Eagle and comes at half the weight and cost.

The Lockheed Martin ALR-56 RWR and Northrop Grumman ALQ-135M high-power jammer, work together to enhance survivability of the F-15K Slam Eagle in hostile skies.

The F-15K is able to carry an array of air-to-ground weapons, including the state-of-the-art TAURUS KEPD-350K and AGM-84H SLAM-ER stand-off cruise missiles, along with various GPS and laser-guided bombs.

In December 2004, eight Korean pilots and WSOs arrived at Seymour Johnson AFB, NC to start their conversion to the F-15. They remained in North Carolina until July of the following year.

On 16 March 2005 Boeing unveiled the premier F-15K Slam Eagle during a ceremony at its plant in St. Louis, Missouri, while a pair of Slam Eagles were shown to the Korean public for the first time at the October 2005 Seoul airshow. A formal induction ceremony for the type was held at Daegu air base on 12 December 2005.

Tragedy struck on 7 June 2006, when during a nighttime training flight an F-15K and its crew were lost in the Yellow Sea off the coast of Pohang, in the southeast of Korea.

Since the crew were experienced aviators, the ROKAF suspected a problem with either the aircraft or its engines caused the crash, and announced this would possibly lead to a reconsideration of the deal to purchase all 40 aircraft. Despite the outcome of the investigation, which blamed G-LOC as the cause of the accident and not the

Should any ROKAF pilot get into trouble and have to abandon their aircraft, the chances are they will be picked up by one of the five long-range HH-47 Chinooks in ROKAF service. (ROKAF)

aircraft or engines, Boeing offered to include an extra F-15K in its bid for the second phase of the F-X programme.

To allow retirement of the last of its F-5A/B Freedom fighters, 20 new jets were needed. The ROKAF initially considered the F-35A, but as this aircraft was not operational yet and too expensive the idea was dropped. As the sole bidder, Boeing won the F-X Phase II contract for a further 21 F-15Ks in April 2008.

The first 40 F-15K Slam Eagles are powered by two General Electric F110 turbofan engines, each developing 29,000lb (13,155kg) of thrust, making it the first time the F110 was used in a twin-engine aircraft. The 21 aircraft procured under the Next Fighter II programme, are equipped with two Pratt & Whitney F-100-PW-229 engines with each engine providing a thrust of 29,100lb (13,200kg). The P&W engines were chosen since these are built under licence by Samsung Techwin and provide commonality with the ROKAF F-16 fleet.

The first three F-15Ks of the new batch, arrived at Daegu Air Base early in the morning of 8 September 2010 after stop-overs in Hawaii and Guam. The last was delivered on 2 April 2012.

On 21 July 2010, while preparing for take off and already on the runway at Daegu Air Base, the backseater of an F-15K accidentally ejected. Repair and replacement of canopy, ejection seat, and parts of the rear cockpit set the ROKAF back USD 12 million.

Following the loss of a second F-15K on 5 April 2018, a total of 59 Slam Eagles remain in use with the three squadrons of the 11th FW at Daegu, and are expected to serve until 2040 at least. The General Electric-powered F-15Ks fly with the 102nd and 122nd FS, while the 110th FS uses the Slam Eagles with the Pratt & Whitney engines.

Boeing CH-47NE and HH-47D Chinook

On 31 December 1991 the ROKAF took delivery of its first pair of HH-47D Chinook helicopters. These were followed by four more in the spring of 1992.

The HH-47D is a specialised, extended-range version of the CH-47D with enlarged fuel tanks and nose-mounted radar. The external rescue hoist, as used on the MH-47 helicopter of the US Army, is also installed above the forward entry door.

Compared to the HH-60G, the HH-47D offers higher speed, more range, and more capacity to evacuate wounded or stranded personnel during CSAR missions. Capability of the HH-47Ds was enhanced during 2006 when they received a nose-mounted FLIR-turret at KAI's Sacheon facility. A Pilot Locator System, provided in kit-form by Israeli company SGD Engineering, was installed in Korea.

In December 2013 the DSCA announced the sale of 14 second-hand CH-47D helicopters to Korea for USD 151 million. These helicopters were stationed at US Army base Camp Humphreys in Korea, and handed over in-country hereby saving nearly USD 14 million in transportation costs.

Since these helicopters have the Honeywell T55-GA-714 engines installed instead of the T55-GA-712 which are standard on the CH-47D, the ROKAF designated their second-hand Chinooks as CH-47NE.

One of five former US Army Chinooks transferred to the ROKAF, CH-47NE serial number 88-095 was one of the first to appear in an overall grey colour scheme.
(Robin Polderman)

The international trend of painting military aircraft grey has also reached the ROKAF. The first CN235 carrying an overall medium grey colour scheme was photographed during April 2021. (YoungKyun Shin)

Five were transferred to the ROKAF and in recent years all CH-47NEs and HH-47Ds received a uniform overall grey colour scheme. During a ceremony at Cheongju air base on 2 March 2016, the 231st SRS was established to operate the CH-47/HH-47 fleet independently from other assets.

The CH-47NE can be equipped with the ERFS II (Extended Range Fuel System), which consists of three crashworthy tanks with a capacity of 800 gallons of fuel each. The system increases the range of the helicopter and makes it suitable to be used as a Forward Area Refuelling Point (FARP).

A plan launched as far ago as 2007 called for the upgrade of the ROKAF and ROKA fleet of Chinooks to CH-47F-standard, incorporating stronger engines, a glass cockpit and upgraded navigation- and communications equipment. At least four feasibility studies were undertaken over the years but no results were achieved. DAPA claims differences regarding the execution of the plan, incorporation of Korean-made equipment and the number of helicopters to be updated were not overcome.

'*It is a chronic problem of most arms introduction projects in Korea that major decision making is overturned several times and the project advancement is prolonged,*' top DAPA official Min Hong-cheol was quoted as saying.

The fleet of five surviving HH-47Ds is currently running close to 30 years old while the ex-US Army CH-47NEs, being rebuilt CH-47C airframes, are over 50.

Their age is reflected in their serviceability: only 41 per cent availability was reached in the first half of 2020.

CASA/IPTN CN235M-100/220 and VCN235M-220

To replace the last of their C-123 Providers the ROKAF signed a contract with the Spanish CASA (now Airbus) factory for 12 CN235M-100 aircraft on 19 August 1992. First deliveries, routing via Hong Kong, were made on 12 January 1994 with the last one arriving only three months later.

In October of 1997 the ROKAF signed a USD 130 million contract for an additional eight CN235M-220 aircraft, to be built by IPTN of Indonesia. The 220 subseries of the CN235 has slight aerodynamic improvements increasing range and structural reinforcements to cater for higher operating weights.

Six standard transports were delivered between December 2001 and April 2002, while two aircraft equipped for the VIP mission, with a luxury interior and improved communications suite, arrived in December 2002. These are dubbed VCN235M by the ROKAF.

The 20-strong CN235 fleet was updated with an Israeli designed airborne electronic warfare suite, missile warning system and cockpit ballistic protection during 2011, following the signing of a USD 29 million contract.

To make room for the incoming fleet of KC-330 and E-737 aircraft at Gimhae, 256 Airlift Squadron and its eight CN235 aircraft relocated to Seoul's Seongnam Air Base during 2016.

A VIP-configured VCN235M aircraft lines up for take off while a standard CN235 awaits its turn. Both aircraft belong to Seongnam-based units, the 257th and 256th Airlift Squadrons, respectively. (SangYeon Kim)

RC-2000 Baekdu (Dassault Falcon 2000S)

To augment the fleet of RC-800 aircraft, the ROKAF purchased two Falcon 2000S aircraft in a contract signed in December 2011. The aircraft were built in 2013 and 2014 respectively, and ferried to the United States from France.

According to DAPA, the first RC-2000 commenced flight testing from Waco, Texas in April 2016. The tests were intended to examine the operability of the aircraft with internal mission equipment in development by Korean manufacturers. US company L-3 Communications Integrated Systems provided the technology to integrate the Korean-built electronics into the aircraft's central mission computer.

Both Hanhwa Systems and LIG Nex1 collaborated with Korea's National Defense Science Institute to develop equipment for the RC-2000. The datalink was provided by Hanwha Systems while LIG Nex1 supplied a communications monitoring system, a long-range EO/IR imaging system and FISINT equipment. The latter is able to pick up metric data from missiles, or signals transmitted between equipment. A Korean publication has stated the electronic signal of a launch button being pushed by North Korean leadership would be picked up by the systems onboard the RC-2000, although this seems a bold claim to make.

In the case of missile launches, the RC-2000 has a main signal detection range of 370km (230 miles) across the peninsula, enough to monitor the DPRK's Tonchangryong missile range, and the Yeongchang nuclear facility, from South Korean airspace. The EO/IR imaging system can even see the flames emitted by the North Korean missile engines.

After the delivery of an initial two examples of the RC-2000, the chances are high another four will enter service with the ROKAF. The type is needed to replace the RC-800, as these airframes become older and harder to maintain.
(Jamie Chang)

The veteran Hawker Siddeley HS.748 still soldiers on with the 256th Airlift Squadron at Seongnam Air Base, its VIP tasks having been taken over by the VCN235M.
(Robin Polderman)

The first RC-2000 arrived in Korea in October 2016. The second example was outfitted by KAL-FSD at its Busan facility and both aircraft were believed to be operational by 2017.

Hawker Siddeley HS.748

Two Hawker Siddeley HS.748 Series 2As were ordered in the early 1970s and delivered in the summer of 1975. The HS.748 was designed by the British company Avro as a DC-3 replacement, before the company was absorbed into Hawker Siddeley during 1963. The HS.748 design stems from the late 1950s, and the aircraft is powered by a pair of Rolls Royce Dart turboprop engines.

Both aircraft delivered were used in the Presidential transport role with the 257th Airlift Squadron until replaced by a pair of VCN235M aircraft. Currently, both examples soldier on with the 256th Airlift Squadron at Seongnam Air Base near Seoul, primarily in a training role.

IAI Harpy

Produced by Israel Aerospace Industries (IAI), the Harpy is an autonomous, loitering, fire-and-forget UAV which was specifically designed to attack radar systems.

The Israelis realised the potential of such an aircraft following its experience during the Lebanon War of 1982. Drones were used to bait Syrian SAM sites to switch on

their radar, after which these radars were targeted by manned aircraft in a SEAD role, requiring a costly aircraft and its crew to get in harm's way. The IDF realised that having an unmanned aircraft do the anti-radar job, migitated the risk for both crew as well as aircraft, and development of a dedicated SEAD UAV was initiated.

The Harpy is propeller-driven and has a low radar cross section, making it hard to detect for the enemy. Its small size – 6ft 11in (2.1m) in wingspan and 8ft 10in (2.7m) in length – helps in staying undetected. It is launched from a mobile transporter by means of a small rocket, and once airborne will not be recovered for further use.

Harpy has a communications range of around 200 km (440lb) and can stay airborne for between two to five hours, using its radar frequency seeker to scan the battlefield for enemy radar systems. This means the UAV is not dependent on real-time intelligence, but can find, identify and attack its targets within an assigned killbox. It will dive into its objective vertically and detonate a 70lb (32kg) warhead in order to shut the radar down permanently. The accuracy of the Harpy has been quoted as around 3.3ft (1m), making it more accurate than an air-launched anti radiation missile and considerably more than an artillery strike.

The fact that this aircraft can attack targets autonomously without a human in control, has raised questions about accountability and laws of armed conflict. This international discussion is still ongoing.

The ROKAF received its first Harpy system during 1999, and used them to equip the 288th EWS, which was established at Wonju-Hoengseong air base in the northern part of the country on 1 July 1999.

KAI KA-1

Following the success of the KT-1, KAI decided to develop the aircraft into an armed close-air-support (CAS), counter-insurgency (COIN) and battlefield reconnaissance platform in order to secure a ROKAF order for the replacement of the Cessna O-2 Skymaster. In November 2003, KAI was given the green light to produce 20 examples of the KO-1 for ROKAF service. To better reflect its role, the designation was changed to KA-1 in 2009.

The KA-1 received a HUD and UFCP to provide the pilot with better situational awareness. The cockpit was equipped with Multi-Function Displays for management of the weapon load on the four underwing hardpoints. Ordnance cleared for use on the

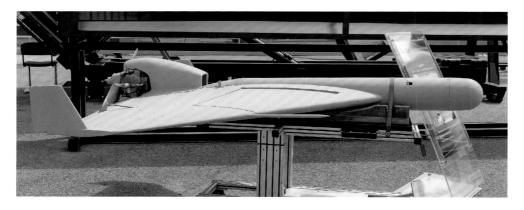

Based at Hoengseong Air Base, not far from the border with North Korea, a single ROKAF squadron has used the IAI Harpy since 1999.
(Archive Robin Polderman)

The KA-1 is basically a KT-1 aircraft modified to perform a light attack role. Twenty are in use within a single squadron at Hoengseong, with this example carrying external fuel tanks and 2.75in (70mm) rocket pods. (ROK MND)

KA-1 are the LAU-131/A 2.75in (70mm) rocket launcher, and the FN Herstal HMP-250 0.5in (12.7mm) gun pod. To extend its range it is able to carry two 415lb (188 litres) external fuel tanks on two of the hardpoints. For identification purposes the KA-1 is equipped with IFF, while it relies on an INS/GPS system for navigation.

On 31 December 2020, KAI received a contract to integrate the Korean-developed Link-K datalink system to to the fleet of KA-1 aircraft. Link-K was developed as an alternative to the US Link-16 system, which is heavily dependent on US restrictions.

The 237th squadron took delivery of the first of 20 KA-1s at Seongnam Air Base during 2005, and relocated to Hoengseong Air Base near Wonju in December 2012.

KAI KT-1

Daewoo Heavy Industries (which would absorb into Korean Aerospace Industries), in cooperation with the Agency for Defense Development, started work on an indigenous training aircraft during 1988. The programme was named KTX-1 (Korean Trainer Experimental), and the new aircraft was developed to provide the ROKAF with a modern basic training aircraft to replace the Cessna T-37C in service at the time. An agreement had been signed with Pilatus aircraft for technical assistance, but with that company wanting to push its PC-9 concept while Korea insisted on a new design, the partnership ended.

Daewoo Heavy Industries utilised CATIA (Computer-Aided Three-dimensional Interactive Application), a 3D design programme by Dassault Systèmes that was not

The southern air base of Sacheon houses all the 84 remaining KT-1 trainers of the ROKAF.
(Robin Polderman)

yet common at the time, making KTX the first trainer aircraft to be developed using this technology.

The maiden flight of the KTX-1 Yeo-Myeong (meaning 'dawn' in Korean) took place on 12 December 1991 at KAI's home base of Sacheon, piloted by Major Lee Jin-ho, a fresh graduate of the Empire Test Pilot School. A total of five prototypes were built and these completed a rigorous flight test programme. During a ceremony on 28 November 1995, the KT-1 received the name 'Woongbi', which loosely translates as 'a great leap', reflecting the fact it is the first completely indigenous Korean aircraft ever developed.

First deliveries of the production version were made during 2000, with all 85 ordered in service during autumn 2003. The aircraft is powered by the ubiquitous Pratt & Whitney Canada PT6A turboprop engine flat-rated at 950hp, which drives a four-bladed Hartzell propeller. The aircraft is equipped with GPS/INS, TACAN and VOR/ILS navigation systems, while the pilots sit on Martin Baker's Mk 16 zero-zero ejection seat also used on the USAF Beechcraft T-6 Texan II fleet. Compared with the T-37C it replaces, the KT-1 achieved a 70 per cent reduction in fuel cost.

All aircraft are painted in a highly conspicuous colour scheme of white with orange and red accents, and serve with the four training squadrons of the 3rd FTW at Sacheon Air Base.

The Air Force Academy has made uses of the KAI KT-100, a military version of the KC-100, since 2016. The introduction of the type allowed the retirement of the Il-103 in May 2018. (AV Kok)

KAI KT-100

On 15 May 2014, DAPA signed a memorandum of understanding with KAI to obtain 23 examples of the KC-100 Naraon light aircraft to replace the fleet of 22 remaining Ilyushin Il-103 trainers.

Development of the Naraon started in 2008, and the prototype performed its maiden flight on 15 July 2011. The KC-100 is a four-seater aircraft powered by a modern Continental TSIOF-550-K FADEC engine, producing 315shp.

The KT-100 is the military version of the KC-100, and in use with the ROKAF Air Force Academy as a flight introductory course trainer. The digital cockpit is equipped with an audio- and video recording system to enhance debrief after the training flight.

The KT-100 has the Privacy ICAO Address (PIA) system installed. This equipment prevents real-time tracking of the geographic location of the training aircraft by non-government entities. For identification purposes the small aircraft is equipped with IFF.

On 11 May 2016, an event was held at Seongmu Air Base to celebrate the arrival of the first two KT-100 aircraft for the Air Force Academy. By the end of that year all 23 had been delivered.

KAI T-50 and T-50B Golden Eagle

Following its experience with the licence-production of the F-16 Fighting Falcon, the Korean aviation industry wanted to put this experience to good use. It had a long

The ROKAF Black Eagles aerobatic team also adopted the T-50 Golden Eagle, and provides a useful promotional tool for the type.
(ROKAF/SMSgt Kwon Hyung)

standing need for a decent advanced trainer that could be further developed into a LIFT and light-attack aircraft, to replace the fleet of older aircraft in use. Preliminary work on the KTX-2 project started in the early 1990s, but the financial crisis that hit Asia in the mid-1990s delayed the project somewhat.

During the summer of 1997, Samsung and Lockheed Martin signed an agreement on the joint development and production of the new aircraft, which saw Lockheed Martin take a 13 per cent share in the development costs, while 70 per cent would be covered by the Korean government. In addition, the US company would provide assistance with the worldwide marketing efforts for the aircraft.

With Lockheed Martin closely involved in the design process, and Korea's experience building the F-16 in mind, it comes as no surprise the KTX-2 design resembles the F-16 in certain areas. The wings, horizontal tails and aft fuselage bear a strong resemblance to the F-16. The KTX-2 features a triple-redundant, digital fly-by-wire flight control system and has an onboard oxygen generating system.

As the aircraft was developed as a pure flight trainer, the decision was made not to equip it with radar.

Seen while turning finals for Gwangju Air Base, this T-50 from the 1st FW is equipped with a centreline fuel tank to extend its range.
(Robin Polderman)

For propulsion the General Electric F404-102 engine was selected, and Samsung Techwin (currently Hanwha Aerospace) obtained a licence to manufacture the engine in Korea.

In late 1999 a public contest was held to find an appropriate name for the aircraft. During the February 2000 Asian Aerospace tradeshow in Singapore, KAI revealed it had chosen the name Golden Eagle. The new trainer would be designated T-50 to commemorate the 50th anniversary of the ROKAF, and the first prototype was unveiled during a ceremony at Sacheon on 13 October 2001.

The prototype performed its maiden flight from Sacheon Air Base on 20 August 2002 with KAI test pilot Hui Man Kwon at the controls . The flight made the Republic of Korea the 12th country in the world to develop and fly a supersonic jet trainer.

A total of four flying prototypes were eventually constructed for a development program consisting of 1,146 scheduled test flights. The first prototype was mainly used to expand the flight envelope and evaluate stability as well as control- and handling qualities, while the second prototype has been used for air loads and high angle-of-attack testing.

The third and fourth prototypes were built with the TA-50 LIFT (Lead-In Fighter Training) in mind, and were equipped with a 20mm gun. The third prototype was used to evaluate the aircraft's avionics while the fourth was used for radar and weapon testflights. Two static test vehicles were also built for structural and ground trials, with durability testing commencing on 22 July 2002.

The first production T-50 for the ROKAF was rolled out at Sacheon on 30 August 2005, and was delivered in October of the same year, while the 50th T-50 for Korea was handed over on 13 May 2010.

The type currently equips two training squadrons with the 1st FW at Gwangju Air Base. Following the loss of one T-50 on 28 August 2013, a total of 49 examples remain in use. The introduction of the T-50 allowed the retirement of the fleet of T-38 Talons, that had been leased from the USAF as an interim solution.

On the production line at Sacheon, the T-50 was followed by the T-50B. Ten aircraft were ordered to replace the A-37B of the Black Eagles aerial demonstration team. The T-50B has an internal smoke system installed, consisting of two oil tanks with a combined capacity of 70 gallons (265 litres), pumps, and necessary piping. Oil is misted into the jet exhaust and immediately oxidises, creating smoke. The seperate oil tanks allow for two different colours of smoke to be displayed. The system is voice controlled by the pilot in the front cockpit. A smoke indication light and remaining oil indicator were added to the cockpit, to aid in controlling the smoke display during the airshows. The T-50B also has four internal and one external camera installed to record in-flight footage, and the jet is equipped with extra spotlights in the wingtip dummy Sidewinders for better visibility. The first aerobatic T-50Bs were handed over to the Black Eagles during March 2010, with the last example arriving in January 2011. Following a maintenance-related crash during 2012, which claimed the life of a Black Eagles pilot, an additional two T-50Bs were ordered. They were delivered to the team during 2016.

The fleet of TA-50 aircraft stationed at Yecheon Air Base is used to provide prospect fighter pilots with lead-in fighter training. More TA-50s are on order.
(Robin Polderman)

Sidewinder-armed FA-50s were used for combat air patrols during the 2018 PyeongChang Olympic Winter Games. (ROKAF)

KAI TA-50

In order to provide future ROKAF fighter pilots with an aircraft to conduct air-to-air and air-to-ground training missions at an acceptable cost, KAI developed the T-50 into the TA-50 LIFT. KAI had recognised the fact student pilots needed to convert to the BAe Hawk LIFT after graduating from flight training using the T-38 Talon. Since the T-50 and TA-50 have almost identical cockpits and flight characteristics, expensive flight hours are saved due to a much faster conversion.

For its role the aircraft received a three-barreled General Dynamics M197 20mm gun, a development of the well-known M61A2 gun, in the left hand strake area.

The US-built AN/APG-67 pulse-Doppler radar was tested in the T-50 LIFT prototype but eventually KAI decided to install the Israeli Elta EL/M2032 radar, which has a range of 120nm (222km) compared to the 70nm (130km) of the American radar system. In 2009, a contract was signed between IAI Elta Systems and Korean company LIG Nex1 for production and further development of the radar.

The TA-50 could be employed as a light combat aircraft and is able to carry the AIM-9L Sidewinder for self defence on wingtip-mounted launchers. The four pylons under its wings can be used to mount a variety of air-to-ground weapons including the AGM-65 Maverick guided missile. A stores management system combined with a MIL-STD-1553 databus allows these weapons to be integrated on the aircraft.

An order for 22 TA-50s was placed in the mid-2000s and the type was used to replace the T-59 Hawk in the LIFT-role at Yecheon's 16th FW. A ceremony for the introduction of the TA-50 was held there on 27 July 2012.

The first FA-50 built for the ROKAF, serial number 13-001, on short finals. The type equips three squadrons; the 103rd and 203rd FS at Hoengseong and the 202nd FS at Yecheon. (Robin Polderman)

On 28 June 2020, DAPA announced a follow-on order for 20 TA-50 Block II aircraft had been placed, with delivery foreseen by 2024. The Block II version is essentially an FA-50 aircraft without the Link-16 transponder system. Reportedly, the introduction of an advanced version of the TA-50 will free up KF-16C/D aircraft for combat roles, after the Fighting Falcons have been upgraded to KF-16V.

KAI FA-50

Further development of the TA-50 resulted in the FA-50 Light Combat Aircraft, aimed at replacing the A-37 and older F-5E/F aircraft in use with the ROKAF. The aircraft received a tactical datalink and an advanced self-protection system, consisting of a Radar Warning Receiver and chaff/flare dispenser to be able to survive over the battlefield. Externally the FA-50 is discernible from the TA-50 by the RWR mounted in the tip of its vertical tail.

As is the case with the TA-50, the IAI Elta Systems EL/M2032 radar was used for the FA-50. The aircraft's internal fuel capacity was expanded to allow for a greater combat range, rumoured to still be only 240nm (448km) with a full weaponload.

The FA-50, dubbed Fighting Eagle, is capable of carrying the same weapons as the TA-50, but has the added advantage of being able to employ precision guided munitions like the 500lb (227kg) GBU-38 JDAM and CBU-105 WCMD.

A contract for the production of the FA-50 was signed in December 2011, with the ROKAF subsequently receiving the first of 60 KAI FA-50 on 20 August 2013, when the

Although primarily used for search and rescue, the HH-32A has an important secondary role as aerial firefighter. The Simplex Aerospace Fire Attack system is attached to the bottom of this HH-32A, the helicopter wearing the new overal grey colour scheme.
(AV Kok)

103rd FS at Hoengseong Air Base took delivery of its first aircraft. Currently, a total of three squadrons operate the FA-50 from the air bases of Hoengseong and Yecheon.

With more and more of its F-4 and F-5 aircraft in the process of being withdrawn, the ROKAF would like the FA-50 to take on the role of these aircraft. An extension to both range and weapon capabilities was deemed highly desirable and a study to determine the details of an upgrade process was initiated in 2019. In connection with the upgrade, Lockheed Martin announced it had successfully tested the integration of the Sniper targeting pod with the FA-50 in October 2019. Further testing and related verification work was completed during the following year.

The British company Cobham was selected to develop and deliver an aerial refuelling system for the FA-50 in December 2020.

Kamov Ka-32A4 (HH-32A)

In 2002 South Korea agreed to accept Kamov Ka-32A4 search and rescue helicopters and Ilyushin Il-103 basic trainers as part of an arms deal to partially offset Russia's USD 2 billion outstanding debt. The Ka-32A4 is the dedicated civil search and rescue variant of the Soviet-era Ka-27 (ASCC Helix) ASW helicopter. The characteristic helicopter features a co-axial rotor system which eliminates the need for a horse-power robbing tailrotor.

The first of seven Kamovs, designated HH-32A in ROKAF service, was delivered on 22 June 2004 to the 235 SRS at Cheongju, replacing the Bell 212 and UH-1N. Before delivery, the helicopters were equipped with an IAI avionics systems package including

navigation systems, weather- and ground survey radar and a digital moving map display allowing them to operate at night and in adverse weather conditions.

As a secondary task the HH-32A can be used as a fire fighting helicopter when equipped with the Simplex Aerospace Model 328 Fire Attack system. This bolt-on package consists of a belly mounted carbon fiberglass tank which holds almost 790 gallons (3,000 litres) of water.

Due to its co-axial rotor, the ROKAF praises the stability of the helicopter in adverse weather and strong winds, while the poor fuel economy, along with a maintenance-intensive engine and other key components are a disadvantage.

On 8 October 2014, one HH-32A was heavily damaged in a non-fatal forced landing. During October 2019, Russian company Rostec offered an upgrade for the HH-32A, consisting of a glass cockpit, improved engines and a new firefighting system, but no contract has been signed to date. The 235th SRS maintains a detachment at the Pilseung range, operating two HH-32A helicopters.

Lockheed C-130H and MC-130K Hercules

In the early 1980s the ROKAF initiated a modernisation programme regarding its tactical airlift capacity. Initially four stretched C-130H-30 were ordered and delivered to South Korea with the first examples arriving on 9 January 1988 following a test and training programme in the United States.

A rather weathered-looking C-130H takes off from Seongnam Air Base. As the MC-130K and CN235 have been seen wearing an overall grey colour scheme after depot maintenance, it is likely the C-130H fleet will follow suit. (Robin Polderman)

In spring 2014, the ROKAF took delivery of four C-130J-30 transports. They serve alongside the C-130H with the 251st Airlift Squadron, which was established on 11 January 1988. (Robin Polderman)

These were followed by eight standard C-130H aircraft handed over to the ROKAF between October of 1989 and March of 1990.

On 24 June 2012 Elbit Systems announced it had been awarded a USD 62 million contract to upgrade the fleet of C-130H and C-130H-30 aircraft. Under the four-year contract the aircraft received advanced electronics and a glass cockpit with Elbit Systems' digital flight displays.

The Israeli company upgraded the 12 C-130 Hercules in close cooperation with Korea Aerospace Industries Ltd. (KAI).

SGD Engineering provided the self-defence suite for the C-130 aircraft, including the ALR-69 RWR, a missile approach warning system and a new countermeasures dispenser system mounted above the main landing-gear wheel bay.

In order to allow its special forces to infiltrate North Korea's nuclear or missile facilities at night or in bad weather it was decided to upgrade three C-130H aircraft for that special role. In the past, South Korea depended on the US military for support of such aircraft.

The upgrade included installation of an EO/IR turret, High Speed Low Level Air Drop Systems (HSSLADS), Multi Role Radar (MMR), SATCOM and DIRCM. The ROKAF decided to designate the aircraft MC-130K and all three are based at Seongnam with the 255th SOS.

Lockheed Martin C-130J-30 Hercules

Three standard C-130Hs were modified as special forces aircraft and were given the local designation MC-130K. They were painted in this grey colour scheme during 2021.
(Jamie Chang)

As part of the Large Transport Aircraft Procurement Program, DAPA sought funding to buy up to 10 transport aircraft for the ROKAF during the late 2000s. Due to budget constraints, only four Lockheed Martin C-130J-30s, the stretched fuselage variant of the Super Hercules, were ordered along with a two-year support package comprising aircrew and maintenance training in December 2010.

The first example took to the skies on 14 August 2013 from Lockheed Martin's Marrieta, Georgia facility, and was delivered to South Korea in April 2014, along with the second aircraft ordered.

The two remaining C-130J-30s arrived for service with the 251st Airlift Squadron at Busan-Gimhae air base on 31 May 2014.

During 2018, with the KC-330 not yet available, the small C-130J-30 fleet was called upon to evacuate South Korean citizens from Saipan Island in the Pacific Ocean following a deadly typhoon.

On 12 May 2020, in the middle of the COVID-19 pandemic, a C-130J-30 flew to Andrews Air Force Base in the US to supply the US Department of Veterans Affairs with a donation of 500,000 protective masks. Earlier, in March of the same year, two C-130J-30s arrived in Myanmar to pick up 80,000 surgical gowns to be used in Korea's battle against the virus. This marked the first time ROKAF aircraft had been mobilised

KF-16C serial number 01-514 of the 20th FW, which began applying tail markings to its fleet of KF-16s during 2017, showing off its air defence configuration consisting of six LAU-129 launchers for AIM-9/AIM-120 missiles and an AN/AAQ-33 Sniper targeting pod attached to the intake for aerial identification. (Hwangbo Joonwoo)

to supply commercial goods after national airlines suspended their routes to Myanmar due to concerns over the COVID-19 virus.

Lockheed Martin (K)F-16C/D Fighting Falcon

In the mid-1970s the Korean government enquired about a possible purchase of 72 General Dynamics (now Lockheed Martin) F-16 aircraft to bolster its air force. In 1978, Washington offered a 60-aircraft deal for the F-16A/B, but this was quickly changed to an offer for the inferior F-16-79, which was powered by the obsolete General Electric J79 engine as flown in the F-4 Phantom and F-104 Starfighter.

After much political wrangling the ROKAF became the first foreign operator of the C/D model of the F-16 Fighting Falcon, when it signed a letter of agreement in December of 1981 for the purchase of 30 F-16C and six F-16D aircraft. The contract, going by the name Peace Bridge I, stipulated delivery of the F-16s to commence during 1986. A ceremony was held at Gunsan after the first two F-16Ds had landed there on 12 April 1986. An introduction ceremony took place on 27 April 1986 at Daegu Air Base, the initial home base of the F-16 fleet belonging to the 161st and 162nd TFS. In terms of air superiority, the introduction of the F-16 gave the ROKAF the edge over the KPAAF again, after the introduction of the MiG-23ML during the early 1980s arguably swung the balance in favour of the North.

An additional four F-16D Block 32 two seaters were ordered in June of 1988 and delivered during 1992.

Shortly after acquiring its first F-16s, Korea launched the F-X programme to obtain 120 extra fourth generation fighters. Since the name of the project resembled the name of a similar Japanese programme named FS-X, it was renamed to Korean Fighter Program (KFP) instead. During December of 1989, the ROKAF made the surprise announcement it had chosen the McDonnell Douglas (now Boeing) F/A-18 Hornet, and in October 1990 a MoU was signed between the United States and Korea. The following month however, Korea announced it had reevaluated its earlier decision and stated it would not be ordering the F/A-18 for the ROKAF.

A number of factors had caused the cancellation of the F/A-18 Hornet. By the time Korea signed the MoU, F/A-18 production had switched to the more expensive Lot 16 F/A-18C jets, increasing the cost of a potential contract. Additionally, the offer presented to the Korean Government stated the August 1988 price in US Dollars. By the time a decision had to be made, in late 1990, the US dollar had increased in value considerably, making the budget insufficient to buy 120 new jets. The Korean demands for transfer of technology, and a larger part of the workshare created another hike in price. In the end, although Korea had a military need for a 4th generation fighter, the desire for a coproduction programme to achieve their aerospace industrial development objectives seemed of greater importance.

When the competition for a new fighter was reopened in early 1991, both the United States Navy and Air Force submitted presentations to the Korean government explaining operating costs of the respective airframes, although the Koreans had already acknowledged that the F-16 was always the less expensive alternative for the Korean Fighter Program.

A total of 11 ROKAF squadrons operate the (K)F-16, each unit having a mix of single-seaters and two-seat variants. Equipped with an AIS pod and AN/ AAQ-33 Sniper, KF-16D serial number 93-105 banks for final approach to Haemi Air Base.
(Hwangbo Joonwoo)

In March of 1991, Korea announced it would sign a contract, codenamed Peace Bridge II, with the US Government for the purchase of 120 F-16C/D Fighting Falcons. Twelve aircraft would be bought off the shelf, a further 36 would be assembled in Korea from knockdown kits, and the remaining 72 would be completely produced in Korea. Next, the ROKAF had to select an engine for the F-16 as it was offered both the General Electric F110 and the Pratt & Whitney F100. Since a variant of the latter engine powered the initial batch of Peace Bridge F-16s, the choice fell upon the P&W F100-229.

The first of 12 KF-16s built by Lockheed Martin in Texas, was delivered to the ROKAF in December 1994. A roll-out ceremony for the first Korean-built F-16 was held at Sacheon on 30 June 1997. In doing so, Korea became the fifth nation to produce F-16s after the United States, Belgium (SABCA), the Netherlands (Fokker), and Turkey (TAI/TUSAS). The last Peace Bridge II KF-16 was delivered to the ROKAF in 2000.

A follow-on contract for 15 KF-16C and five KF-16D aircraft under the name Peace Bridge III was signed on 27 July 2000. These aircraft allowed the 111th FS, based at the PACAF air base of Gunsan, to relinquish its F-5E/F aircraft in favour of the KF-16.

Within the ROKAF the F-16 is employed as a multi-role platform. It can be used in the air defence role carrying AIM-9 and AIM-120 missiles, perform SEAD with the AGM-88 HARM, or attack targets with a variety of PGMs. After the withdrawal of the RF-4C Phantom, the task of tactical reconnaissance was also bestowed upon the F-16. The 159th TRS at Jungwon Air Base was formed out of the 159th FS during 2014. The unit operates 10 RF-16Cs, named Saemae, specifically wired to carry the available reconnaissance pods of Israeli and Korean manufacture. A new reconnaissance wing, the 39th RW, was established during a ceremony at Jungwon Air Base in November 2020, and the 159th TRS now reports to the new wing.

The ROKAF ordered the Lockheed Martin Tactical Systems AN/ALQ-165 Airborne Self-Protection Jammer (ASPJ), to be installed on its fleet of F-16s. A ROKAF F-16 equipped with the AN/ALQ-165 was testflown at Edwards Air Force Base for integration and verification trials during 1997, after which the system was installed on the remaining F-16s in Korea.

In May 2009 the US Defense Security Cooperation Agency (DSCA) announced it had received a request from South Korea to support the upgrade of 35 surviving F-16C/D Block 32 aircraft to allow employment of GBU-31 JDAM (through the installation of the MIL-STD-1760 databus), and the AIM-120 AMRAAM. Additionally, an Improved Data Modem, and Secure Voice capabilities would be added.

The Improved Data Modem (IDM) is a device that interfaces with the F-16's mission computer and existing on-board radios to provide a data-link capability. It allows transmission of images and target information to and from a range of sources, including other jets, UAVs and FACs by means of either analog, digital, and/or digital-secure communications.

Work on the fleet, dubbed Peace Bridge Upgrade, was completed in 2016 at a cost of USD 250 million.

Another upgrade for the Block 32 fleet was announced on 30 March 2020 by the DSCA. The ROKAF would like Mode 5 IFF and Link 16 Tactical Datalink to establish a better interoperability with other USAF and ROKAF assets. The upgrade would include ARC-238 radios, AN/APX-126 Combined Interrogator Transponders and KY-58M secure voice modules and is estimated to cost close to USD 200 million.

Currently 27 F-16C and seven F-16D Block 32 aircraft remain in use with the 161st and 162nd FS at Jungwon Air Base.

A contract between Lockheed Martin and the South Korean government to upgrade 134 ROKAF KF-16C/D Block 52 aircraft was signed on 18 November 2016, after an earlier deal between the ROKAF and BAE Systems fell through. The upgrade envisions the installation of an active electronically scanned array (AESA) radar and essentially brings the aircraft up to the F-16V standard offered by the same manufacturer. The first two aircraft, a KF-16C and KF-16D, were upgraded at Lockheed Martin's Fort Worth facility. The single seat aircraft, serial number 92-021, performed its first flight after modification in August 2019 and relocated to Edwards AFB in California soon after. Here it was joined by the two seat KF-16, serial number 92-046, which had performed its first flight after upgrade at Fort Worth on 8 September 2020.

These upgrades will ensure the F-16 stays the backbone of ROKAF airpower in the future, with the Fighting Falcon currently equipping 11 squadrons flying from the air bases of Gunsan, Haemi and Jungwon.

Lockheed Martin F-35A Lightning II

The ROKAF flirted with the idea of acquiring the F-35 for the second phase of its F-X programme, but eventually the timeline and purchase price was deemed unrealistic and a second batch of F-15K Slam Eagles was ordered.

As the third phase of the project loomed, the question arose if the ROKAF would select either the F-35A, more F-15Ks, or another jet altogether.

In the early 2010s there was still hope the KF-21, Korea's indigenous 4.5 generation fighter, would be ready in time to participate. It soon transpired this hope was in vain, as the KF-21 timeline slipped considerably. The F-35 was back on the radar.

As DAPA desperately tried to stay within its USD 7.3 billion budget cap, it soon became painstakingly clear that 60 F-35s were simply too expensive and would mean a massive budget overrun.

Additionally, there were question marks regarding the delivery schedule, as the ROKAF required its first aircraft to be in service in 2016, to replace the veteran F-4E Phantom II. With the order being processed through the United States' FMS programme, it means there usually is no compensation for delays in the delivery schedule.

When Lockheed Martin, Boeing and Eurofighter presented their formal bidding documents to South Korea for the 60-aircraft contract on 18 June 2012, the Dassault Rafale and Sukhoi T-50 (Su-57) had already been eliminated from the competition.

As expected, the price of both the Lockheed Martin F-35 and Eurofighter Typhoon offers were well over USD 7.3 billion each, and DAPA saw no other choice than eliminate them from the competition as well.

The sole bidder once again turned out to be Boeing, offering the Silent Eagle, an F-15 with low observable features. Compared to the F-15K the F-15SE offered two additional hardpoints for a total of either four AIM-9s, four AIM-120s or two AGM-88 missiles. It would have an digital electronic warfare system with 360 degrees jam capability, an AESA radar, and an advanced cockpit with single pane large area displays. Its canted tails would give it higher range and greater lateral stability while the conformal weapon bays (scheduled to be designed, developed and manufactured in Korea),

The 40th F-35A for the ROKAF will take to the skies from Fort Worth in late 2021 or early 2022. Pictured here is serial number 19-007, on short finals for home base Cheongju. (Hwangbo Joongwoo)

would give the aircraft some stealth capabilities. Last but not least it would have digital fly-by-wire flight controls, giving the aircraft enhanced performance and handling.

Boeing claimed the F-15SE would provide 85 per cent platform compatibility with the F-15K already in use, and would be a low-risk solution due to a logistics support and maintenance capability already in place in-country.

The choice for the Silent Eagle at the conclusion of the F-X programme sparked controversy in the South Korean political arena, with high ranking officials claiming the F-15SE is insufficient as a long-term investment to protect South Korean airspace at a time of escalating military tensions with the DPRK, along with China developing its own fifth-generation fighter in the form of the Chengdu J-20.

What followed was a long line of internal delays and abortive negotiations which eventually led to a rejection of the Boeing bid in September 2013. DAPA clearly had its heart set on a 5th generation fighter, and the accompanying technology transfer to go with it. Additionally, a stealth fighter able to penetrate enemy airspace undetected to take out essential targets was something extremely high on the ROKAF's agenda.

The tender was reopened but this time the guidelines had been revised to favour the F-35; the initial contract for Phase III had shrunk from 60 to 40 aircraft, with another 20 to be purchased at a later date.

The Republic of Korea and the US government signed a Letter of Offer and Acceptance for the purchase of 40 F-35A Lightning II jets on 30 September 2014 under the Pentagon's FMS programme. Total acquisition costs are estimated at around USD 7 billion. The contract included the offer of 25 technologies used on the F-35A to support South Korea's indigenous KF-X fighter programme.

The first F-35A for the ROKAF, serial number 18-001, was rolled out during a ceremony at the Lockheed Martin facility in Fort Worth, Texas on 28 March 2018. The aircraft was flown to Luke AFB, Arizona to join the 944th Operations Group Detachement 2. This unit, known as the Ninjas, is a team of Reserve and active duty Airmen, instructor pilots and contractors responsible for executing the F-35 FMS programme and providing training for ROKAF, but also JASDF and Israeli Air Force pilots.

On 20 July 2018, Major Kiyun Jung became the first Korean pilot to fly the Lightning II, when he took to the skies from Luke AFB flying the first F-35A destined for the ROKAF.

The Korean Air Force announced it had chosen the name Freedom Knight for the F-35A, after it held a competition among its service members in early 2020. A ROKAF spokesman added: '*The nickname reflects the military's hope for the advanced fighters to serve as a loyal knight that protects the freedom of South Korea's noble value of free democracy*'.

The first pair of F-35s destined for Korea took off from Luke AFB on 22 March 2019, and arrived at Cheongju Air Base exactly a week later. In a ceremony held at Cheongju on 17 December 2019, the ROKAF declared IOC (Initial Operating Capability) for its fleet of F-35s, meaning it has attained a limited combat capability on its way to Full Operational Capability (FOC). At the end of 2020, the ROKAF had received 24 of its 40 F-35A aircraft, with at least 13 more scheduled for delivery in 2021.

In a report to the National Assembly on 7 October 2019, DAPA stated it would launch the second part of the F-X Phase III programme during 2021. South Korea aims to acquire another 20 F-35A Freedom Knights at a cost of USD 3 billion, with deliveries complete around 2026.

On 12 April 2020 the US Government cleared a USD 675 million follow-on package for the ROKAF fleet of Freedom Knights, consisting of spare engines and parts, ground support equipment, weapons and training.

McDonnell Douglas F-4E Phantom II

Operational experience in Vietnam led to the development of the F-4E which differed from the F-4C/D by means of an internal gun, better radar and RWR equipment, more powerful engines and increased fuel capacity. Following on from its experience with the F-4D, the ROKAF ordered 19 examples of the F-4E Phantom II, with deliveries starting on 20 September 1977 to equip the 151st TFS at Daegu. These are the only ROKAF Phantoms equipped with the TISEO (Target Identification System Electro Optical) system built on the inboard leading edge of the port wing. The United States assigned the code name 'Peace Pheasant' to the acquisition of these F-4E fighters.

An F-4E two-ship, each jet carrying four inert Sidewinders, poses for the camera high over the Republic of Korea. The first Peace Pheasant II Phantoms will be withdrawn from use in November 2021, with final withdrawal scheduled for 2024. (ROKAF)

A further batch of 18, code named Peace Pheasant II, were ordered with deliveries starting in June 1979. Among these was the 5,068th and final F-4 Phantom built in the United States (not the last Phantom ever built as production continued in Japan for another year). Sadly, the last US built Phantom, serial 80-744, was lost in a crash in the early 2000s. The fleet of 37 new-built Phantoms received, only spent a short time at Daegu after delivery from the United States before moving to Cheongju Air Base where, on 1 September 1978, the 17th TFW had been formed.

To replace aircraft that were lost in crashes, a total of five former USAF Phantoms were received between 1985 and 1986.

When the ROKAF commander visited Washington during 1985, he was told additional F-4E aircraft would not be available until some time after 1990. However, after the 497th TFS at Daegu Air Base disbanded, and the 36th TFS at Osan replaced its F-4E aircraft with new F-16C/D Block 30 models, the much coveted Phantoms did become available a little bit sooner then first anticipated. A total of 15 former 51st TFW machines changed ownership during 1989. These were followed by nine additional PACAF examples during 1990, as the 90th TFS at Clark Air Force Base in the Philippines got rid of its F-4E Phantoms. Further deliveries included almost 20 aircraft of the 141st TFS of the New Jersey Air National Guard. Between early 1989 and late 1991, a total of 53 E-model Phantoms were received, bringing the total in ROKAF service to 95. The former USAF Phantoms were transferred under the MIMEX (Major Item Material Excess) programme, and therefore these aircraft were known as 'MIMEX F-4' in ROKAF service.

The ROKAF had been trying to obtain the state-of-the-art Global Hawk since early 2005, but its bid was turned down by the United States. Under the Missile Technology Control Regime, the Global Hawk is classed as a Category I system, meaning it is considered technology of the greatest sensitivity, and could potentially be used as a delivery system for WMDs.

In August 2008, it was reported that South Korea could buy the Global Hawk, despite the MTCR that was previously thought to block any such transactions.

In December 2014, the ROKAF awarded a USD 657 million contract to Northrop Grumman for four RQ-4B Block 30 UAVs, two spare Rolls-Royce North American F137-RR-100 turbofan engines and associated ground control equipment. Follow-on contracts for additional support and equipment raised the total cost of the deal to USD 1.6 billion.

The Block 30 version of the Global Hawk is a multi-intelligence platform equipped with EO/IR sensors, SIGINT sensors and a SAR and is able to reach an altitude of 60,000ft (18,288m).

The RQ-4s with its advanced radar and sensors will be capable of gathering communication and electronic information regarding, but not limited to, the North's ballistic missile and nuclear weapons development. It can be operated day or night and acquire intelligence regardless of weather conditions.

As part of an off-set programme, Korean companies Firstec and KJF (Korean Jig and Fixture) were chosen to manufacture components, including wire harnesses, for the Korean Global Hawk project. Final assembly of the Korean Global Hawks took place at the Northrop Grumman facility in Palmdale, California.

A new multi-hangar complex was built at the north-west side of Sacheon Air Base to house the small fleet of Global Hawks, with the first example arriving there on 23 December 2019.

A second Global Hawk flew to Korea in mid-April 2020 and the final two examples had been received by September of the same year.

The Global Hawks are operated by the 131st Reconnaissance Squadron, the former RF-4C unit, and form part of the newly established 39th Reconnaissance Wing.

The 206th FS, established on 15 February 1978, is not only responsible for air defence of the south-western part of Korea, the squadron has also served as a combat readiness training unit since 2004. Northrop-built F-5E serial number 61-646 is seen returning to Gwangju Air Base with smoke pods attached to its underwing pylons.
(Robin Polderman)

Northrop F-5E/F and KF-5E/F Tiger II

The ROKAF became one of the earliest users of the F-5E/F Tiger II when it received its first F-5E on 27 August 1974. A total of 126 F-5E single seat and 20 F-5F dual seat were received through the MAP programme, with the final example arriving in mid-1979. A core group of ROKAF pilots were trained at Williams AFB in Mesa, Arizona, and some of its F-5 aircraft were used there before being shipped to Korea. An interim upgrade programme initiated in 1976 saw the fleet being retro-fitted with RWR sensors on nose and aft fuselage. The delivery of the F-5s allowed the retirement of a large number of F-86 Sabres.

The rapid growth in Korea's economy during the 1970s fuelled the development of its aviation industry. An initial wish to start licence building the General Dynamics F-16 was refused by the US Government, but the less advanced F-5 was offered instead. The initial contract for 36 single seaters and 32 two seaters, agreed to in 1980, was changed to 48 F-5E and 20 F-5F at the end of 1982.

A clean KF-5F taking off from a snowy Suwon Air Base. The jet carries the markings of the 207th FS that was established in 1979 as part of the 8th TFW. The squadron moved to Suwon and was disbanded in 2014.
(ROKAF)

Licence production was to be undertaken by the Hanjin Corporation (now KAL-FSD) at its facility on the west side of Busan airport, with Samsung building the J-85 jet engines after obtaining a licence from General Electric.

The Korean-built Tiger II aircraft are designated KF-5E/KF-5F and have the 'shar-knose' radome along with larger Leading Edge Extensions (LEX). In ROKAF service the Northrop-built F-5s retain their black noses making them easily distinguishable from the grey painted Korean-built KF-5 radomes.

The first Korean-built Tiger II aircraft, KF-5F 10-594, took off from Busan on 9 September 1982 for its maiden flight. The last one, KF-5E 10-625, was handed over to the ROKAF at the end of October 1986. In Korean service the KF-5E/F aircraft that rolled of the Busan productionline were named Jegong which loosely translates as 'Skymaster', and they were used to equip three squadrons (the 101st, 201st and 207th) of the 10th Fighter Wing at Suwon Air Base.

The F-5 fleet is used as a multi-role platform, employing the AIM-9L for air defence, while in the air-to-ground role the AGM-65 Maverick, Hydra 70 rockets and KGGB guided bomb are some of the weapons that can be used.

On 18 June 2010, Lieutenant Colonel Park Jeong-wu and First Lieutenant Jeong Seon-gung of the 105th FS flying out of Gangneung Air Base lost their lives when the F-5F they were piloting plunged into the East Sea. The crew had apparently tried to eject but at too low an altitude. Following the month-long investigation into the cause of the crash, the ROKAF decided to replace the ejection seats of its fleet of (K)F-5E/F fighters. Between 2011 and 2013, a total of 150 F-5 aircraft received new Martin Baker US16T ejection seats. Earlier, during 2005, the US16T seat had been chosen by the USAF Air Education and Training Command to upgrade the escape system on their fleet of T-38 Talons, and this seat proved to be fairly easy to adapt to the F-5 airframes in use with the ROKAF.

Over the past few years the ROKAF has progressively phased out its oldest Northrop-built F-5E/F airframes, despite instigating life extension upgrades in the mid-1990s and around 2003. Beginning in 2020, the ROKAF started to concentrate the older airframes at Gwangju's 206th FS, which doubles as the F-5 training unit. This will eventually leave the Gangneung and Suwon-based Tiger II squadrons operating the KF-5E/F only. The Northrop-built aircraft are scheduled to be replaced by the KAI KF-21 from 2026, while the Korean-built examples should be replaced by the same aircraft from 2030.

A total of 37 F-5E/F and 55 KF-5E/F remained in service with the ROKAF at the end of 2020. The Suwon-based pair of squadrons fly the KF-5E/F exclusively, while both squadrons belonging to the 18th FW at Gangneung Air Base fly a mix of F-5E/F and KF-5E/F. A single squadron based at Gwangju, the 206th FS, doubles as the F-5 training unit and currently only has Northrop built examples in the inventory.

Raytheon RC-800B Baekdu (SIGINT) and RC-800G Geumgang (IMINT)

The Baekdu/Geumgang project, initiated by South Korea during 1991, was a plan for the acquisition of both a communications monitoring (SIGINT) aircraft as well as an

The RC-800B SIGINT has proven expensive to operate as the aircraft get older and spare parts become harder to obtain. However, the type is needed to gather intelligence on the northern neighbour.
(Robin Polderman)

Four examples of the RC-800G have been in use since 2000 for IMINT missions, with the aircraft flying close to the DMZ.
(Robin Polderman)

imagery collecting (IMINT) aircraft. Israeli firm Rafael offered a modified Cessna Citation for the missions, while Thompson of France proposed the Dassault Falcon. The US-based company E-Systems chose the Raytheon Hawker 800XP (Extended Performance) for its bid, a variant of the Hawker with superior performance in range and payload.

In June 1996 E-Systems, that had been bought by Raytheon the year before, was awarded the contract. The ROKAF had decided it wanted the guarantee of a US Government-backed FMS sale, although this was the most expensive of the three bids and initially had been deemed the least suitable.

The names Baekdu and Geumgang were apparently chosen to reflect the range of the intelligence equipment onboard the two types of aircraft. Both are mountains located in North Korea, at a distance from the MDL of 178 miles (330km) and 11 miles (20km), respectively. Mount Baekdu is on the border between China and North Korea and even features prominently on North Korea's national emblem.

The US DoD assigned the codenames Peace Krypton (IMINT) and Peace Pioneer (SIGINT) for the respective programmes.

RC-800G IMINT

Raytheon Aircraft in Wichita, Kansas assembled the first Hawker 800XP for the ROKAF in late 1997, after which it was flown to the Lockheed Martin facility in Goodyear, Arizona. A total of four aircraft were equipped with a synthetic aperture radar (SAR) and associated equipment like workstations, to collect reconnaissance imagery of selected areas during missions either day or night. The SAR, built by US company Loral, has a resolution of 6in (30cm) and is alledgedly able to detect football-size objects on the ground south of Pyongyang. The system is able to peek into North Korea up to 100km (62 miles) north of the DML.

The RC-800G collects FTI (fixed target imagery) as well as MTI (moving target indicator) data, with the latter being a mode of operation of the SAR to discriminate a target against ground clutter, and to determine if it is moving or not.

The Geumgang-system consists of the AE (Aircraft Element – the RC-800 itself) and a CEES (Central Exploitation Equipment Subsystem). This is the imagery collection point that receives all data transmitted real-time via an imagery data transmission system onboard the aircraft.

The system is also able to utilise a MEES (Mobile Exploitation Equipment Subsystem).

The CEES and MEES include facilities such as a data server, computers, ground datalink, and workstations for mission planning and exploitation.

Over the years, the ROKAF has awarded contracts to Lockheed Martin for system sustainment.

This involves maintenance of the aircraft fleet as well as providing support- and test equipment for both the aircraft, and its fixed and mobile ground stations. The company also provided software development and software upgrades as needed to modernise the reconnaissance system.

RC-800B SIGINT

The four Baekdu aircraft were modified at the Raytheon E-Systems facilities in Greenville, Texas at a cost of USD 135 million, including the airframes themselves. For their signal intelligence role, they were outfitted with US made equipment that can be used

The sliding door and large step on both sides identify this VH-60P as a Korean-built helicopter.
(Robin Polderman)

to intercept and record communications, such as phone and radiocalls by the North Korean leadership or the KPA. As part of the contract, Raytheon E-Systems also provided the Republic of Korea with a support facility.

Both the RC-800B and RC-800G operate between 40-50km (25-31 miles) south of the MDL at an altitude of 33,000ft (10,060m). The aircraft can, depending on wind-conditions, remain airborne for up to five hours.

The fleet of Baekdu/Geumgang aircraft is based at Seongnam near Seoul, and operated by the 296th Reconnaissance Squadron.

All data collected while airborne is fed to Military Unit 5679, the code name for a unit within the Korean Armed Forces Intelligence Command. The Koreans claim the fleet of RC-800 aircraft has better intelligence-gathering performance than the Osan-based Lockheed U-2 Dragon Lady aircraft of the USAF.

Both types of the RC-800 have been in operational use since 2000.

Sikorsky/Korean Air HH-60P and VH-60P Black Hawk

In late 1990, three VIP-configured VH-60P Black Hawks for the ROKAF rolled off the Sikorsky production line in Stratford, USA. In the same year, Korean Air and Sikorsky signed an agreement for licence production of the Black Hawk in Korea. This agreement saw the Korean company built around 150 HH/UH/VH-60P helicopters, the majority of which were destined for service with the ROKA. The Korean version of the Black Hawk is based upon the UH-60L with some modifications.

In 1991 the VH-60Ps were followed by a small number of Sikorsky-built UH-60Ps, destined for the ROKAF as utility and search and rescue helicopters and painted gloss dark blue.

A radar-equipped HH-60P CSAR
Black Hawk in its element over
South Korean waters.
(ROKAF)

In need of a CSAR helicopter in case the cold war with North Korea went hot, the ROKAF sent its UH-60Ps to KAL for conversion into HH-60P. Between 1995 and 2000, the Black Hawk fleet received a TACAN system, GPS, HF/DF radios, a rescue hoist and AN/ASC-15B console.

The AN/ASC-15B functions as an airborne and ground commandpost, providing tactical voice/data communications in both secure and nonsecure modes. It is able to recieve and relay communications via satellite. The HH-60Ps also received a pair of 1,900lb (861-litre) fuel tanks mounted on stub wings.

During the early 2010s, with assistance from Elbit Systems, a number of HH-60Ps were equipped with an EO/IR-turret and a nose mounted weather radar while others only received the turret. A further modification saw the addition of RWR modules on nose and tailboom as well as a chaff/flare dispenser, but again not all Black Hawks received these modifications making the 13 HH-60Ps in service with the ROKAF somewhat of a mixed bag. At an unknown date, SGD Engineering of Israel provided a pilot locating system to aid in (C)SAR missions. In summer 2012, the first HH-60P in an overall matt grey colour scheme emerged.

The ROKAF became one of the
first military users of the VH-92,
when it ordered three examples
for the VIP role in 2005. They
serve with the 257th Airlift
Squadron at Seongnam Air Base
in Seoul.
(Robin Polderman)

Further to the trio of VH-60Ps bought from Sikorsky, another five Black Hawk helicopters were modified for the VIP-role, with KAL-ASD starting conversion work on
the UH-60Ps in June 2002. It necessitated structural improvements due to the installation of seats, while additional soundproofing material was added along with improved
communications equipment. After completion they received the same white/blue colour scheme as the earlier VH-60Ps. The new VIP helicopters retained their original
sliding passenger doors contrary to the sideways-opening doors on the Sikorsky-built
VH-60P, and as such the Korean-built VIP-version is easily distinguishable from the
original US-built VH-60P.

Some sources report the VH-60s as being converted back to UH-60P standard for
use as escort helicopter whenever the president travels by VH-92. One Black Hawk will
carry members of the Presidential Guard, while the other carries a medical team from
the 15th SMW.

The 233rd SRS operates the HH-60Ps and some of the VH-60Ps from Cheongju, while
maintaining a search and rescue detachment at Haemi Air Base, near the west coast of
Korea. The remaining few VH-60Ps are in use with the 257th Squadron at Seongnam.

Sikorsky VH-92

On 6 May 2005 Sikorsky (now Lockheed-Martin), announced it had won a contract for the delivery of three S-92A Helibus helicopters to the ROKAF for the presidential mission. The S-92A was selected over the Agusta-Westland EH101 in a competition conducted by the ROKAF, DAPA and the Korean MoD. The S-92 was developed by Sikorsky to provide the offshore industry with a reliable helicopter and first flew in December of 1998. It has some commonality with the H-60 Black Hawk family, with both types sharing the same flight control system.

The first VH-92 for the ROKAF rolled off the production line in Stratford, Connecticut, during 2006. After some factory test flights, it was flown to the US Navy test airfield of China Lake in California, still in primer and carrying US civil registration N8064Q. During February 2007, the helicopter's countermeasures system was tested using the ranges situated near China Lake.

The three VH-92, as the VIP version of the S-92A was dubbed, were handed over to the ROKAF during a ceremony at the Seoul Airshow on 16 October 2007, taking over the VVIP role of the VH-60P. The trio of helicopters had arrived in Korea the month before.

In February 2016, defence company Heli-One announced they had won a contract to upgrade the VH-92's navigation systems. The contract involved the installation of EO/IR cameras and upgrades of existing moving map-systems to the latest EuroNav7 version. The installation of these features was aimed at safer operation in adverse weather conditions

All three VH-92s currently serve with the 257th Airlift Squadron, the ROKAF's dedicated VIP squadron at Seongnam Air Base near Seoul.

ROKAF ARMAMENT, WEAPONS AND STORES

With the United States being the long-standing, principal ally of South Korea, it comes as no surprise that the majority of its weapon stock is of US manufacture. In the past two decades, however, spurred by an ambitious Korean aviation and defence industry, the ROKAF has introduced indigenous weapons and systems to equip its fleet of combat aircraft. Additionally, much to the suprise of many in the aerospace business, the ROKAF recently decided to choose weapons of European manufacture when it comes to air-to-air missiles for its indigenous KF-X fighter.

The ROKAF took note of American lessons from Operation Desert Storm in 1991. During that conflict in the Gulf, precision-guided munitions (PGM) inflicted 42 per cent of the damage upon Iraqi targets, even though these weapons constituted less than 10 per cent of the total tonnage of ordnance employed. This statistic showed that PGMs will reduce the number of combat sorties required and, in doing so, the risk of fighter pilots being lost to enemy fire. Over the past three decades, the ROKAF has invested in these so-called smart weapons in the form of laser and GPS-guided munitions, including expensive air-launched stand-off missiles.

Should the cold war with North Korea turn into an armed conflict, the ROKAF will be tasked with taking out a large number of targets including nuclear facilities, ICBM launch sites/TELs, as well as command bunkers. In many cases these facilities will either be hardened, located underground, or both, and will most likely be very well defended. This necessitates not only weapons that can penetrate a substantial layer of concrete, but also have a large stand-off range and are immune to jamming.

Air-to-air missiles

AIM-7M Sparrow
Currently the only aircraft in ROKAF service carrying the radar-guided AIM-7 is the dwindling fleet of F-4E Phantom II aircraft. It is understood that the upgrade (PBU) on the Block 32 F-16s has seen the Sparrow replaced by the AIM-120 on these aircraft.

The Sparrow was designed by US company Sperry during the 1950s and the design was progressively updated over the years. Although the external dimensions of the Sparrow remained relatively unchanged from model to model, the internal components of newer missiles represent major improvements with vastly increased capabilities.

The AIM-7M version, featuring improved low-altitude performance and reliability, is better suited for electronic countermeasures environments. It also features digital controls and an active radar proximity fuse triggering a significantly more lethal warhead.

The AIM-7M is capable of attacking aerial targets at a range of 70 km (44 miles).

An F-4E comes in to land carrying at least one AIM-9 Sidewinder on the underwing weapons pylons and a pair of AIM-7 Sparrows on the aft fuselage stations.
(AV Kok)

AIM-9P3/L/M/X/X-2 Sidewinder

The Sidewinder is probably the most widely known air-to-air missile in the Western world. More than 110,000 examples have been produced, and different versions of the AIM-9 have scored at least 270 aircraft kills around the globe. The first version of the AIM-9 entered service as long ago as 1956. Over the past six-and-a-half decades, the missile has seen almost constant improvements. Korea received its first Sidewinders, in the form of the AIM-9B, during 1958.

The ROKAF fleet of F-4E and (K)F-5E aircraft make use of the AIM-9P3, which first entered service during the mid-1970s. The AIM-9P3 was expressly developed for export, and is based on the US-standard AIM-9J/N. Compared to older variants of the Sidewinder, the AIM-9P3 has an all-aspect capability. More than 21,000 AIM-9P missiles were built and exported outside of the United States.

The development of the subsequent AIM-9L incorporated the lessons learned from several conflicts in which older Sidewinder variants saw use.

This version was the first to incorporate an active laser proximity fuse. Laser beams are transmitted around the missile and, when reflected by the target, these beams bounce back and are picked up by a photo diode, which triggers detonation. Following the introduction of the AIM-9L in 1974, the ROKAF also acquired the AIM-9M, which features an almost smokeless rocket motor along with improved guidance and counter-countermeasures.

The AIM-9M can be distinguished from the AIM-9L by its larger photo diodes and an arming key that is not removable. The ROKAF uses these missiles on its fleet of (K)F-16C/D, F-15K, and FA-50/TA-50 aircraft.

After the United States moved away from the AIM-132 ASRAAM project in 1996, it continued development of a much upgraded variant of the Sidewinder, the AIM-9X. Korea became the first international customer for the AIM-9X when it signed a contract

A Yecheon-based FA-50 with captive AIM-9s on the wingtips.
(AV Kok)

with Raytheon in 2002, as part of a weapons package for the F-15K. Further AIM-9X Sidewinders were ordered in 2009.

The Mach 2.5-capable AIM-9X is equipped with a high off-boresight (HOBS) seeker. Thanks to its jet-vane steering it can manoeuvre at up to 50G and, in conjunction with the Joint Helmet Mounted Cueing System (JHMCS), the X-variant has a much wider attack envelope in comparison with older Sidewinder variants.

Test firing of a new version of the Sidewinder commenced in November 2008. The AIM-9X Block II, or AIM-9X-2, is an upgraded variant with a datalink enabling it to be used in near-beyond-visual-range engagements. The rumoured range of the AIM-9X Block II is 27km (17 miles). The Block II also has a new rocket motor battery, redesigned fuse, and improved onboard processors. DAPA first ordered 76 examples of the Block II AIM-9X in 2014, with follow-on orders for 60 and 115 missiles in February 2017 and October 2020 respectively. The AIM-9X and X-2 are carried by the F-15K, (K)F-16C/D and F-35A.

AIM-120 AMRAAM

During the 1980s, the Hughes Aircraft Company designed an Advanced Medium-Range Air-to-Air Missile (AMRAAM) to replace the AIM-7 Sparrow in service at the time. The first variant, the AIM-120A, was fielded in autumn 1991.

When compared to the Sparrow, one of the most significant advantages is the active homing radar seeker. Upon detection of an aerial target, information about its location and speed is fed into the missile's inertial navigation system (INS) through the aircraft's interface. Following launch, the datalink between the missile and aircraft periodically updates the information regarding the target. Once within range, the missile guides itself towards the target using its built-in active homing radar, and no longer relies on target data from the launch aircraft.

The F-15K is a true multi-role aircraft as evidenced by this General Electric powered example carrying four AIM-120C AMRAAM missiles and a pair of AIM-9X Sidewinder AAMs, alongside a Sniper pod for visual identification.
(AV Kok)

The ROKAF ordered 88 examples of the AIM-120A for its fleet of Block 52 KF-16C/D aircraft, the first of these missiles entering service during 1997. These were quickly followed by 737 AIM-120Bs, a slightly improved version with a WGU-41/B guidance section and updated electronics. Both the AIM-120A and AIM-120B have a range of roughly 65km (40 miles).

The AIM-120C has an improved seeker allowing high-angle, off-boresight launch, and can be easily distinguished from the A and B models due to its clipped wings and control surfaces.

Between 2006 and 2014, the ROKAF received 200 examples of the AIM-120C-5, mainly to equip the F-15K Slam Eagles of the 11th FW.

The ROKAF was cleared to buy 120 examples of the AIM-120C-7/C-8 during October 2019, for use on the F-35A. Additional AIM-120C-8 missiles were ordered in March 2021. The AIM-120C-8 is also known as the AIM-120D and features extended range, rumoured to be in excess of 160km (100 miles), when compared to the 100km (62mile) range of the C-7 variant. It also offers GPS-assisted guidance as well as improved resistance to countermeasures.

The AIM-120 AMRAAM is powered by a high-performance rocket motor using reduced-smoke, solid-fuel propellant, and flies at speeds of up to Mach 4.

IRIS-T

The Diehl Defence IRIS-T short-range infrared air-to-air missile was developed within a European cooperation programme consisting of Germany, Greece, Italy, Norway, Sweden and Spain. German defence company Diehl Defence, part of the Diehl Group,

is the prime contractor in the IRIS-T programme, and has produced the missile since 2005.

The combination of thrust vectoring and aerodynamic control provides the missile with extremely high agility. The wide employment envelope of IRIS-T allows targets to be engaged behind the aircraft, as well as the interception of incoming enemy missiles.

For target tracking the missile uses an imaging infrared (IIR) seeker head in conjunction with intelligent image processing. Target designation is accomplished by the launch aircraft's radar or via the pilot's helmet sight. The IRIS-T has a range of 25km (15.5 miles) and flies at speeds of up to Mach 3.

The IRIS-T also has an air-to-surface capability. In 2016, the Royal Norwegian Air Force for the first time demonstrated this missile's capability to engage sea targets, during a test firing.

The IRIS-T will be the short-range air-to-air missile carried on the ROKAF fleet of KF-21 aircraft.

The IRIS-T short-range missile (on wingtip) and Meteor BVRAAM (underwing) have both been purchased by the ROKAF for the KF-21 Boramae. (Robin Polderman)

Meteor BVRAAM

The Meteor is an active radar guided, beyond-visual-range air-to-air missile (BVRAAM), with a range of over 100km (62 miles) and able to travel at speeds of up to Mach 4. Full-scale development of the Meteor began in 2003, by a group of six European partners led by defence company MBDA, together with Airbus, BAE Systems and Leonardo. The ramjet propulsion system, a solid-fuel, variable-flow, ducted rocket, provides the missile with thrust all the way to target intercept. The Meteor can be network-enabled through a two-way datalink, allowing either the launch aircraft or an offboard third

A TA-50 taking off with a pair of AGM-65 Mavericks. The white example with transparent seeker head is an EO-version of the Maverick, while the opaque seeker head of the grey missile indicates the IR version. Both missiles are missing the rear fins, indicating a training role on this particular mission. (via Robin Polderman)

party to provide mid-course target updates or retargeting. To ensure destruction of the target, the missile is equipped with both impact and proximity fuses, and a fragmentation warhead that detonates on impact or at the optimum point of intercept to maximise lethality.

In November 2019, MBDA announced it had signed a contract with DAPA for the integration of the Meteor on the KF-21 fighter. The contract includes integration support to KAI, transfer of know-how, and manufacture of test equipment for the KF-21 integration and trials campaign. The missile should become operational with the first batch of KF-21 aircraft, scheduled for delivery to the ROKAF around 2026.

Air-to-ground missiles

AGM-65A/B/D/G Maverick

The ROKAF is a long-standing user of the Hughes (now Raytheon) AGM-65 Maverick air-to-ground missile. Development of the Maverick started during the Vietnam War as a subsonic replacement for the AGM-12 Bullpup, with first deliveries of the AGM-65A to the US Air Force in August of 1972.

The initial version of the missile uses an electro-optical (EO) guidance system, to display an image of the target on a screen in the aircraft's cockpit. Following launch, the missile homes in on its target by constantly comparing the locked target image with the EO camera image.

The AGM-65B has enhanced optics which increase image resolution, thereby allowing the missile to be used at greater range from the objective and/or acquire smaller targets.

The AIM-65D is basically a B-model that uses an infrared seeker for night and all-weather employment.

Fielded in the early 1990s, the AIM-65G has a heavyweight penetrator warhead along with an IR seeker and a digital autopilot. The Maverick uses a two-stage solid-propellant rocket motor and has a range of 18km (11 miles) under ideal circumstances.

The latest batch of Mavericks for the ROKAF, consisting of 89 AGM-65Gs, was requested during January 2017 with proposed delivery before the end of 2018. The contract was worth USD 70 million.

The ROKAF uses the AGM-65 on the F-4E, (K)F-5E/F, (K)F-16C/D, and FA-50/TA-50. The ROKAF has both the single-rail launcher (LAU-117) as well as the three-rail launcher (LAU-88) in its inventory.

AGM-84L Harpoon Block II

The AGM-84 Harpoon over-the-horizon anti-ship missile has been in service since 1977, and many variants have been produced. The land attack SLAM and SLAM-ER versions are descendants from the Harpoon missile family.

The current version in production by Boeing, the AGM-84L Block II, has a GPS/INS system installed for more accurate mid-course guidance. The navigation system, along with the software and mission computer, were taken from the SLAM-ER missile, while

This F-15K carries an ATM-84, the training version of the AGM-84 Harpoon, under the wing, with GBU-38s and a single GBU-31(V3) on the fuselage stations.
(Robin Polderman)

the inertial measuring unit finds its origin in Boeing's Joint Direct Attack Munition (JDAM) programme.

The Harpoon missile uses an active radar for terminal guidance, and requires minor modifications to the launch aircraft including a software adjustment, as well as an electronic hardware component that allows the weapons management system to communicate with the weapon. The missile is capable of executing both overland strike and anti-ship missions. It has a range in excess of 124km (77 miles) and is fitted with a 500lb (227kg) high-explosive warhead.

In ROKAF service the AGM-84 Harpoon has been noted fitted to the F-15K and KF-16C.

AGM-84H SLAM-ER

The day/night, all-weather, over-the-horizon, high-precision AGM-84H SLAM-ER (Stand-off Land Attack Missile – Expanded Response) uses a combination of GPS, IR and INS to reach its target. The weapon, propelled by a small turbojet engine, is capable of hitting moving as well as stationary targets. In autonomous 'fire-and-forget' mode the weapon can strike its target using GPS updates alone.

In the final stages of flight, the pilot or WSO in the launch aircraft can select and refine the precise impact point using a screen cursor on the cockpit display. Should the prime target already be destroyed, the missile can be redirected through the datalink to a target miles away.

The AGM-84H has a range of 270km (168 miles), and a CEP of between 1-3m (3.3-9.8ft). The 1,400lb (635kg) weapon is equipped with a 500lb (227kg) warhead, and equires the AN/AWW-13 datalink pod to receive mid-course updates.

The AGM-84H was developed during the mid-1990s and the ROKAF became the first foreign customer for the weapon in August 2005. During a test off the coast of California in early 2006, a ROKAF F-15K succesfully fired a SLAM-ER. Within the

The AGM-84H SLAM-ER is a deadly weapon, able to strike targets 270km (168 miles) away with almost pinpoint accuracy. The CATM-84H-1A training version is seen loaded onto an F-15K, with inert versions of the AIM-9X and AIM-120C attached to the same pylon. (AV Kok)

An F-16D PBU, mostly likely assigned to the 162nd FS as this is the main F-16 OCU, comes in to land carrying a CATM-88. This version is the training variant of the AGM-88 HARM, and is often flown without the characteristic fins.
(Jamie Chang)

ROKAF inventory of fighter aircraft, only the F-15K Slam Eagle is cleared to employ this weapon.

AGM-88 HARM

Raytheon's High-speed Anti-Radiation Missile, or HARM, is intended to engage enemy ground radar equipment. The missile uses a fixed antenna in the nose to detect radar emissions and is able to precisely locate the source of the emission.

The HARM can be used to destroy a preplanned target; in this case, the weapon will be launched in the direction of the objective at a predetermined point, and the seeker will home in on the enemy radar once in range. The missile can also be programmed to launch against a threat, once the launching aircraft is picked up by an enemy radar system, for example.

Additionally, the missile's seeker can be used to find targets of opportunity. However, with the HARM Targeting System (HTS), a podded enhanced emission detector, not made available to the ROKAF, the effectiveness of the weapon is somewhat reduced. The ROKAF therefore regularly teams up with PACAF units which fly the F-16 with the HTS system.

The missile uses a smoke-less, solid-propellant rocket motor, and travels at supersonic speeds. Upon detonation the target is showered with thousands of preformed metal fragments.

The AGM-88, and its LAU-118 launch rail, are in use with the ROKAF fleet of KF-16C/D aircraft of the 20th FW at Haemi.

One of the reasons the ROKAF is keeping the F-4E in service until 2024 is seen under the wing of this 153rd FS F-4E. The AGM-142 Popeye stand-off missile and associated AN/ASW-55 datalink pod are carried by the F-4E exclusively. (Jamie Chang)

AGM-142 Popeye

During September 1997, Korea signed a Foreign Military Sales deal worth USD 100 million for the purchase of 116 AGM-142 stand-off guided missiles. Following a two-year evaluation, the AGM-142 was chosen over a variant of the AGM-130.

The AGM-142 missiles for the ROKAF were produced by PGSUS (Precision Guided Systems United States), a joint-venture comprising Lockheed Martin and the Israeli company Rafael, with production lines operating in Alabama and Florida. Rafael had developed the AGM-142 in the early 1980s, and the design was reportedly influenced by Israeli experience with the AGM-65 Maverick.

A total of 36 ROKAF F-4Es were modified to employ the AGM-142. The particular version(s) delivered to ROKAF is a matter of some speculation. Both Popeye 1 (AGM-142A) as well as the C and D variants of the missile are reportedly in use, while other sources mention versions specifically adapted for ROKAF F-4s, these being the AGM-142G and AGM-142H. The difference between these versions of the Popeye missile mainly lie in the method of obtaining its target: either EO or IR seeker heads can be used.

Employment of the AGM-142 requires the AN/ASW-55 datalink pod to be carried on the aircraft.

The missiles have a CEP of around 3m (10ft) and a range of about 80km (50 miles). The Popeye's 750lb (340kg) blast-fragmentation warhead is triggered by a tail-mounted impact fuse, and the missile is powered by a solid-fuel rocket motor.

During September 1997, the ROKAF reportedly ordered 116 examples of the missile in both the Popeye 1 variant, for use on the F-4E, and the lighter AGM-142B Popeye 2 for the KF-16C/D. Deliveries commenced during 1999, but it is fairly certain the Popeye 2 version for the F-16 was never received.

TAURUS KEPD 350K

The first KEPD 350K stand-off missiles for the ROKAF were handed over during a ceremony in October 2016. TAURUS Systems, a joint venture between MBDA Deutschland and Saab Dynamics, developed and produced the weapon.

South Korea initially ordered 170 examples of the missile from the German and Swedish manufacturers but, after yet another North Korean nuclear missile test in late 2016, decided to order 90 more.

The TAURUS KEPD 350K is an upgraded version of the KEPD 350E missile already in use with some European air forces.

The 5m (16ft 3in) long, 3,100lb (1,400kg) missile uses low-level terrain-following flight to approach its target. The KEPD 350 is equipped with both GPS and INS navigation systems. This fail-safe system allows the missile to continue on its planned flight-path even without GPS availability.

The weapon can hit locations at a range of more than 500km (310 miles), which is far enough to strike any target in the DPRK while still being launched from within South Korean airspace.

The missile has a dual-stage warhead and can be used to destroy heavily fortified (underground) objects, as it is able to penetrate up to 6m (20ft) of concrete. The weapon can be programmed to scan the area for a three-dimensional image of its target. Once

The F-15K Slam Eagle is currently the only aircraft in ROKAF service able to carry and fire the TAURUS KEPD 350K long-range stand-off missile. (MBDA)

its objective has been identified, the missile pops up and then dived straight down onto its target.

Within the ROKAF, the TAURUS KEPD 350K is carried exclusively by the F-15K Slam Eagle.

The ROKAF has expressed the need for a lighter version of the missile, still being able to hit targets 400km (250 miles) away, for use on its fleet of FA-50 aircraft. This version is currently under development, and will also be used to arm the KF-21.

Air-to-ground bombs

Mk 82/Mk 84

In use since the Vietnam War and produced in massive quantities, the Mk 82 500lb (227kg) and Mk 84 2,000lb (907kg) unguided, general-purpose bombs need little introduction. The majority of the Mk 82/Mk 84 bombs carry a tritonal explosive load, consisting of 80 per cent TNT and 20 per cent aluminium powder.

The Mk series of bombs become precision-guided munitions when coupled with a laser guidance and/or GPS guidance kit.

The Mk 82 is able to be used by any combat aircraft in ROKAF service, including the KA-1. In many cases the Mk 82 serves as a training weapon to provide pilots with their first taste of a live weapon drop.

Four FA-50 aircraft carrying Mk 82 freefall bombs on TERs, plus AIM-9M Sidewinders loaded on the wingtips. (KAI)

The Mk 84 is capable of being dropped from the F-4E, (K)F-5E/F, F-15K and (K)F-16C/D, although the use of PGMs has generally superseded these earlier weapons.

CBU-58/B

For use against troop concentrations and soft-skinned vehicles, the CBU-58/B cluster weapon contains 650 BLU-63/B submunitions in a SUU-30 dispenser. The submunitions are spherical with a prefragmented case and contain titanium pellets for increased incendiary effects.

Upon release from the aircraft, the arming wire is withdrawn from a fuse, initiating the arming and time delay process. Following fuse ignition, the couplings keeping both halves of the dispenser in place unlock, allowing the weapon to break up in flight and dispense its deadly load of submunitions. Due to its shape, the bomblets start spinning. This in turn will arm a fuse making the bomblet detonate on impact with the target or the ground.

The 800lb (363kg) weapon can be dropped at speeds of up to 625kts (1,150km/h) and is carried by the (K)F-5E/F and FA-50 aircraft.

CBU-100 (Mk 20 Rockeye II)

The CBU-100 (also known as the Mk 20 Rockeye II) is a US-built cluster bomb which is employed primarily in the anti-tank role. The weapon weighs 490lb (222kg) and carries 247 examples of the Mk 118 Mod 1 bomblets. The bomblets each weigh 1.3lb (600g) and have a high-explosive shaped-charge warhead.

A KF-5E poses for the camera with Mk 82 bombs under the wings and AIM-9P Sidewinders on the wingtips. Exhibited in front of the aircraft are, left to right, top to bottom, a CBU-58B, Mk 82 Snakeye high-drag, Mk 82 low-drag, LAU rocket pod, AIM-7M Sparrow, AIM-9P Sidewinder, AGM-65 Maverick and CBU-100 Rockeye. Curiously, the AIM-7 missile on display is not carried by the ROKAF F-5 fleet. (ROK MND)

A flight of ROKAF F-16 aircraft dropping the CBU-100 cluster weapon during a firepower demonstration. (ROK MND)

The arming wire attached between the bomb and the aircraft triggers the Mk 339 or FMU-140 fuse upon weapon release, and also initiates the folding-fin mechanism to stabilise the dispenser.

Between 1.2 and 4 seconds after release, depending on the settings selected, the fuse initiates a linear shaped charge cutting the dispenser case in half, releasing the bomblets for free flight so they spread over the targeted area.

With the ROKAF, the CBU-100 has been seen on the (K)F-5 and (K)F-16 aircraft. They are easily distinguished from the similar-shaped CBU-58 and CBU-105 due to their white colour.

CBU-105B/D

The Wind Corrected Munitions Dispenser (WCMD) Sensor Fuzed Weapon is a tactical area weapon for use against concentrations of enemy vehicles or personnel.

The 1,000lb (453kg) dispenser has a payload of 10 BLU-108 submunitions, each containing four skeet-shaped copper disks totalling 40 target-seeking projectiles. The weapon's active laser and passive IR sensors are programmed to detect the shape of a vehicle or its IR signature.

When falling towards its target, a small explosive charge cuts open the dispenser, allowing the submunitions to be ejected using compressed air. A parachute is used on each of the BLU-108s to slow its descent. Upon detection of the target a charge

An F-4E returns to base carrying a GBU-12 laser-guided bomb on the left-hand inboard wing station and a Pave Tack targeting pod on the centreline station.
(Robin Polderman)

The Paveway II laser-guidance kit transforms a free-fall 2,000lb (907kg) Mk 84 bomb into a GBU-10.
(Robin Polderman)

detonates, penetrating the vehicle at the topside, where the armour is generally the thinnest.

The CBU-105 is employable from all altitudes and in adverse weather conditions.

The ROKAF received 367 CBU-105s for use on its F-15K, (K)F-16C/D and FA-50 fleet following a contract signed in June 2012.

GBU-10/B and GBU-12/B Paveway II

Following the first successful drop of a laser-guided weapon in 1965, the US Air Force directed funds for further development of these bombs in a programme dubbed Paveway I. Different versions of the Paveway I were used during the war in South East Asia, with great success, starting in 1968.

The Paveway II family of laser-guided bombs was developed based on lessons learned during the Vietnam War. One of the improvements made was the inclusion of folding fins, which allows for better storage and handling, as well as improved ground clearance when installed on an aircraft.

A guidance kit transforms the 500lb (227kg) Mk 82 low-drag general-purpose (LDGP) bomb into a GBU-12 laser-guided precision weapon. The 2,000lb (907kg) Mk 84 LDGP or BLU-109 penetrator adds a guidance kit to convert it into the GBU-10.

Both the GBU-10 and GBU-12 have a CEP of around 9m (30ft) and are guided towards their intended target by use of a laser beam that bounces off the target. The laser seeker in the nose cone detects the reflected laser energy when close enough to the target, and the on-board computer subsequently directs the weapon towards the source. Since its introduction in 1977, more than 100,000 Paveway II guidance kits have been delivered and production is still ongoing.

A GBU-24 Paveway III, still missing its forward fins, loaded under the wing of a USAF F-16C.
(US ANG/MSG Carl Clegg)

Designed specifically to destroy bunkers, the GBU-28 has been in ROKAF use since the early 2010s. Pictured is a Lakenheath-based F-15E dropping the weapon over a test range in the United States.
(USAFE/TSgt Michael Ammons)

Within the ROKAF, the GBU-10/12 is used on the F-4E, F-15K, (K)F-16C/D and F-35A (GBU-12 only).

GBU-24/B Paveway III

To allow delivery at lower level, the Paveway III family of laser-guided weapons was developed. A new guidance and control unit enables the weapon to fly a smoother and therefore more efficient flight path. This is achieved due to controlled guidance, whereas the Paveway II family uses full control deflection to alter the weapon's path, limiting range and accuracy.

Ultimately only the 2,000lb (907kg) version was produced, as the GBU-24. The ROKAF uses the version based upon the BLU-109 penetrator, which is able to pierce a concrete layer of up to 3m (10ft). In case of war the GBU-24 will likely be used to take out hardened aircraft and artillery shelters.

The weapon has a CEP of 3m (10ft) and, when dropped at altitudes over 30,000ft (9,144m), a range of around 30km (19 miles).

GBU-28/B Paveway III

While Korea was in the process of signing a deal with Boeing for 40 examples of the F-15K, DAPA also tried to secure a contract for the delivery of the GBU-28, a so-called bunker-buster weapon. However, officials in Washington refused, as the GBU-28 is classified as a high-end strategic weapon and the export of the 4,700lb (2,131kg) bomb was therefore prohibited, so as not to upset the balance in the region.

When North Korea conducted a second underground nuclear test during May 2009, the United States finally agreed to supply the weapon to the ROKAF.

The GBU-28 was developed, produced, tested and deployed operationally in a timespan of little over three weeks in early 1991, when the USAF needed a weapon to target the various underground military bunker compounds in Iraq.

The USD 63.5 million deal for 150 examples of the GBU-28 for the ROKAF was finalised in November 2009, with deliveries of the weapon complete by 2013.

'*The deployment of GBU-28s will significantly improve the country's deterrence against North Korea's weapons of mass destruction*', a DAPA official was quoted as saying after the signing of the contract.

If armed conflict were to break out on the Korean peninsula, the laser-guided GBU-28 bombs would likely be loaded onto F-15K Slam Eagles for use against North Korean missile- and aircraft shelters as well as underground command posts sheltering the DPRK regime's leaders.

Additionally, the weapon is ideally suited to destroy the KPA's artillery hidden in tunnels and caves north of the DMZ.

The GBU-31(V3)/B consists of a GPS kit mated to a 2,000lb (907kg) BLU-109 penetrator bomb, seen here being loaded on a ROKAF F-16.
(ROK MND)

Last but not least, the GBU-28 could be employed to target elements of the DPRK's nuclear programme, suspected to be hidden underground in the north-eastern part of the secretive country.

GBU-31(V3)/B and GBU-38B JDAM

A new programme to develop an all-weather, low-cost family of precision-guided munitions was intitiated during 1991, as the Joint Direct Attack Munition (JDAM). After evaluation, the proposal from McDonnell Douglas (now Boeing) was chosen, and further testing of the new weapon commenced. In December 1998 the GPS-guided weapon reached initial operating capability with the USAF.

The ubiquitous 500lb (227kg) Mk 82 forms the basis of the GBU-38, while the GBU-31(V1)/B consists of a 2,000lb (907kg) Mk 84 bomb body. The penetrator version uses the BLU-109 bomb body and is designated GBU-31(V3)/B.

The electronic control unit, INS unit and GPS receiver are located in the weapon's tail section. The control unit steers the weapon using its tail fins (three moveable, one fixed). To enhance gliding capability and increase stability, strakes are fitted to the bomb body (GBU-31) or on the nose (GBU-38). After launch the inertial guidance kit directs the weapon, aided by periodic updates from the GPS system.

To allow for employment in GPS-degraded conditions, the weapon can use the INS system only. This decreases the CEP from 4.8m (16ft) to around 30m (100ft).

To increase its stock of GPS-guided weapons, the ROKAF ordered additional GBU-31 guidance kits in a March 2021 contract worth USD 415.6 million.

The weapons are carried by the F-15K, (K)F-16C/D, F-35A (GBU-31 only) and FA-50 (GBU-38 only).

Two inert GBU-39 SDBs attached to a BRU-61 rack are prepared for installation on a USAF F-15E.
(USAF/A1C Kimberly Barrera)

GBU-39/B SDB1

The Small Diameter Bomb (SDB) is a 250lb (113kg) high-precision weapon developed to minimise the risk of collateral damage. Four weapons are carried on a single BRU-61 dispenser rack. The GBU-39 is a Boeing design and was first fielded by the USAF during 2006.

The weapon is GPS-guided and receives target coordinates either in the ground or in the air through the aircraft's interface. Coordinates for a GPS-guided weapon can be generated using a targeting pod such as the AN/AAQ-14 or AN/AAQ-33 Sniper.

The SDB was designed from the outset to be resistant to GPS jamming, but still uses INS as a back-up targeting system.

Several GBU-39s can be released simultaneously to strike different targets. Due to its excellent gliding capability provided by folded wings which open after release, the small GBU-39 has a range close to 80km (50 miles) when dropped from higher altitude.

The ROKAF acquired the GBU-39 as part of a weapon package for the F-35A, although the weapon can also be employed by its F-15 and (K)F-16 aircraft. The F-35A has the provision to carry the BRU-61 both internally in its weapons bay, as well as externally on a weapon pylon, making it theoretically possible to carry 24 precision-guided weapons on a single jet.

GBU-54 and GBU-56 LJDAM

The downside to any GPS-guided munition is the fact it can not be employed to engage moving targets. To allow for greater flexibility during missions it was decided to combine both GPS and laser targeting into a single weapon. Boeing was chosen to design the weapon and the 500lb (227kg) GBU-54 was introduced during 2007. Essentially, the GBU-54 is a GBU-38 JDAM with added laser guidance capability, to produce the Laser Joint Direct Attack Munition (LJDAM). A GBU-54 consists of a standard Mk 82 bomb with the Boeing guidance kit added.

A ROKAF ordnance specialist checks the GBU-54 LJDAM attached to the fuselage station of an F-15K Slam Eagle. (USAF/SSG Shawn Nickel)

The GBU-56 is the 2,000lb (907kg) version of the LJDAM, combining either a BLU-109 or Mk 84 dumb weapon with laser and GPS targeting capability. The GBU-56 became operational with the USAF during 2011.

During Red Flag 17-1, at Eielson AFB in the United States, the F-15K Slam Eagle employed the GBU-54 for the first time when attacking targets on the vast training ranges of Alaska.

Korean GPS Guided Bomb (KGGB)

The KGGB consists of a mid-range GPS/INS guidance kit and a Mk 82 500lb (227kg) general-purpose bomb. The guidance kit turns a standard free-fall bomb into an accurate weapon. The KGGB has a large stand-off range thanks to its excellent gliding capabilities provided by its wings, which fold open after release. When dropped from altitudes in excess of 30,000ft (9,144m) the weapon has a range of more than 100km (62 miles). Produced by Korean defence company LIG Nex1, the weapon is capable of manoeuvring to attack targets at the optimum angle.

The KGGB can be mounted on an aircraft without any modification to existing hard and/or software. Mission information is fed into a portable pilot display unit (PDU), which is carried in the cockpit and used to communicate with the bomb. The KGGB has been tested for use on the ROKAF fleet of F-4E, (K)F-5E/F, F-15K, (K)F-16C/D, and FA-50 aircraft and has been in use since 2013.

SPICE 2000

The Israeli firm Rafael Advanced Defense Systems developed and produced the SPICE 2000 guidance kit to convert standard 2,000lb (907kg) Mk 84 LDGP bombs into precision stand-off strike weapons. Mission information is fed into the weapon on the ground or onboard the aircraft, with the weapon plotting a route towards the target using its own navigation systems.

The indigenously designed KGGB GPSINS weapon has been in ROKAF use since 2013.
(AV Kok)

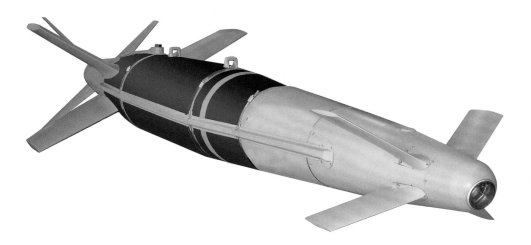

Israeli company Rafael supplied
the ROKAF with the SPICE 2000
EO guidance kit to turn freefall
Mk 84 bombs into weapons
with pinpoint accuracy.
(Rafael Advanced Defense
Systems)

The bomb can be employed as far away as 80km (50 miles) from the intended target
due to its excellent gliding capabilities. Target acquisition is performed using scene-
matching algorythms through an advanced EO seeker. The SPICE 2000 then hits at the
predefined impact angle and azimuth. Thanks to its EO system, the weapon is insensi-
tive to GPS jamming.

The ROKAF was reported as having ordered the guidance kits during 2015, with
the first deliveries taking place the following year. The SPICE 2000 is employed by the
ROKAF's fleet of (K)F-16C/D aircraft.

Guided Graphite Bomb

In August 2020, the ADD announced it had selected companies tasked with developing
a graphite bomb, or so-called 'black-out' weapon.

This type of non-lethal bomb is filled with graphite filament that, upon explosion of
the warhead inside, will break up and form a cloud of fine particles in order to short-
circuit electrical installations like power stations, overhead power lines or distribution
stations.

A computer-generated image
of the Guided Graphite Bomb,
currently under development for
the ROKAF.
(Poongsan Corp)

The outer shell of the bomb will be built by Poongsan, with Hanwha Systems
responsible for the fuse, and LIG Nex1 providing the guidance kit. The ROKAF hopes
to start testing the bomb in 2025.

Air-to-ground rockets

Hydra 70

The 2.75in (70mm) Folding-Fin Aircraft Rocket, or FFAR, has been in use since the
late 1940s. The Hydra 70 is an upgraded version of the rocket still in use today, with an
effective range between 0.5 and 8km (0.3 and 5 miles).

The Hydra 70 is available with different warheads depending on mission. Some
of these warheads allow them to be used to create a smoke curtain or to illuminate
targets.

The AN/AWW-13 datalink pod used to guide the AGM-84H SLAM-ER is also used by the US Navy, as evidenced by this photo of an example being uploaded to a P-3C Orion.
(USN/PH3C Shannon R. Smith)

ROKAF ordnance specialists lay out a display of Hydra 70 rockets alongside a LAU-61 launch tube in front of an F-5E.
(ROK MND)

The LAU series of pods was designed to carry the rockets. Both the LAU-3/A and LAU-61/A hold 19 rockets, while the LAU-131/A holds seven.

The Hydra pods used by the ROKAF are compatible with the (K)F-5E/F, (K)F-16C/D, FA-50/TA-50 and KA-1.

Targeting and reconnaissance systems

AN/AWW-13 datalink pod

The AN/AWW-13 is used to communicate with the AGM-84H SLAM-ER missile after launch. The pod transmits radio-frequency signals to the missile inflight, to allow slewing and designation of the track point of the missile. The datalink in the SLAM-ER sends the seeker imagery back to the AN/AWW-13 datalink pod on the controlling aircraft. The pod then relays this imagery to the cockpit video display.

For a photo of this pod see page 115 top.

AN/ASW-55 datalink pod

This 1,907lb (865kg) datalink pod is used to communicate with the AGM-142 Popeye/ Have Nap missile. Footage from the missile's EO or IR seeker is transmitted via the datalink pod to a display in the F-4's cockpit. The pilot or WSO in the aircraft remotely guides the missile into its target. The pod also has the provision to record and store in-flight footage recorded by the missile.

For a photo of this pod see **AGM-124 Popeye** on page 102.

AN/AVQ-23 Pave Spike targeting pod

The Westinghouse Pave Spike uses a laser designator coupled to an EO seeker for targeting, which limits the pod to daytime use only. Compared to earlier targeting pods in

The AN/AVQ-23 Pave Spike pod loaded on the left-hand forward fuselage station of a USAF F-4D. (USAF)

use, the Pave Spike has the advantage of not taking up a valuable air-to-ground weapon station. The pod is suspended from the front left Sparrow well on the F-4E. Another advantage is its weight; 420lb (209kg), or less than a third of the weight of a Pave Tack pod also carried on the Phantom. The pod first saw service with the USAF during the Vietnam War, and is still carried on ROKAF Phantoms today.

AN/AVQ-26 Pave Tack targeting pod

Pave Tack is a laser designator pod used for precision navigation, target location and target designation. Weighing around 1,385lb (629kg) the Pave Tack pod uses an EO/IR system to provide a clear view of targets in day, night, or adverse weather. A video image is transmitted to a display in the F-4's cockpit meaning the pod can function as a reconnaissance asset if needed.

The large turret at the rear of the pod contains an IR camera, laser rangefinder and laser designator. The latter system allows the Phantom crew to designate a target for a laser-guided weapon. The turret rotates in both pitch and roll, allowing the crew to continue designating a target even as the aircraft flies away from it.

The ROKAF ordered an initial batch of eight pods in 1984 for delivery in 1987. It is unknown if additional pods were subsequently received from surplus USAF stocks.

The Ford Aerospace AN/AVQ-26 Pave Tack is still in use with the ROKAF's dwindling fleet of F-4E Phantom II aircraft.

For a photo of this pod see page 107 top.

LANTIRN navigation and targeting system

The LANTIRN (Low Altitude Navigation and Targeting Infrared for Night) system consists of an AN/AAQ-13 navigation pod and AN/AAQ-14 targeting pod.

A complete LANTIRN system, consisting of both the AN/AAQ-13 navigation pod (left-hand side) and AN/AAQ-14 targeting pod, seen carried by an KF-16C.
(Robin Polderman)

A KF-16C comes in to land carrying the AN/AAQ-33 Sniper targeting pod on the right-hand intake station and an ALQ-200 ECM pod under the centreline. (Robin Polderman)

The system was designed for both the F-15E and F-16C/D, to allow these aircraft to effectively identify and target enemy assets and also fly at low altitude during night and in adverse weather. The LANTIRN system was first fielded in 1987.

The AN/AAQ-13 uses a terrain-following-radar and a FLIR camera to provide visual clues concerning terrain and obstacles. An IR image of the terrain ahead of the aircraft is displayed on the head-up display.

The AN/AAQ-14 pod provides target identification and recognition as well as laser designation for PGMs. The pod's IR sensor provides the pilot or WSO with an IR image of the target on a cockpit display. The built-in laser rangefinder is used to designate the target for the delivery of guided munitions.

Both podded systems are still in use with the KF-16C/D squadrons of the ROKAF, even after the introduction of the Sniper ATP.

AN/AAQ-33 Sniper ATP

In 2001, Lockheed Martin won the competition to provide the USAF with an Advanced Targeting Pod (ATP).

The system features a high-end CCD camera able to identify targets, on the ground or in the air, at a much greater range than previous targeting pods. For low-light or

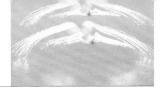

adverse weather conditions an IR camera was added. The pod is able to send target imagery to other aircraft or ground stations via a datalink.

In 2009, Lockheed Martin demonstrated the benefits of the Sniper's capability by successfully flying the pod on ROKAF F-15K and KF-16C/D aircraft with a common Sniper pod software load. This capability allows operators maximum flexibility by being able to deploy the pod on various aircraft types, without the need to change software. In April 2011, the first AN/AAQ-33 pods were delivered to the 11th FW at Daegu to replace the AN/AAQ-14. Subsequently, the ROKAF placed a follow-on order for the Sniper ATP during December 2013.

In October 2019, Lockheed Martin declared it had completed a fit check of the Sniper ATP on the KAI FA-50. The fit check verified the engineering, physical connections and interfaces, as well as validated upload and download procedures of the pod. The pod was expected to have been fully integrated on the FA-50, including completion of a flight test programme, by the end of 2020.

In addition to the F-15K and FA-50, the Sniper ATP is also carried by the (K)F-16C/D.

AN/AAS-42 TIGER Eyes navigation pod

TIGER Eyes was designed as an all-weather navigation, terrain-following, and long-range infrared search and track (IRST) podded system for the F-15K Slam Eagle in use with the ROKAF. The pod is an evolution of the AN/AAQ-13 navigation pod still in use on the ROKAF F-16 fleet. Lockheed Martin chose the IRST system used on the F-14D Tomcat for integration in the pod. A passive long-wave infrared sensor system searches for and detects heat sources within its field of view. The IRST system allows the F-15K to assess and engage long-range airborne targets without using the radar system.

Below: The AN/AAS-42 TIGER Eyes pod, with its shiny IRST sensor clearly visible. The system is designed to serve as a pylon, with the AN/ AAQ-14 LANTIRN targeting pod hung underneath. (Archive Robin Polderman)

Bottom: A fully loaded F-15K carrying the LANTIRN system, a AN AAS-42 TIGER Eyes pod, multiple GBU-38s, a GBU-31(V1) ,as well as CATM-84H SLAM-ER and CATM-120B training missiles. (Robin Polderman)

Rarely photographed, this RF-16C is returning from an intelligence-gathering sortie along the DMZ carrying an ARD300K TAC ELINT pod, as well as live AIM-9 and AIM-120 missiles.
(Anonymous)

An RF-16C returns from a reconnaissance sortie carrying the ELBIT Condor2 pod on its centreline station.
(Archive Robin Polderman)

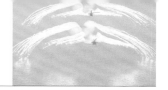

TIGER Eyes sparked some controversy when the United States accused the ROKAF of breaking the seals on the system, to copy the technology for its own use.

Elbit Systems-ISTAR Condor2 reconnaissance pod

In April 2017, Elbit Systems revealed a USD 82 million deal for an unspecified number of Condor2 pods, under a contract signed with an 'undisclosed Asia-Pacific country'. As the pod has been observed being carried by ROKAF F-16Cs recently, it is believed South Korea was the signee of the contract.

The Israeli-built Condor2 is an EO/IR LOROP system that provides simultaneous high-resolution visible and IR reconnaissance images. The long focal length electro-optical camera is able to cover wide areas in a short time span. Thanks to its EO/IR camera, the system can be used both day and night.

Compared to conventional photo-pods the Condor2 enables photography at higher altitudes, up to 50,000ft (15,240m), as well as longer stand-off distances, rumoured to be in excess of 80km (50 miles). The system can be operated at speeds up to Mach 1.4. These advantages greatly reduce the risk from ground threats such as the North Korean arsenal of anti-aircraft missiles.

The Condor2, carried on the F-16's centreline station, is capable of onboard mission data recording but can also make use of a wide-band datalink for real time image transmission to a (mobile) image exploitation station.

The fully autonomous target covering, thanks to precise geo-referencing, allows the pilot to fly a pre-planned route without worrying about operation of the pod. The pilot is able to override the system if a target of opportunity presents itself.

The Condor2 pod allows the ROKAF to peer over the border into North Korea, while remaining on the safe side of the DMZ.

ARD-300K TAC-ELINT pod

The ARD-300K is an indigenous electronic intelligence (ELINT) system which gathers signals transmitted by air defence radars and missile systems. The pod has LPI (low probability of intercept) radar signal collection/analysis, high-frequency, and millimeter-wave threat detection. The pod is able to pinpoint the locations of enemy radar transmissions and has a secondary function as a HARM targeting system.

The pod can send real-time data to ground stations through a datalink. Development of the pod was initiated by the Agency for Defense Development, and it was built by Hanwha Systems (a joint venture between Samsung and French company Thales). The pod is carried on the centreline of the RF-16C and entered service on 30 December 2013.

TAC-EO/IR reconnaissance pod

This reconnaissance pod was developed by LIG Nex1 in cooperation with the ADD, and is normally carried on station 5B, the right-hand intake mount on the RF-16C. Through the EO/IR seeker, intelligence imagery is collected day or night, and transmitted real-time to ground receivers using an onboard datalink system.

Due to its manoeuvrability, high speed, improved situational awareness, and ability to fly low, a manned fighter aircraft equipped for reconnaissance is sometimes a better option than a slower and higher flying drone.

A Suwon-based F-5E returns to base in an interesting configuration consisting of the A37U target tow system (the TDU-10/B DART having been discarded after use) and live AIM-9P Sidewinders. (Robin Polderman)

The exact range of the TAC EO/IR pod remains a well guarded secret, as is the number of pods delivered to the ROKAF since its induction on 30 December 2013.

Miscellaneous systems

A/A37U-15 towed aerial target system

The A/A37U-15 system was developed to provide pilots with a system for air-to-air gunnery training. The system consists of the TDU-10/B DART towed aerial target, and the RMU-10/A reel pod which houses 2,200ft (671m) of armoured tow cable. If the target system is flown with the target in the tow position, the maximum speed is 450kts (roughly Mach 0.9) at loads of 2.5G. Minimum speed for reeling out the DART is 200kts (370km/h) at an altitude of between 1,000 (305m) and 20,000ft (6,097m).

The DART is covered in radar-reflecting material, hence the silver colour, to permit the use of radar gun sights. The system is still in limited use on the ROKAF (K)F-5E/F.

AGTS-36 Aerial Gunnery Target System

The AGTS-36, manufactured by US company Meggitt Defense Systems, was developed in the early 1980s to replace the A/A37U-15 target system. The AGTS-36 is a reeling machine attached to a weapon pylon and houses the TDK-39 Aerial Gunnery Tow Target, which is reeled out 2,000ft (600m) behind the towing aircraft.

The TDK-39 target is compatible with the operating airspeeds and manoeuvre capabilities of modern fighter aircraft. It is a reusable solid-body target specifically designed for manoeuvres up to 5G and speeds up to Mach 0.9.

The TDK-39 houses a real-time Doppler scoring system (RADOPS), consisting of a telemetry transmitter and antenna. A receiver module is installed in the reeling machine, and scores are transmitted in real time to the towing pilot for transmission to the shooter after each pass. The TDK-39 target houses an internal mechanism for deploying a 30ft (9m) string-sleeve known as the Visual Augmentor (VA). This VA is the actual aim point of the engagement and is discarded after the TDK-39 is recovered and secured onto the AGTS-36 reeling machine. The Doppler scoring system is optimised for 20–30mm munitions and firing rates up to 7,200 rounds per minute.

In ROKAF service the AGTS-36 is carried by the F-5 and F-4E, but is also compatible with the F-15 and F-16.

AIS instrumentation pod
The Airborne Instrumentation Subsytem pod is carried during simulated air combat and large-scale exercises organised by the ROKAF. The pods are frequently carried during operations at Cheongju Air Base since a ground station and debriefing facility is located there. The pod provides the link between the ground station and the aircraft by transmitting data, consisting of aircraft location, altitude, attitude, speed and other parameters. To collect data for transmission, the pod is equipped with an air data sensor, a UHF antenna, INS and a radar altimeter.

Not one but two AIS instrumentation pods carried on an F-4E. The absence of external fuel tanks is a clear indication it has been involved in simulated air combat.
(Robin Polderman)

The AN/ALQ-88 ECM pod is still in limited use on the remainder of the ROKAF F-4E fleet. The now-retired F-4D also carried the pod, as evidenced by serial number 68-759.
(Robin Polderman)

▶ Right side, top: as well as a pair of external fuel tanks, this KA-1 also carries the HMP-250 gun pod.
(AV Kok)

A KF-16D participating in a Red Flag – Alaska exercise carrying an ALQ-200 ECM pod on the centreline station.
(USAF/SrA Ashley Nicole Taylor)

The AIS pod has the shape of an AIM-9 Sidewinder and is carried on the same launchrail.

AN/ALQ-88K ECM pod
An indigenous electronic self-defence pod used on the F-4E and F-16C/D, the AN/ALQ-88K is still in limited use with the remaining F-4E Phantom II squadron despite the introduction of the newer ALQ-200K system. The pod is carried in the left forward Sparrow bay on the F-4E.

ALQ-200K ECM pod
Korean defence company LIG Nex1 manufactures the ALQ-200 pod, development of which started in 2000. The system was designed as an externally mounted pod that enhances the survivability of aircraft flying missions over enemy territory in future electronic warfare environments by jamming SAMs, AAA radars and the systems of enemy aircraft. After collecting, measuring and analysing the direction of radio-frequency signals emitted by enemy missiles and radar, it sends jamming signals to the direction of threats to block enemy radars from tracking data or to increase the error rate of guided missiles.

Initially designed for use on F-4E and (K)F-16C/D aircraft, the system was later adapted for use on the F-15K Slam Eagle. Deliveries of the pod to operational units started in 2005. The number of pods received by the ROKAF is a closely guarded secret.

SUU-20B/A practice bomb and rocket dispenser
The SUU-20 dispenser was designed to train pilots in delivering unguided bombs and rockets. In use since the early 1970s, the ROKAF continues to employ it on its fleet of

A ROKAF armourer checks the safety switches on a SUU-20 dispenser attached to the wing pylon of a KF-16D. (Robin Polderman)

A KAI test pilot puts a T-50 through its paces at an airshow. To accentuate the manoeuvres, the wingtips are fitted with smokewinders.
(Robin Polderman)

fighter aircraft. The dispenser holds six BDU-33 or Mk 106 practice bombs, as well as four 2.75in (70mm) unguided training rockets.

HMP-250 gun pod

Built by Belgian defence company FN Herstal, the 250lb (114kg) HMP-250 contains a 12.7mm (0.5in) M3P machine gun which was specifically designed for aerial operations. The pod contains 250 rounds of ammunition, enough for more than 15 seconds of continous firing, and is used on the KA-1 aircraft of the 8th FW at Hoengseong Air Base.

Smoke generators

To show off the capability of its T-50 family of jets during displays, KAI makes use of smokewinders built by Sanders Aeronautics of the United States. The smokewinder is a completely self-contained smoke system that mounts directly onto a standard 16S210 Sidewinder launch rail. They are of slightly larger diameter than a standard AIM-9 and contain both a fuel and oil tank. A sparkplug ignites fuel that is dispensed from the back of the device, which is then 'extinguished' by the oil, which generates the smoke.

The ROKAF uses a different way of generating smoke during fly-overs, using a system consisting of two tubes welded to a mounting plate which, as an assembly, is attached to a weapon pylon. Air flows in via small holes on the front side of the tube, passing the smoke-generating pyrotechnic device, with smoke emitting from the back. The device can be triggered by the pilot from the cockpit.

The system is rather maintenance-intensive, as residue pouring from the pipes sticks to pylons and other parts of the jet, requiring a thorough cleaning after use.

As the system can be installed on any weapon pylon, it is able to be carried by all fighter aircraft in use with the ROKAF.

Surface-to-air missile systems

MIM-104F Patriot PAC-3

The Patriot is manufactured by Raytheon and derives its name from the AN/MPQ-53 radar used on the weapon system — Phased Array Tracking Radar to Intercept of

An MIM-104 missile fired from a ROKAF Patriot system. (ROK MND)

Target. The first examples of the Patriot system were delivered to US forces in 1983. The Patriot was designed as an anti-aircraft SAM but, through constant upgrades, has established itself as the prime anti-ballistic missile system in the Western world.

The ROKAF received its first Patriot PAC-2 system second-hand from the German military on 22 November 2008, purchasing a total of six batteries consisting of 48 fire units and 192 MIM-104 missiles.

The Republic of Korea signed a Letter of Offer and Acceptance on 13 March 2015 for the upgrade of its Patriot missile system to the more advanced PAC-3 configuration. This upgrade addresses nearly every aspect of the missile, allowing the country to defend itself more effectively against the threat of incoming ballistic missiles.

Korea updated some of its systems to PAC-3 Cost Reduction Initiative (CRI) standard and others to PAC-3 Missile Segment Enhancement (MSE) standard. While the CRI has a range of 12 miles (20km), a more powerful dual-pulse motor currently allow the MIM-104F SME missiles to intercept ballistic missiles at a range of 30km (19 miles) and a speed of Mach 5.

ROKAF personnel scramble towards an indigenously developed Cheon Gung I SAM system parked on top of a hill. (ROKAF)

To better protect its precious fleet of fifth-generation F-35A aircraft, the ROKAF decided to relocate a Patriot PAC-3 battery to Cheongju, home base of the stealthy fighter, during April 2020. With ballistic missile development north of the DMZ ongoing, it is believed North Korean SRBMs now have the range to reach Cheongju. Earlier in 2020, a Patriot battery was moved closer to Seoul in order to protect key facilities against the SRBM threat North Korea poses.

KM-SAM (Cheon Gung I and Cheon Gung II)

The National Defense Research Institute started development of an indigenous air defence system in 2011. The KM-SAM system is produced by Korean defence company LG Nex1 in cooperation with Almay-Antez and Fakel, both of which are Russian companies, and based on technology that is used in the Russian S-400 SAM system. The medium-range KM-SAM was fielded in 2015 after several test firings had proved successful, and the system replaced the MIM-23 HAWK system, which was withdrawn from use in July 2021 after 39 years in service.

Each Cheon Gung battery consists of a multifunction radar attached to a firing control system and a TEL carrying eight missiles. The KM-SAM has an effective range of 40km (25 miles) and can intercept targets at altitudes up to 15,000m (49,000ft).

Where the HAWK could only intercept one target at a time, the KM-SAM is capable of tracking and targeting up to six targets simultaneously.

The KM-SAM was designed with the modern battlefield in mind, meaning it is virtually immune to jamming from electronic warfare systems currently in use. The last of 24 Cheon Gung I systems was delivered to the ROKAF in April 2020.

Korea continued development of the Cheon Gung to create a PAC-3-level ballistic missile interceptor system to counter one of the main threats from the DPRK. In order to make the weapon capable for that mission, the missile's maximum altitude was increased to 20,000m (66,000ft). The first of seven Cheon Gung II systems was delivered to the ROKAF in November 2020.

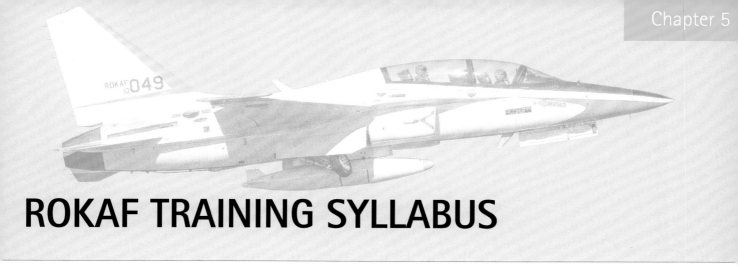

ROKAF TRAINING SYLLABUS

Korea established an Aviation Academy at Gimpo, near Seoul, on 14 January 1949. Later renamed to Air Force Academy (AFA), it had to relocate a few times due to the outbreak of the Korean War. After having resettled in Seoul during 1959, the AFA moved to its current location just south of the city of Cheongju in December of 1985. Female students were allowed to enroll in the Air Force Academy starting in 1997, and the first female pilot graduated back in 2002.

To train conscripts, NCOs and officers not enrolled in the AFA, the ROKAF set up a training centre at Jinju, which doubles as the headquarters of the Education and Training Command. It was established as the Air Education Unit at Daegu on 1 April 1951 and finally settled in the town of Jinju, following an earlier relocation to Daejon, in 1988.

Future aircraft technicians receive their technical training here, with a number of withdrawn aircraft, including some F-4s and F-5s, in use as instructional airframes. A couple of replica aircraft shelters were constructed in order to teach tow tractor drivers the art of safely manoeuvring an aircraft inside, as realistically as possible.

Flight training

Training a skilled South Korean fighter pilot costs more than USD 4 million and could take up to eight years, including four years of college education at the Air Force Academy, two years of pilot training, and three to four years of sharpening skills at one of the ROKAF's operational squadrons.

During the summer months of their first year at the academy, cadets learn to fly paragliders as an introduction to flight. Following theoretical training regarding weather, equipment and basics of flight, cadets will fly together with an instructor on short, low altitude paraglide hops, for their first taste of flight. After the student has developed enough skill for landing, take off, and is deemed safe to fly solo, he or she continues training at Sungmu Bong, located 430m (1,410ft) above sea level.

Throughout their time at the academy, cadets are subject to pilot aptitude testing for which the ROKAF developed Pilot Aptitude Research Equipment (PARE). Cadets use this equipment to improve in the fields of perceptual capacity, multi-tasking, spatial orientation, hand-eye coordination, stress tolerance and resilience. PARE can be used by all year groups, but fourth-year cadets have priority.

Computer-based simulators are used by cadets to familiarise themselves with the cockpit instruments and the basics of aircraft control.

Since 2001, the joint commissioning ceremony has also included female graduates. (ROK MND)

When in their third year, cadets undergo centrifuge training to develop a physical ability to gravitational velocity, the so-called G-tolerance.

Cadets at the academy perform a familiarisation flight in the KAI KT-100 Naraon at Seongmu Air Base, a mere stonethrow away from the academy grounds, during their first and second year. Two more familiarisation flights are undertaken during the fourth year. After a flight in the right-hand seat of the KT-100, the student moves to the left seat in an attempt to take on the roll of pilot-in-command on their second flight, under close supervision of the instructor.

The 23 KT-100 trainers in use at Seongmu, belong to the 212th Flying Training Squadron (212th FTS) which was founded in 1970. To enhance the cooperation between the 212th FTS, the maintenance and logistics department, and the unit responsible for the simulator and PARE systems, the 55th Flight Training Group was established on 6 March 2014.

Following graduation from the AFA, the cadets are commissioned in the rank of second lieutenant. Only then will they start their elementary flight training with the 212th FTS, which will take 12 weeks to complete.

Obtaining the Red Scarf

To raise morale among its pilots, the ROKAF decided to reintroduce the red scarf which was commonly worn in the 1950s. Korean fashion designer Andre Kim was requested to come up with a design, to which he agreed without accepting a fee. The 3 July was designated 'Day of the Pilots' in Korea, and on this day in 2008, the first redesigned red scarfs were handed out to pilots during a ceremony in Seoul, in the attendance of

With the introduction of the KAI KT-100, all fixed-wing training aircraft, from basic to lead-in fighter training, are made in Korea.
(KAI)

Football player Koo Ja-cheol, who competed in the German Bundesliga for VfL Wolfsburg, Mainz 05, and FC Augsburg, was appointed honorary ambassador of the ROKAF in 2012 and as such had the privelege to fly in the back seat of an F-15K. For the occasion he received the famous red pilot scarf.
(ROKAF)

veteran pilots of the Korean War. Subsequently, red scarfs were distributed to all active duty and retired ROKAF pilots.

Clearly, for all student pilots, obtaining the red scarf is their prime objective, for it being a symbol of successful graduation.

Besides graduating the AFA, there are other ways to becoming a pilot in the Republic of Korea Air Force. Students which have a college degree and pass entry tests are eligible to enroll in the 15-week Basic Officer Training course in Jinju. These so-called 'short-term' officers will have a chance to undergo elementary flight training at Seongmu following flight screening and entry test. While in college, students are

Two Cessna 172s from Korea Aerospace University during another MPC sortie at Jungseok airfield.
(Hwangbo Joonwoo)

A pair of KT-1 trainers takes to the sky at the southern air base of Sacheon. Four squadrons at the base make use of the fleet of 84 KT-1 aircraft. (Robin Polderman)

able to follow an ROTC (Reserve Officer Training Corps) programme, similar to that practised in the United States, to prepare them for military service, partially in their spare time.

Students at the Korea Aerospace University (KAU), majoring in Flight Operations can enroll in the Military Pilot Course (MPC), which takes up two years. Upon graduation the new pilots will be contracted to fly with the ROKAF for 13 years before continuing their career as an airline pilot. The university operates flight training centres at Goyang, Jungseok and Uljin. The MPC takes place using the university's Cessna 172 Skyhawk aircraft at Jungseok airfield on the southern island of Jeju.

Flight Practice Section 1 of the MPC basically finishes the Private Pilot Licence (PPL). The second section of the training is oriented towards instrument flight certification.

Besides the Korea Aerospace University, the Cheongju, Chodang, Hanseo, Jungwon and Kyungwoon Universities all offer similar flight training courses and are in posession of their own training aircraft.

Basic flight training

Following successful completion of elementary flight training, the AFA graduate commences basic flight training. The student pilot will spend 36 weeks at Sacheon Air Base, flying approximately 80 hours in the KAI KT-1 Woongbee trainer.

Student pilots who graduated from one of the previously mentioned civil universities are already in posession of a PPL, and basic flying training for them is shortened to a 22-week curriculum.

Student pilots will go through formation flying, perform navigation and instrument flights and will practice flying in the darkness. The advantage of the KT-1 compared to the T-37C which was previously used in this stage of training, is the Head-Up Display. This allows for better situational awareness of the student, and improves the usefulness of the aircraft during spin training. The KT-1, having a modern cockpit, equipped with four multifunction displays, prepares the students for more advanced trainers.

On completion of the basic flying stage, a selection is made to determine which students will become either a helicopter or transport pilot, or who will progress to fast jet training.

Pilots chosen to fly transport aircraft or helicopters, remain at Sacheon for another 21 weeks of KT-1 training following which another selection is made. Pilots destined to fly fixed wing aircraft proceed to either the CN235/HS.748 (25 weeks) or C-130H (27 weeks) for conversion training, before being posted to their operational fixed wing

Three Bell 412 helicopters, used in the VIP role until replaced by newer aircraft, soldier on in the training role from Cheongju Air Base.
(SangYeon Kim)

squadron. Future helicopter pilots transfer to Cheongju for 35 weeks of rotary training using both the Bell 412 and H-60 Black Hawk.

The ROKAF takes care of basic training of the Navy's fixed wing pilots as well. Students from the Naval Academy will fly the KT-1 at Sacheon, before returning to a ROK Navy air station to continue their career on the Reims-Cessna F406 or P-3CK Orion.

Advanced flight training

Next step in the training syllabus for future fighter pilots consists of 30 weeks at Gwangju air base with the 1st FW, flying the KAI T-50 Golden Eagle jet trainer. The first squadron to operate the T-50, the 203rd FTS, was established at Gwangju in June 2005. Initially it consisted of eight instructor pilots who had never flown the T-50 before, but they were actively training new pilots less than 18 months later. After the 203rd FTS moved to Hoengseong Air Base in April 2013 to become an FA-50 squadron, the 216th FTS took its place. Before being assigned to Gwangju, the 216th FTS operated the T-59 Hawk from Yecheon Air Base.

The other training unit located at Gwangju is the 189th FTS, a former T-38A squadron, and together the two squadrons operate the 49 remaining T-50 Golden Eagles and train roughly 140 student pilots per annum.

The T-50 is used in the advanced flight training course to teach student pilots basic flying abilities in jet-powered flight. The handling characteristics of the T-50 are improved due to its digital fly-by-wire flight control system.

The aircraft was designed with a large tail, flaperons, and rudder to make the T-50 easier to control at lower speeds, and therefore very suitable for low-speed approaches.

Before being assigned to fly the P-3CK Orion with the ROK Navy, pilots will need to report to the ROKAF for flying training on the KT-1.
(Robin Polderman)

Seen taking off from Gwangju on a training sortie, T-50 serial number 10-049 was the penultimate T-50 trainer delivered to the ROKAF during 2010.
(Robin Polderman)

These features makes an aircraft easier to land than most fighters, including the T-38 it was destined to replace. Many students have landed the T-50 without instructor assistance on their first flight. A student's first sortie in the T-50 is a front-seat familiarisation flight, with the student at the controls most of the times, often including the take-off and landing. This is made possible thanks to a thorough theoretical training system in place, with the student learning to operate the aircraft from engine start to engine shut down without ever having to leave the ground.

Modern training systems

The student pilots will spend their first seven weeks at Gwangju in a ground training squadron, before continuing to the flying portion of the training at one of the two based T-50 squadrons. The theoretical portion of the training is conducted in the T-50 Integrated Training Center which is also located at Gwangju Air Base. Instruction to students heavily relies on computer-based training systems, and they can work in individual sessions at their own pace. The same systems are also used to track the performance of the student throughout the training syllabus.

Student pilots learn to operate the T-50 using two different simulators: a full mission trainer and a procedure trainer. The latter consists of a cockpit with five displays to allow the student pilot to practice engine start-up procedures as well as go through various emergency drills.

To prepare students for the task ahead, KAI has developed a number of state-of-the-art simulators for the T-50. (KAI)

Following the initial batch of 22 TA-50 aircraft, another 20 examples were ordered for lead-in fighter training. They will most likely also be based at Yecheon, alongside the first batch of TA-50s. (KAI)

The full mission trainer is a full dome simulator used for training an entire flight from start to finish.

The simulator building houses a control room where instructors monitor student performance on both simulators. Using their control screens, instructors can change the weather, turn day into night, and introduce malfunctions resulting in emergency situations. The system also allows for multiple aircraft to be simulated in order to

create more complex scenarios. A network is used to connect flight simulators, so students can practice the art of air combat or fly in formation. Contrary to a real aircraft, any mistakes made in the simulator can be quickly corrected by the flick of a switch.

The ROKAF claims the introduction of the T-50 has led to a reduction of training time by 20 per cent, a reduction in training cost by 30 per cent, and an increase in student skill level by 40 per cent. This is not in the least thanks to the state-of-the-art ground-based training systems in use. Students are able to advance much faster through the primary stages and time saved is used to introduce the students to tactical flying.

Before the introduction of the T-50 the student pilot flew 60 hours on the Northrop T-38A Talon followed by an additional 44 flight hours on the F-5E and F-5F prior being posted to an operational squadron. The use of the T-50 eliminated both the T-38 and F-5E/F steps in the training curriculum for fighter pilots and has eliminated 10 sorties from the training syllabus.

LIFT and CRT

Following succesful graduation at Gwangju, pilots will transfer to either the TA-50 for lead-in fighter training (LIFT) or straight to the FA-50, (K)F-5, F-15K or KF-16 for combat readiness training (CRT), taking anywhere between 26 weeks (TA-50) to 30 weeks (F-15K).

Pilots assigned to follow a CRT course will fly a number of back seat sorties before transferring to the front seat. After being declared safe to fly, it will take considerable time before the new pilot has mastered the weapons platform he or she now controls. The acquisition of a new batch of TA-50s should free up aircraft like the KF-16D for operational sorties, instead of being used for CRT training by the 157th Fighter Squadron.

Training at Nellis

Red Flag is arguably the world's premier aerial combat training exercise. Following lessons learned in the Vietnam War, where USAF pilots scored only marginally better than their Vietnamese adversaries, a new training programme was initiated. Statisitics showed that if a pilot survived his first 10 combat missions, his probability of survival for remaining missions increased substantially. The USAF reasoned that if it could replicate those first 10 missions by providing training in a highly realistic combined air, ground and electronic threat environment, this would significantly improve the combat effectiveness, survivability and confidence of its pilots during real conflicts.

The first Red Flag exercise was organised at Nellis Air Force Base in Nevada during 1975 and the exercise still takes place there three times a year. Red Flag missions are flown over the vast 4,500sq mi (11,690km^2) Nevada Test and Training Range (NTTR), in use as bombing and gunnery range.

The NTTR houses many targets such as mock airfields, vehicle convoys, tanks, parked aircraft, bunkered defensive positions and missile sites. These targets are defended by a variety of simulated enemy air and ground threats to give participating aircrew the most realistic combat training possible.

The NTTR is heavily instrumented allowing the Red Flag Measurement and Debriefing System to monitor and record the air war in real time. It provides a way to digitally reconstruct the manoeuvers flown during Red Flag missions afterwards, and makes it possible to integrate the activity of ground-based threats to create a complete picture. The Mission Commander and participating aircrew can use the info provided in the after-action debrief as a valid base to evaluate their own decisions and assess the lessons learned.

Since 1975, a total of 29 countries, including South Korea, have joined the United States in these exercises.

The ROKAF's lack of budget for overseas training, curtailed any large scale participation in Red Flag exercises at Nellis. However, the Koreans found a clever way around the budgetary problems by limiting the size of the participating detachment and, more importantly, by using aircraft that were already in the United States waiting

Red Flag 08-4, in August 2008, saw six brand-new F-15K Slam Eagles participate. These flew to Nellis directly from the Boeing factory in St Louis. (Robin Polderman)

for delivery to the ROKAF. This diminished the cost of flying aircraft from Korea, supported by aerial refuelers, half way across the globe to participate. It also saved expensive training missions to teach its participating pilots the art of air-to-air refuelling before ferrying their aircraft overseas.

The ROKAF participated in a Red Flag exercise for the first time during March of 1979. Three brand new F-4E Phantom II aircraft were ferried from the McDonnell Douglas factory in St. Louis, Missouri, to Nellis AFB. These aircraft formed part of the second batch of Phantoms, codenamed Peace Pheasant II, that the ROKAF had purchased. A total of six Phantom crews participated in this edition of Red Flag.

During August 1979 four factory fresh Northrop F-5F two seaters, straight from the Northrop facility in nearby California, were present at Nellis to participate in Red Flag. At the conclusion of the exercise the aircraft were disassembled and flown to South Korea on USAF C-5 Galaxy transports.

The whole process was repeated in the spring of 1980, with the same number of F-5F aircraft along with 17 participating ROKAF pilots.

When the ROKAF obtained second-hand F-4 aircraft out of the MIMEX programme, some of these aircraft were flown to Nellis to join Red Flag exercises before being ferried to their new homeland. In October 1983, three F-4Ds participated and this detachment hit the news in Korea when it transpired that one of its pilots, Colonel Lee Young-soon, had claimed a USAF F-15 during a simulated dogfight over the NTTR.

Four second-hand F-4E Phantoms and 17 aircrew participated in the August 1990 edition of Red Flag.

When a follow-on order for four F-16D Block 32 had been placed, it allowed the ROKAF to plan participation in another edition of the exercise. All four two-seaters spent three weeks at Nellis in January 1992 before crossing the Pacific.

The Red Flag editions 08-4 and 12-2, in August 2008 and January 2012 respectively, each saw six F-15K Slam Eagles participate, straight from the Boeing facility in St. Louis.

From the desert into the cold

On 15 June 1991, Mount Pinatubo on the Philippines erupted, forcing the closure of Clark Air Base, used by the United States. The Cope Thunder series of exercises, which were held at Clark since 1976, moved to Eielson AFB in Alaska. USAF officials viewed Eielson AFB as the most logical choice, as the 353rd Combat Training Squadron based there already controlled and maintained three major military flight training ranges in the area. The Cope Thunder exercise was re-designated Red Flag-Alaska (RF-A) in 2006 and is organised three times a year on average.

The exercise takes place in the Joint Pacific Alaska Range Complex over both Alaska, as well as a portion of Western Canadian airspace. The entire airspace is made up of extensive Military Operations Areas, reserved airspace, and training ranges, for a total airspace of more than 67,000 sq mi (173,500km^2). The range complex holds one conventional bombing range and two tactical bombing ranges containing more than 500 different types of targets and 45 threat simulators, both manned and unmanned. The Red Flag-Alaska series of exercises is frequented by PACAF units from Alaska, Japan and Korea, along with their allies from the region.

Since its first participation in Red Flag-Alaska, during 2013, the ROKAF has been back almost every year. The F-15K Slam Eagles flew to Eielson to participate in RF-A 13-3 (September 2013), RF-A 17-1 (October 2016), RF-A 19-1 (October 2018) and RF-A 21-2 (June 2021).

Both in September 2014 (RF-A 14-3), and in August 2015 (RF-A 15-3), six F-16D aircraft participated, with the 20th FW along with members of the 38th FG taking part in the 14-3 edition.

On 1 June 2017, six KF-16D aircraft of the 20th FW took off from Haemi Air Base in the very early morning on their way to Eielson AFB for participation in RF-A 17-2. The 10-hour non-stop flight was supported by USAF tankers but aerial refuelling went wrong and the six-ship had to divert to Yokota Air Base in Japan. This diversion caused quite a stir given the history between the two countries.

After the problems with the tanker had been resolved, the F-16s continued their journey towards Alaska on the following day.

The 19th FW along with the 39th RG sent some of their pilots to Eielson for participation in RF-A 19-2, from 6 to 21 June 2019, as observers.

Both of the ROKAF's C-130 squadrons have also participated in RF-A. The 251st AS was sent to participate with two C-130H aircraft in RF-A 17-1 and returned to Eielson with a C-130H-30 in early 2019 for RF-A 19-2. Both the Seongnam-based 255th SOS, as

During Red Flag – Alaska 19-1, held in October 2018, ROKAF photographers managed to capture the Northern Lights dancing above these Pratt & Whitney powered F-15K Slam Eagles. They belong to the 110th FS, which was established at Suwon in 1966 and was equipped with the F-5 before moving to Daegu in 1972 for conversion to the F-4D. The unit recieved the F-15K in 2010 and celebrated 100,000 accident-free flight hours on 4 August 2021.
(ROKAF)

well as the Gimhae-based 251st AS, sent a C-130H Hercules aircraft to Eielson for participation in RF-A 19-1. During the exercise, the C-130s inserted and extracted special forces using the remote airfields on the training range and practiced cargo drops.

Sharpening skills overseas and in-country

In the 2000s, the ROKAF C-130s regularly showed up at McChord AFB, Washington, to participate in the bi-annual Air Mobility Rodeo exercise.

The USAF Air Mobility Command restructured the Air Mobility Rodeo into a new exercise named Mobility Guardian. Whereas the Rodeo focused on the best performers from each air force and was set up as a competition, Mobility Guardian is an exercise with a complex training scenario that focuses on interoperability and not competition.

One of the main focal points of the Mobility Guardian exercise is to help build better relationships between different nation's airlift and air mobility forces for better cooperation should the need arise.

The first edition was held in summer 2017 and the ROKAF participated with a C-130H of the 251st AS.

ROKAF F-16D PBU serial number 85-585 of the 19th FW, carrying an indigenous ALQ-200 pod on the centreline, blasts off Eielson's runway during Red Flag – Alaska 15-3. (Barry Griffiths)

In 2016, the Royal Air Force deployed some of its Eurofighter Typhoons to Korea for participation in Exercise Invincible Shield alongside fighter aircraft of the USAF and ROKAF.
(ROKAF/CMSgt Kim Kyeong Ryul via USAF)

Exercise Max Thunder is a bilateral exercise that trains PACAF and ROKAF pilots to work closer together to defend the Republic of Korea against a hostile force. The exercise is held twice a year, using either Gwangju Air Base and hosted by the ROKAF, or Gunsan Air Base hosted by the US Air Force. The North Korean government always complains about large-scale joint exercises taking place, as it views them as a preparatory move for invasion.

The official USAF response to the North's criticism, claims the exercise '*it is not tied to any real-world events or specific threats, but solely serves the purpose of enhancing interoperatibility between the USAF and ROKAF*'.

A series of Buddy Wing exercises are held throughout the year at different USAF or ROKAF air bases across Korea, bringing together single squadrons of both air forces for bi-lateral training and the exchange of skills. During the exercises, ROKAF fighter pilots, maintainers and support personnel are integrating with USAF airmen concerning mission planning, briefing, execution and debriefing. The Buddy Wing exercise usually lasts a single week and the experience gained during these exercises comes at a very low relative cost. The programme is easily planned, does not require excessive amounts of manpower from the parties involved and helps amplify regularly scheduled training for all participating squadrons. The first Buddy Wing exercise was held in 2013, to help prepare the ROKAF for its inaugural participation in Red Flag – Alaska that same year.

A ROKAF F-16 approaches a US Air Force KC-135 from the 909th Air Refueling Squadron over the ocean. Regular aerial refuelling training is needed in order for ROKAF pilots to successfully cross the Pacific for participation in the Red Flag – Alaska exercise.
(USAF/SrA Maeson L. Elleman)

In February 2014, the ROKAF sent a CN235 along with 20 personnel to Andersen AFB on Guam for exercise Cope North. This marked the first time the Koreans participated in the exercise, which is held bi-annualy since 1978.

The Korean aircraft participated in the disaster relief portion of the exercise along with Australian, Japanese and USAF assets. The ROKAF returned to Guam for Cope North during 2016.

A rare opportunity occurred in November 2016, when the ROKAF participated in the Invincible Shield exercise together with the USAF and the British Royal Air Force. For the occassion, a detachment of RAF Typhoons deployed to Osan Air Base.

The partnership between No. 77 Squadron of the Royal Australian Air Force at RAAF Williamtown and the 102nd FS at Daegu was cemented during 2016, when some ROKAF pilots spent a week at Williamtown interacting with their Australian colleagues and taking the opportunity for backseat rides in F/A-18B and Hawk Mk 127 aircraft.

Training to take top honours

Each autumn, the ROKAF stages the Boramae Aerial Shooting competition, where fighter pilots are judged on their air-to-air and air-to-ground shooting skills, as well as on their ability to perform an intercept on another aircraft. Although listed as a live-firing competition, transport and helicopter pilots also participate, as there is a cargo, and search and rescue competition running simultaneously.

The first Boramae competition was held in 1960, simply named Air Force Shooting Competition, and was given its current name, which means Hunting Hawk, in 1994.

Major Jae-Seok Han, a KF-16 pilot of the 123rd FS out of Haemi Air Base, became the ROKAF Top Gun of 2020. Scoring 965 out of the 1,000 available points, he received a presidential reward as well as a cash prize for his achievement.

In addition, Major Iseri, a CN235 pilot of the 258th AS won the transport part of the competition, while Major Kwak Myung-seok, a HH-60P pilot of the 233rd SRS, won the search and rescue competition. Pilots who compete in the Boramae event for the first time are eligible to win the 'Rookie of the Year' award. In 2020, KA-1 pilot Captain Yu-hwan of the 237th FS won the award.

The 121st FS of the 20th FW and 203rd FS of the 8th FW scored the same amount of points and therefore shared the honours as best overall fighter unit.

The 2020 competition ran from 7 October to 13 November, with 130 fighter pilots along with 30 helicopter and transport pilots participating. For the competition, the ROKAF made use of the ranges at Gangwon and Gyeongsangbuk. The 2020 edition was the 61st time the event took place.

The Buddy Wing series of exercises sees small groups of ROKAF and USAF aircraft plan and fly missions together from a single base. Here, a ROKAF KA-1 waits until a USAF A-10C has taken off.
(USAF/SrA Stephenie Wade)

Test pilot training

In 1990, the first ROKAF test pilot was trained at the Empire Test Pilot School at Boscombe Down, United Kingdom, in preparation for the test flight programme of the KTX-1.

Having graduated test pilots in its ranks, allowed the ROKAF to establish a dedicated test unit, and the 281st Flight Test Squadron was born in 1991. The unit expanded into the 52nd Test and Evaluation Group in December of 1999, and calls the air base at Sacheon home.

The National Test Pilot School in Mojave, California, has trained test pilots for both the ROKAF and Korea Aerospace Industries. Another civil entity, the International Test Pilot School based at London International Airport in Ontario, Canada, has upgraded ROKAF flyers into test pilots since 2011.

A total of five Korean pilots were trained at the USAF Test Pilot School (USAFTPS) at Edwards AFB, California, with the last one graduating in 1993. Test pilots assigned to the 52nd TEG have made exchange visits to the USAFTPS on a regular basis. Student test pilots assigned to the school travel to Korea to fly Korean-built aircraft as part of their TPS curriculum, while in turn ROKAF test pilots visit the USAFTPS to fly the T-38C and F-16C/D over Edwards' test ranges.

ROKAF Fighter Weapons School

The 29th Tactics Development Training Flight Group (29th TDTFG), often referred to as the 29th Tactical Fighter Weapons Group (TFWG), provides the ROKAF with its own Topgun or Fighter Weapons School. Additionally, the unit has the responsibility to develop tactics and provide aggressor pilots for local flying exercises. The unit's motto is: *'One Shot! One Kill!'*.

A ROKAF delegation of test pilots visiting the USAF Test Pilot School at Edwards AFB. (USAF/Joseph Gocong)

The 29th TDTFG was established at Suwon Air Base on 15 October 1979 and moved south to its current home base of Cheongju on 7 April 1981.

Pilots selected to participate in the ROKAF Fighter Weapons Instructor Course spent five to six months at Cheongju for academic training and a variety of air-to-air and air-to-ground missions.

The 191st Tactics Training Squadron (191st TTS) was established in 1988 to set up tactical training for ROKAF fighter pilots through exercises and various other training courses. The squadron has a big part in the organisation of the Soaring Eagle exercise, which is held twice a year, usually at Cheongju Air Base.

During exercise Soaring Eagle, ROKAF fighters carry AIS pods in order to collect information regarding the aircraft's attitude, altitude, position and speed.

The information received through the datalink feeds a software network that not only provides real-time monitoring of the simulated air combat, but also allows post-mission debrief through the reconstruction of manoeuvres and tactics.

For this purpose, the 29th TDTFG has a large Air Operations Center at Cheongju, where data is recorded and four large displays show the simulated air war unfold in real time.

During large scale exercises a Range Training Officer (RTO) is in charge, who monitors flying operations and ensures that the actual events are proceeding according to plan.

The RTO might receive information from the aircrews that force changes to the plan and may require redirection of the participating aircraft.

Unforseen issues, such as an aircraft dropping out due to a malfunction, being one of the likely scenarios that has to be dealt with, in order not to jeopardise the effectiveness of the whole mission for the remainder of the airborne package.

Pilots qualified as element lead and with three to four years experience in the squadron are eligible to be trained as RTO.

Seen during Exercise Soaring Eagle 2011, two F-5s of the 10th FW line up on runway 24L at Cheongju, while an F-4E has just commenced its take-off roll on the parallel runway. (ROKAF)

Chapter 4

ROKAF bandits

A second squadron subordinate to the 29th TDTFG is the 192nd Tactics Development Squadron (192nd TDS) which has been tasked with the development of air-to-air tactics to deal with enemy aircraft. It has been giving particular attention to slow- and low flying aircraft in order to be able to deal with the KPAAF An-2 fleet or UAVs crossing the border from the North.

Thanks to the 192nd TDS a number of flight manuals have been revised. The unit provides consultation on the tactical development of fighter aircraft to fighter squadrons and fighter wings throughout the ROKAF.

A select group of pilots from the 29th TDTFG have studied the KPAAF and its behaviour extensively, and have learned to simulate the tactics employed by the north in a very effective way. They have also taken into the account the lessons learned from the Korean evaluation of the MiG-19 and MiG-21.

In May 2011, during a Max Thunder exercise at Kunsan Air Base, the ROKAF employed the aggressor pilots of the 29th TDTFG for the first time. Pilots of both the 191st and 192nd acted as aggressor pilots during this and subsequent exercises.

On 2 January 2014, a dedicated Adversary Flight (literally 'virtual bandit unit') was established at Cheongju under the wings of the 29th TDTFG. As the colours of the 192nd, yellow and blue, are used in the Adversary's unit patch, the nucleus of the unit was most likely formed by pilots of that squadron.

A pair of Pratt & Whitney powered F-15K Slam Eagles of the 110th FS dropping Mk 82 bombs during a training mission. The squadron was the last unit to fly the F-4D and received the F-15K during 2010. (USAF)

The Adversary Flight of the 29th
TFWG borrows KF-16C aircraft
from operational squadrons
when needed. This example,
carrying six LAU-129 launchers
and an AN/AAQ-33 Sniper
targeting pod, is firing a flare in
self defence during a simulated
dogfight.
(AV Kok)

MODERNISATION OF THE ROKAF 2021–2035

The Armed Forces of South Korea have attempted to transform themselves into an independent military. The resulting modernisation efforts have been shaped by a series of defence reform plans that have largely been driven by the actions of its northern neigbour, the DPRK, but are also influenced by the rivalry with Japan and, to a lesser extent, China and Russia.

Recent conflicts have shown that technology provides the means for rapidly eliminating opposing forces by making use of accuracy, intelligence and flexibility. This precision in airpower has subsequently resulted in a diminished need for large standing armies. For Korea, modern air capability is now the predominant instrument of national security, and to maintain the edge the ROKAF has over its neighbours, considerable investments are needed.

Defence Blueprint 2021–2025

The Korean MND presented the 2021–2025 defence blueprint in Seoul on 10 August 2020. One of the major bullets of the plan is the transformation of the Korean Armed Forces from a manpower oriented organisation to a technology oriented organisation. A reduction of 55,000 personnel is planned, from 555,000 in late 2020 to 500,000 in 2022, although this should only marginally effect the ROKAF, as most reductions in personnel are planned for the ROK Army.

Conscription is still a thing in South Korea, where male citizens between the age of 18 and 35 are to perform compulsory military service, which translates to 22 months if selected to serve within the ROKAF. The number was reduced from 24 months during 2020, to help alleviate the burden of military service borne by the youngsters who face enough challenges in education and employment as it is.

The defence programme outlined in the blueprint, calls for a budget of slightly over USD 253 billion to be spent over the years 2021-2025, with an annual increase of 6.1 per cent taken in consideration. Some 33 per cent of the budget will be used on force improvement, meaning acquisition of new material as well as research and development. The remaining 67 per cent is budgeted for force sustainment, and includes operating and supporting existing assets.

When focusing on 2021, the defence budget for South Korea was set by the National Assembly at 52.8 trillion Won (USD 48 billion), a 5.4 per cent increase compared to 2020. This amount is only slighter lower than the 52.9 trillion Won the Ministry of

Except for some minor modifications, no upgrades have been performed on the fleet of HH-47D Chinooks. As the acquisition of newer helicopters to replace them appears to be cheaper, this is an option that might be pursued by the ROKAF. (Hywell Evans)

Defense asked for, mainly due to some of the arms acquisition programmes having been postponed.

The budget allocated to national defence has seen a steady rise from almost 21 trillion Won in 2005 to the 52.8 trillion Won it is now. The increase signals the growing security uncertainties Korea faces and the need to boost its self-defence capabilities amidst non-traditional challenges, such as infectious viruses. The COVID-19 virus has seen ROKAF aircraft being used to deliver masks and to collect surgical gowns, while Chinook helicopters were used to deliver vaccines to remote locations.

Due to costs associated with combating the pandemic, the defence budget had to be somewhat reduced, including slashing USD 250 million from the F-35A budget. This should not affect delivery of the F-35s as Seoul was ahead of scheduled payments, and will start negotiations to pay any remaining amounts at a later date.

The defence blueprint also revealed Korean plans to develop its own version of the Israeli-produced Iron Dome interceptor in the coming five years.

The interceptor system will be developed to counter the North's rocket artillery, which is a threat to capital Seoul should a conflict erupt. Following development and testing the new air defence system is expected to be fielded in either the late 2020s or early 2030s.

A two-ship of FA-50s breaks for the camera while ejecting flares. Proposed upgrades for the FA-50 fleet will increase the endurance of the aircraft as well as its effectivity as a fighter. (ROKAF)

CH-47NE/HH-47D replacement

The lengthy project to update the fleet of CH-47D and HH-47D Chinook helicopters of the ROKAF and ROKA, is expected to be stopped to allow for acquisition of a new helicopter to replace them.

According to DAPA, ordering a new helicopter is 131.3 billion Won (USD 112.5 million) cheaper than an upgrade of the existing fleet. However, incorporating Korean-made mission equipment might cause an increase in price and a possible delay in delivery of six months.

Korea has expressed a desire to order 22 examples of the CH-47F Chinook. A Letter of Offer and Acceptance (LOA) between DAPA and Boeing was not expected to be signed before summer 2021, with a targeted delivery date 42 months after a firm order has been placed. How many of the 22 helicopters will be diverted to the ROKAF is still unclear.

T-50/TA-50/FA-50 upgrades

A performance improvement contract to install an IFF system on the T-50 and TA-50, as well as an upgrade of the IFF and Link 16 (tactical datalink) on the FA-50, was signed between DAPA and the ROKAF in December 2020. The deal, worth 110 billion Won (USD 94.3 million), should see IFF added to the fleet in 2023, while the upgrade on the systems of FA-50 will be completed by 2025.

The datalink system, used to share tactical data between assets, will significantly improve the pilots's situational awareness and the effectivity of the FA-50 over the modern battlefield.

In June 2020, the ROKAF and the ADD jointly published a report containing a list of upgrades it intended to research in order to enhance the range and combat capabilities of the KAI FA-50. The report was labeled 'Emergency Notice', indicating an upgrade of the FA-50 fleet is urgently needed. The ongoing retirement of older F-4E and F-5E/F aircraft is reason for concern. Due to its limited range, rumoured to be around 450 km (280 miles), and its incomplete arsenal of Precision Guided Munitions, the ROKAF deems the FA-50 to be underperforming. It cannot penetrate deep into enemy airspace or operate without fighter escort.

The report details a number of options that need to be researched in order to establish the most suitable way to utilitze the FA-50 fleet to its full potential.

There have been several options under consideration for increasing fuel capacity and operational range of the FA-50. The aircraft has seven internal fuel tanks, five in the fuselage and two in the wings, holding 4,675lb (2,654 litres) of fuel. Additionally, it is capable of carrying three 1,000lb (569-litre) external fuel tanks, but these will take up some of the precious hardpoints on the jet. Some of the options under consideration were the development of larger external fuel tanks, the addition of a conformal fuel tank, and creating room for more internal fuel.

Introducing an air-to-air refuelling (AAR) capability was ultimately selected as the best available course of action. Following modification, the FA-50 will be able to take on fuel via the hose-and-drogue method. The fleet of KC-330 Cygnus aircraft carrying the underwing refuelling pods is capable of supporting this procedure.

KAI selected the UK-based Cobham Mission Systems for the FA-50 Aerial Refuelling upgrade on 3 December 2020.

To increase the aircraft's effectiveness, not only the number but also the types of PGMs integrated with the FA-50 Fighting Eagle need to be increased. As far back as 2015, the German-Swedish company Taurus announced they were working on a smaller version of their TAURUS KEPD-350K, carried on the ROKAF F-15K fleet. The version, dubbed K2, was under development specifically for the FA-50, but the project seems to have been abandonded in the project stage.

Following delivery of the GBU-39 Small Diameter Bombs to the ROKAF, this type of weapon has a high chance of being integrated on the FA-50. Connected to the wish for more PGMs is the need to integrate a targeting pod. In October 2019, a Lockheed Martin Sniper Advanced Targeting Pod (ATP) was succesfully tested on the FA-50's centreline hardpoint. The ATP-capable FA-50s will be designated as Block 10 airframes.

In order to carry out BVR engagements, a medium- to long range air-to-air missile capability is needed. Following requests from export customers operating the FA-50, this option was already actively being studied by the aircraft's manufacturer, Korea Aerospace Industries, using the designation FA-50 Block 20. Connected to the introduction of new weapons is the ability to carry them. The ROKAF would like to see the number of available weapon pylons increased, while still carrying three external fuel tanks.

For better survivability the ROKAF would like an increase in the speed, manoeuvrability, and maximum G-load, although without a more powerful engine and a major

redesign of the aircraft, this will be either be too difficult or prohibitively costly to achieve.

After thorough research, the ADD will compile a report determining each option's priority and will assess feasibility and costs. Subsequently, a roadmap detailing an FA-50 upgrade is expected to be published during late 2021.

Large Aircraft Procurement Program – second phase
In the late 2000s, DAPA sought funding to purchase up to 10 additional transport aircraft, with the Airbus A400M, Boeing C-17A and Lockheed C-130J-30 under consideration. Eventually, budget constraints limited the number of aircraft purchased, and only four C-130J-30s entered service during spring 2014.

The acquisition of new transport aircraft remained on DAPA's radar nevertheless, and the second phase of the programme was initiated during 2018. The ROKAF announced it would like to increase its capacity of rapid force deployment, the support of peacekeeping operations, as well as emergency relief over longer distances. Following a study on required operational capability and programme expense, a strategy to move forward will be presented during 2021. The required budget will be secured from the National Assembly during 2022, following which a tender notice for at least four new transport aircraft will be published in the same year.

In late 2018, the Korean Times newspaper disclosed South Korea and Spain had entered negotiations to exchange four to six A400M transports for up to 50 Korean-made trainer aircraft (20 T-50 and 30 KT-1). On 30 January 2020 however, the Spanish Air Force signed a contract for 24 Pilatus PC-21 trainer aircraft, making it extremely unlikely additional aircraft from Korea will be sourced.

With four examples of the C-130J-30 already in service, it is no surprise that this aircraft is on the shortlist for a follow-on order under the Large Aircraft Procurement Program. Alternative aircraft including the A400M are also being considered.
(Robin Polderman)

Based upon the Bombardier Global 6500, Saab's GlobalEye is one of the two contenders for a ROKAF contract for two AEW&C aircraft. Saab will go head-to-head with Boeing, which hopes to sell two additional E-737 aircraft to Korea. (Saab)

AEW&C expansion

After the introduction of the four Boeing E-737 Peace Eyes, it quickly transpired additional AEW&C aircraft were needed. With the Yellow Sea and China to the west, the East Sea and Japan to the east as well as south, and its unpredictable neighbour to the north, the extra capacity is needed for round-the-clock surveillance and to establish a Command and Control (C^2) umbrella over South Korean territory. The ability to provide robust C^2 with these AEW&C aircraft presents a significant advance for ROKAF intradependence, mitigating the need to rely on USAF assets.

The need for extra capacity was reflected in the Long-Term Requirement Paper, published in 2016 and was once again underlined in the 2021-2025 Defense Blueprint.

The main discussion will focus on whether to purchase additional E-737 aircraft, or to select a different AEW&C airframe altogether, with the Saab GlobalEye likely the only other contender for the contract. The GlobalEye consists of Saab's Erieye ER (Extended Range) radar, along with an extensive sensor suite, mated to a Bombardier Global 6500 airframe.

The additional two aircraft could be obtained by direct acquisition or through an open tender, with the exact method of procurement likely to be announced during 2021.

With Korean firm KAI having the experience of fitting out three of the four E-737 airframes currently in use with specialised AEW systems, this could be an advantage for the Boeing product. There is a slight caveat however, as the order book for the 737 has been filled for a few more years to come, meaning a possible delay for the ROKAF. One option could be to source second-hand Boeing 737-700s, as the British Royal Air Force did for their E-737 programme.

The KT-1 has been in use since the year 2000 and the fleet is heavily uitilised for training new pilots. Looking ahead, the ROKAF has initiated development of its replacement, to be fielded around 2035. (Hywell Evans)

Parallel to the acquisition of the new aircraft, the ROKAF would like to upgrade the IFF and Link-16 equipment on its current fleet of E-737 aircraft, for which it reserved USD 433 million in its budget. In early August 2021, KAI announced it had signed an initial USD 15.6 million contract with Boeing to upgrade the mission systems on all four aircraft currently in service. It is anticipated further upgrades to the fleet will be carried out by the KAI/Boeing joint venture. Funding for the acquisition programme of the two new aircraft, an estimated USD 1.32 billion, will be likely secured in 2022, with the new aircraft expected to enter service before 2025.

KT-X development

To be able to replace the current fleet of KAI KT-1 trainer aircraft, in use since 2000, a new trainer is being sought by the ROKAF. Preliminary research has begun during 2021, and funding for the project should be acquired in 2025. A conceptual design by Korea Aerospace Industries is expected to be proposed to the ROKAF in the second half of 2021, and is anticipated to be unveiled at the ADEX Seoul airshow in October 2021.

Development of the indigenous aircraft in the performance class of the Pilatus PC-21 is set to begin in 2026. It should be powered by an engine producing around 1,600hp and have a state-of-the-art avionics suite. Total budget required for the KT-X project, which includes research, development and production, is somewhere in the region of USD 1 billion. Reportedly, the ROKAF would have a slight preference for a subsonic jet aircraft instead of the proposed turboprop aircraft.

The new KT-X trainer should begin replacing the current fleet of KT-1 aircraft during 2035.

The ROKAF is looking to improve its ISR capability to keep track of the movements of its neighbours, especially in the North. A requirement for four additional SIGINT aircraft has been identified to replace the RC-800 now in use, and it is highly likely these will be purchased in the shape of the Falcon 2000S, dubbed RC-2000 in ROKAF service. Although KAI has indicated it is also working on developing an ISR aircraft, the sole bidder to date appears to be Korean Air. (SangYeon Kim)

ISR capability improvement

One of the most important programmes currently running within the ROK Armed Forces is the expansion of its ISR capability. In addition to the RF-16, RC-800, RC-2000, RQ-4 Global Hawk as well as various satellites, Korea would like to add additional ISR aircraft, dedicated military satellites, and indigenously developed UAVs.

In the timeframe between 2021 and 2026, the ROKAF would like to add add four new Baekdu ISR aircraft, most likely the proven Falcon 2000S (RC-2000) already in the inventory. A budget of USD 650 million has been reserved for the project, which will help increase the missile detection capability considerably. Assisted by ISR aircraft and satellites, Seoul would like to have real-time imagery and signal intelligence available 24/7, covering the whole Korean peninsula and the KADIZ.

During April 2021, the president of KAI announced his company was working on developing an ISR aircraft. This will most likely entail the conversion of an off-the-shelf business jet into an ISR platform, following KAI's experience with fitting out the E-737 AEW&C for the ROKAF. If this project is related to the pair of Baekdu aircraft to be purchased, or KAI will be competing for an additional future contract altogether, has not been specified. A request for tender was issued by DAPA on 30 June 2021.

Seoul's intelligence-gathering capabilities were revealed after North Korea killed a stranded South Korean citizen on 24 September 2020. Information, accidently leaked during a press release, confirmed South Korea and the US have access to around 75 per cent of North Korean military communication at all times.

The secretive 777 Command, also known as Unit 5679 of the ROK Armed Forces, reportedly cooperates closely with the US National Security Agency to record an average of 77,000 minutes of North Korean voice communication per day. The accidental release of this information might have alerted Pyongyang and forced them to change protocols regarding communication within the KPA.

39th RW establishment

Such is the emphasis the Korean Ministry of National Defense places on its ISR capability, that the establishment of a dedicated ROKAF Reconnaissance Wing was not only outlined in the Defense Plan, but was also promptly executed. On 3 November 2020, the 39th Reconnaissance Wing stood up at Jungwon Air Base, to control the various ISR assets on strength with the ROKAF.

The creation of a seperate wing managing the ISR aircraft of the ROKAF, is seen as a major boost to the key defence capabilities required for the transfer of OPCON from the United States to the Korean side.

As technology evolves, the importance of the 39th RW will grow, and it is likely it will expand in terms of squadrons and available assets.

F-35B STOVL

It is a long standing ROKN wish to own an aircraft carrier, as it will greatly enhance the naval air power and prestige of the Republic of Korea. After the introduction of various frigates, destroyers and an amphibious assault ship over the last two decades, the time was deemed right for an aircraft carrier.

Hyundai Heavy Industries (HHI) shipyard won the conceptual design order for the new light aircraft carrier project, named CVX, in October 2019.

A US Marine Corps F-35B Lightning II assigned to Marine Medium Tiltrotor Squadron 164 (Reinforced), 15th Marine Expeditionary Unit (MEU), takes off from the flight deck of amphibious assault ship USS *Makin Island* (LHD 8). (USMC/Cpl Patrick Crosley)

Contrary to the *Dokdo*-class amphibious assault ships that were constructed earlier, the new light aircraft carrier will have a suitable flight deck to facilitate F-35B aircraft, and will also be larger in size. The carrier will need enough room to accommodate around 20 Short Take-Off and Vertical Landing (STOVL) F-35s along with eight ROKN helicopters.

It is a big burden for the ROKN, budget and manpower-wise, to operate both the fighter jets as well as the ship. The cost of the ship is estimated at USD 1.83 billion, while the F-35B aircraft and helicopters will set the Korean taxpayer back an additional USD 2.7 billion, with an additional annual operating cost of USD 180 million.

A joint military system has frequently been discussed among high ranking officers of both services, making the decision to assign the F-35B aircraft to the ROKAF inventory fairly easy.

The ship is expected to be commissioned with the ROKN in 2030, but a date for the introduction of the F-35B has not been announced. As the ROKAF hopes to acquire an additional 20 F-35A aircraft on top of the 40 being delivered, it is likely a combination-deal for the F-35A and F-35B will be negotiated.

Initially the ROKAF had hoped to replace its remaining squadron of F-4E Phantoms with a squadron of F-35As during 2024. As a contract is not expected to be signed before the end of 2021, delivery of the F-35s is not foreseen before 2025. If this means the modest Phantom fleet will remain in service until the new jets arrive, remains to be seen.

ISTAR-K – the Korean JSTARS

In April 2007, several high ranking ROKAF officers gained approval to fly on a rare but insightful USAF E-8 Joint Surveillance Target Attack Radar System (JSTARS) mission over Korea. The JSTARS aircraft regularly deploy to Osan Air Base, and the mission was used to impress upon them the value of the JSTARS C^2 capabilities.

Using a modern intelligence, surveillance, target acquisition and reconnaissance (ISTAR) aircraft, the ROKAF will be able to provide its battle field commanders and decision makers with ground surveillance to support military operations and targeting to contribute to the delay, disruption and destruction of enemy forces.

Realising the need for such an aircraft due to the increasingly complex security environment on the Korean peninsula, the ROKAF issued a requirement.

The ISTAR-K (K for Korea) could be used to search and track TEL (Transporter Erecter Launcher) vehicles, the mobile launchers used by the North Korean surface-to-surface (ballistic) missiles. The high resolution radar onboard the aircraft would produce target information in the form of images or video. The cost of the ISTAR-K programme was budgeted at 2 trillion Won (USD 1.7 billion) for four aircraft, training and support. The ROKAF would like to introduce the first ISTAR-K in operational service in 2023, although this seems rather optimistic.

On 15 October 2019, US defence company Raytheon signed a collaboration agreement with Korean Air at the Seoul International Aerospace and Defense Exhibition to pursue the ROKAF's ISTAR programme. Under the agreement, Raytheon will be the prime contractor and provide multiple-intelligence (Multi-INT) technologies for the aircraft. The Aerospace Division of Korean Air (KAL-ASD) will deliver design, logistics and life cycle support services. Multi-INT technology synthesises data from a variety of sensors, including radar, multifunction EO/IR, and signals intelligence suites, to create

a comprehensive picture of the battlefield. The HISAR-500 AESA radar intended to be integrated with ISTAR-K, features a Ground Moving Target Indicator (GMTI) radar, a Synthetic Aperture Radar (SAR), as well as an Inverse Synthetic Aperture Radar (ISAR).

According to the company, the combination of multiple different sensors and advanced communications systems will give Korean military leaders the information they need, when they need it. In close cooperation with Bombardier, Raytheon and Korean Air will modify Global 6500 business jets to meet ROKAF's specific mission needs.

The ROKAF has been wanting to aquire an aircraft with similar capabilities to the E-8C JSTARS for a long time. The development of a dedicated ISTAR-K aircraft is ongoing. In the meantime, the E-8C aircraft are regular guests at Osan Air Base.
(Northrop Grumman)

KF-16 upgrade

In December 2010, a defence project committee attached to the ROK Ministry of National Defense initiated a project for the upgrade of the ROKAF's KF-16 fleet.

DAPA set up the acquisition process according to Foreign Military Sales (FMS) regulations, meaning the US government would be responsible for business selection as well as quality assurance.

After assessment, DAPA chose BAE Systems' offer, which turned out to be a competitive commercial bid, which is not allowed according to FMS regulations. DAPA subsequently reported that the USD 1.7 billion price of the contract had been agreed upon with the US Government, which was not the case, as Washington valued the contract at USD 2.4 billion, citing the company's lack of experience with projects of this magnitude. The considerable increase in cost led to a cancellation of the BAE contract by the US government, on behalf of DAPA, in early November 2014, which effectively meant a delay of four years and the loss of USD 89 million that had already been paid to BAE. By that time, two ROKAF KF-16s had already arrived at the BAE Systems facility at Fort Worth-Alliance airport.

The F-16V can be distinguished from the ROKAF (K)F-16 fleet by virtue of the IFF antennas, the so-called bird slicers, in front of the cockpit. Unmodified aircraft have these attached to a separate bracket on top of the panel, while on the upgraded aircraft they are integrated in a more aerodynamic way. This upgraded aircraft, serial number 92-046, is seen during weapons tests over the Edwards AFB range complex in California. (USAF/Ethan Wagner)

After the cancellation, Lockheed Martin tried to land the deal and, after approval by the US State Department, the company was awarded an initial USD 1.2 billion contract in late 2016 to upgrade the ROKAF's fleet of 133 KF-16s to KF-16V configuration.

The capabilities of the KF-16 took a giant leap following the installation of the Joint Helmet Mounted Cueing System II (JHMCS II) helmet-mounted display, as well as an AN/APG-83 Scalable Agile Beam Radar (SABR). The APG-83, built by Northrop Grumman, is an AESA radar capable of detecting multiple targets. It features the Big Synthetic Aperture Radar (Big SAR) mode, which enhances situational awareness by mapping a large area, all-weather, day and night. Compared to the previous radar installed on the F-16, the SABR has air-to-air and air-to-surface modes with substantially increased ranges and can operate both modes simultaneously. Around 95 per cent of the AN/APG-83's mode suite comes directly from the AN/APG-81 radar in the F-35A, including robust electronic protection to counter the most advanced threats. Given its capabilities, it comes as no surprise the AN/APG-83 SABR is classed as a 5th generation radar system.

The KF-16V received an upgrade to its avionics systems, including the addition of a large-format Center Pedestal Display (CPD). The upgrade also incorporates a new Modular Mission Computer with a higher computing power able to generate full-colour high resolution images for the 6in × 8in (15cm × 20cm) CPD. It allows the pilot to display AESA radar data, detailed targeting pod footage, tactical moving maps, an air-to-air situation overview or flight instrument data.

For self-protection the jet is equipped with the BAE Systems AN/ALR-56M Advanced Radar Warning Receiver system, which is continously detecting and intercepting RF signals in various frequency ranges. The system integrates with modern jamming and countermeasures equipment and is programmable in order to have the latest threat library always available.

For IFF purposes, the BAE Systems AN/APX-126 Combined Interrogator/Transponder (CIT) is installed. The system operates well beyond the pilot's visual range, having a range of over 100nm (185km). It uses Mode 5 and Mode S to positively identify friendly forces and has a high resistance against jamming. For enhanced safety, the Auto Throttle system including Automatic Ground Collision Avoidance System (GCAS) was incorporated.

All these features arguably make the ROKAF fleet of KF-16s the most advanced fourth generation fighters on the globe.

The first ROKAF KF-16V, serial number 92-021, made its maiden post-upgrade test-flight from Fort Worth in August 2019. It took up residence at Edwards AFB in California to start operational testing with the 412th TW later that year. It was joined by the second KF-16V, two-seater 92-046, during 2020.

On 26 February 2021, the two-seat KF-16V flew a successful weapon seperation test over the Edwards ranges, dropping a GBU-39 SDB carried under the wing.

Externally, there seem to be very few differences between the standard and the upgraded F-16. On the KF-16V variant, the 'bird slicer' IFF antennas in front of the canopy are larger and more integrated with the fuselage.

In 2020, a total of 10 ROKAF KF-16s were modified to V-standard in-country, with two squadrons fully converting to the type during 2021. Upgrade work is expected to be completed by 15 November 2025, and the ROKAF plans to keep the KF-16V in service until at least 2039.

Black Hawk upgrade

Not mentioned in the Defense Blueprint but on DAPA's agenda nevertheless is an upgrade to the UH-60 Black Hawk fleet of the ROKAF, ROK Army and ROK Navy. US company Northrop Grumman has offered its Integrated Mission Equipment Package, originally designed for the UH-60V, which is the ongoing upgrade of the US Army fleet of UH-60L helicopters.

The upgrade provides the helicopter with new avionics and a fully digital cockpit. The open, plug and play architecture allows integration of readily available hardware and software, enabling rapidly and timely capability enhancements in the future.

Black Hawk pilots operating the upgraded version will benefit from improved situational awareness and mission safety as well as decreased workload. The upgrade would extend the life of the Black Hawk fleet, which is currently around 30 years old, and would lead to a higher interoperatibility with the US Army UH-60M fleet deployed in-country. Northrop Grumman has stated the ROKA fleet of Black Hawks can be easily operated for another 5,000 flying hours, or 20 years, following upgrade.

Northrop Grumman has stated it supports authorised technology transfer and expansion of capabilities in Korea for the benefit of local economy and labour market. Any upgrade provided by the US manufacturer would be performed in Korea through a partnership with either KAI or KAL-ASD. This would allow the Korean aerospace industry to expand its aircraft upgrade business across the global market.

Although DAPA pushed for the replacement of the Black Hawk with the indigenous Surion, the capabilities the H-60 brings to the battlefield cannot be overlooked and it is likely the type will be upgraded and kept in service. A dedicated ROKAF SAR Team, a well-trained special forces unit also based at Cheongju, flies on the Black Hawk aircraft during certain (C) SAR missions. (ROKAF)

DAPA pushed for the replacement of the Black Hawk fleet with the indigenous KAI Surion helicopter, but it is unlikely this option will be pursued. While complete replacement would be the most costly course of action, the Surion also does not have the capabilities the Black Hawk brings to the battlefield.

F-15K upgrade

The ROKAF has reserved funds under the Defense Plan 2021-2025 to equip its Slam Eagles with, amongst other upgrades, an AESA radar. With the Raytheon APG-82(V)1, which was chosen for the USAF new F-15EX aircraft, being the most advanced radar currently available, it is highly likely the ROKAF would like the same system to be installed in its F-15K fleet. Additionally, an announcement made in May 2020 revealed a budget of USD 242 million had been allocated for an upgrade package consisting of IFF Mode-5, the latest version of Link-16 and a new anti-jamming GPS system.

Boeing reportedly proposed an complete F-15K upgrade to the ROKAF, which will include a new Digital Electronic Warfare System (DEWS), improved targeting and navigation pods, a large full-colour touch display in the cockpit, and the JHMCS II helmet mounted display.

The upgrade package would cost approximately USD 4.46 billion, which was met with great scepticism in Korea. This equates to roughly USD 75 million to upgrade one fourth-generation fighter, while a brand new 5th generation F-35A can be had for less

than USD 10 million more. Realising this offer was not really worthy of consideration, Boeing revised its proposal. In April 2021, details of the new offer to Korea came to light. The cost of upgrading the 59 Slam Eagles is reduced, but only if the ROKAF takes delivery of 20 examples of the F-15EX for an additional sum. Total cost of the package has not been exactly disclosed, but is rumoured to be close to USD 4.8 billion.

As news in the Korean press broke regarding the high costs associated with operating the F-35A, many officials have openly questioned the need for an additional 20 stealth fighters. If the F-15EX would be bought instead of the intended second batch of F-35As, it would not only be Lockheed Martin that would object. The F-15EX, because of its classification as a 4.5 generation fighter, falls in the same category as the KF-21, but there are a few differences that put the new Eagle ahead of its competitor. The KF-X is not capable of employing air-to-ground munitions until at least 2030, when the Block II version is rolled out. Besides that, the payload capacity of the F-15EX is increased. But cutting the number of KF-21 to be ordered and purchase a squadron of F-15EX instead was not really on DAPA's agenda. It is clear the Korean decisionmakers are facing somewhat of a dilema.

F-16 PBU replacement
On 25 May 2020 the ROKAF announced that F-16 PBU serial number 84-373, an F-16D Block 32, had reached 10,000 flight hours during which it had travelled an estimated

Besides an upgrade package for the F-15K, the ROKAF might opt for a squadron of F-15EX jets in a combination deal. This would undermine plans to acquire additional F-35s on top of the 40 already ordered. The first F-15EX destined for the USAF, serial number 20-0001, is seen on its delivery flight to Eglin AFB in Florida.
(USAF/TSgt John McRell)

F-16D PBU 84-373 of
the 19th FW received a
commemorative logo on the
tail fin when it reached 10,000
flight hours. This jet was the
fourth F-16D delivered to the
ROKAF.
(Jamie Chang)

4 million nautical miles (7,400,000km). With the aircraft in ROKAF service since early 1995, a little math leads to an average of 250 flight hours per year. With an anticipated life limit of 12,000 flight hours, this would mean a possible retirement around 2028. It is likely the ROKAF would like to defer the retirement of their oldest F-16s until the KF-X has replaced the KF-5E/F, scheduled to be completed around 2032. Although the KF-X has been classified as a 4.5 generation fighter jet, its open architecture allows room for upgrade to a 5th generation aircraft, should the need arise. With the F-16 being the workhorse of the fleet, the ROKAF needs to carefully weigh its options, as it would like an aircraft with roughly the same operating costs.

Air base modernisation through relocation

On 28 August 2020, the Korean Ministry of Defense finalised a decision to relocate Daegu Air Base to a rural location in North Gyeongsang province.

The air base doubles as the civil airport of Daegu and has been in use since the Korean War. It was upgraded from a military airstrip to a military air base in 1958 and has been used by both the USAF and ROKAF since.

The location of the air base places limitations on urban development in the area, and has also been the subject of longstanding noise complaints.

A completely new air base will be built on a 5.9 square miles (15.3km^2) stretch of land inbetween the counties of Gunwi and Uiseong, located 12.5 miles (20km) from the city of Daegu.

Fast jets and UAVs

In 1980 Korean Air was chosen to licencebuilt the KF-5E/F aircraft, named Je-gong in ROKAF service, after a bold request to build the F-16 was denied by the US Government.

Initially, 36 KF-5E single seat and 32 KF-5F dual seat aircraft, a total of 68 aircraft, were to be produced, but the contract was changed to 48 KF-5E and 20 KF-5F in November of 1982. The first locally produced Tiger, KF-5F 10-594, making its maiden flight from Busan-Gimhae airport on 9 September 1982, with the last example rolling off the production line in October of 1986.

In March 1991, Korean Air Aerospace Division (KAL-ASD) finally gained permission to licence build the F-16 for the ROKAF. Dubbed KF-16, the first example was produced in June of 1997.

Between September 1990 and December 1999, KAL-ASD undertook final assembly of the UH-60P/HH-60P helicopters for ROKA, ROKAF and ROKN use.

A pair of locally produced KF-5 aircraft, a single-seat KF-5E and dual-seat KF-5F, returning to Suwon Air Base, each carrying an AIS instrumentation pod on the right-hand wingtip as well as a SUU-20 dispenser on the centreline. The 10th FW at Suwon is one of the oldest fighter unit in ROKAF, having been established on 28 September 1951.
(AV Kok)

KF–16D serial number 01–526 turning finals for home base Haemi, with three more aircraft about to break overhead the air base for landing. The 20th FW was established on 2 December 1996 to operate the locally produced KF–16 aircraft. (Hwangbo Joonwoo)

The company also manufactures the fuselage and canopy for the KAI KT-1 basic training aircraft.

KAL-ASD had been working on an unmanned, remote controlled version of the MD500 since 2013, when it entered talks with Boeing. An initial Memorandum of Understanding between both parties resulted in the signing of a Memorandum of Understanding concerning technology transfer and cooperation in September 2016. This MoU formed part of the offset agreement reached between the two companies following the signing of a contract for 36 Boeing AH-64E Apache Guardian helicopters for the ROKA.

The Korean Unmanned System – Vertical Helicopter (KUS-VH) first flew from the helipad of the Goheung research institute on 30 July 2019. The UAV was developed for high-risk military missions and will be armed with either a gun pod, AGM-114 Hellfire missiles or unguided Hydra rockets. The KUS-VH could be operated in the armed scout role alongside the Apaches. Through the Manned-Unmanned Teaming (MUM-T) ability already built-in the AH-64E, its aircrew could control the sensors and weapons onboard the nearby KUS-VH.

As the roughly 200 MD500s in ROKA service are scheduled to be replaced over the coming years, ample helicopters should be available for conversion into drones.

A contract between KAL-ASD and the Korean Army has not been signed yet, and the company, with assistance from Boeing, is also actively searching for customers for its KUS-VH on the international market. As future projects, KAL-ASD intends to convert UH-1H and UH-60 helicopters, and eventually F-5 fighter jets into UAVs.

Since 2011 KAL-ASD has been working on a Unmanned Combat Air Vehicle (UCAV) with stealth capabilities. The programme is known under the designation KUS-FC, and the company flight tested a subscale demonstrator during 2015. The Kaori-X, as the demonstrator is called, allowed Korean Air to test the flight dynamics of its design, before commiting to a full-scale version.

Korean Light Helicopter

In an ongoing drive to improve the reconnaissance capabilities of the ROKA, it signed for 12 Eurocopter BO105CBS-5 helicopters during the late 1990s. A co-production agreement was reached between Eurocopter and KAI, and the helicopters were to be assembled in Korea under the project name Korean Light Helicopter (KLH). KAI also offered the KLH for export, but as the first BO105 already flew in the 1970s and more modern helicopter types were available on the worldwide market, the company did not chalk up any orders.

The helicopters for the Army were fitted out with a non-standard (Korean-produced) mission equipment package, prompting the new type designation BO105CBS-5-KLH.

This equipment package consists of the Nighthawk Sight System (EO/IR surveillance) and a Target Acquisition and Designation Sight (TADS) similar to that used on the AH-64 Apache. Additionally, the type was fitted out with a new transmission system and improved rotorblades. Plans to equip the KLH with the LOGIR (Low Cost Guided Imaging Rocket), a joint US-Korean weapon developed initially for the Korean Navy, seem to have been disbanded. The dozen BO105s entered service with the ROKA shortly after the turn of the century.

The Korean Light Helicopter project was rather short-lived, with only 12 Bo105 helicopters assembled by KAI and delivered to the ROK Army. The example pictured carries LAU rocket pods on its stub wings. (Robin Polderman)

The KUS-FS prototype in flight. The UAV is in the same class as the American MQ-9 Reaper. (Hwangbo Joonwoo)

KUS-FS: MALE UAV

Development of the KUS-FS (Korean Unmanned System - Fixed-wing Strategic) MALE (Medium Altitude, Long Endurance) UAV started in 2008. A prototype was revealed at the Seoul Airshow 2019, following which DAPA announced development of the UAV would be completed by June 2020 with deployment to an operational unit expected in 2021.

Two prototypes were built by KAL-ASD but exactly how many have been ordered by the ROKAF for use by the 39th Reconaissance Wing is currently unknown, although a need was identified for 10 examples.

The KUS-FS operates at medium altitudes (10,000-30,000ft/3,048-9,144m) with a flight duration of at least 30 hours. It uses a Hanwha Systems EO/IR system for intelligence gathering but is also equipped with a LIG Nex1 synthetic-aperture radar. The latter system is able to create high-resolution 2D images from 3D objects or terrain and can see through cloud layers. It has four underwing hardpoints to allow the employment of precision guided munitions.

KAL-ASD: an overhaul leader

Korean Air uses its depot maintenance facilities at Busan-Gimhae airport to overhaul various types of aircraft in service with the South Korean and United States Armed Forces. To date, KAL-ASD has performed maintenance or modification on more than 3,500 military aircraft. The first USAF F-4 Phantom to be enrolled in Program Depot Maintenance by Korean Air entered the facilities in 1978, and since then the company has evolved to become the leader in the Asia-Pacific region when maintenance of US military aircraft is concerned. The contracts signed allowed Korean Air to gain experience, and in doing so expand its business in military aircraft modification and other maintenance and performance improvement projects.

During August 2007 Korean Air inked a contract to perform the Common Configuration Improvement Program on 100 USAF F-16s based in the Pacific Region between 2007 and 2013. While in depot the aircraft underwent the Falcon-STAR programme, which provides structural improvements to prolonge the life of the fleet, enhance aircraft availability and improve flight safety.

A new contract regarding the lifespan extension of the PACAF fleet of 90 F-16s was signed in November 2020. The deal is worth around USD 257 million and is expected to run until September 2030. Work done will be corrosion prevention after disassembly and replacement of some of the structural parts to allow the aircraft to fly for an additional 4,000 hours. The contract will be executed in close cooperation with KAI, which will undertake work on PACAF F-16s at its Sacheon facility.

Since 1984, KAL-ASD has conducted depot maintenance for almost 900 F-16 fighter jets.

In December 2019, the US Department of Defense announced it had awarded a USD 213 million contract to KAL-ASD for work on the A-10C aircraft fleet based in Korea. The contract runs for 10 years, until 31 December 2029, and all work will be carried out at the overhaul facilities in Busan-Gimhae.

Additionally, the United States Air Force contracted with Korean Air for the maintenance of its F-15 and C-130 aircraft stationed in Japan. The company also performs the 1,200 flight hours depot level inspection on the PACAF HH-60G Pave Hawk fleet, in use for search and rescue.

Left: A pair of US Marine Corps CH-53E helicopters undergoing maintenance in the KAI facility. (KAI)

Right: A ROKAF F-16D undergoing depot maintenance. (KAI)

The KT-1 was a success, with KAI producing 85 aircraft for the ROKAF at Sacheon plus 84 ordered for export to various countries around the globe. More international sales might follow.
(Robin Polderman)

The US Army in Korea flies its (R)C-12 aircraft as well as its Black Hawk and Chinook helicopters to Busan-Gimhae for maintenance with Korean Air.

The US NAVSUP (Naval Supply Systems Command) Fleet Logistics Center Yokosuka awarded a USD 278 million, eight-year contract to Korean Air Lines on 10 December 2020.

The contract detailed depot-level aviation maintenance and support for the CH-53E Super Stallion and MH-53E Sea Dragon helicopters of the US Marines Corps and US Navy.

The Fleet Readiness Center Western Pacific has limited organic capability to provide full depot-level repair for this type of helicopter. Signing a commercial contract for maintenance work to be done in theater has significant benefits as it reduces downtime as well as eliminating the need of flying or transporting the aircraft back to a maintenance facility in the continental United States. KAL-ASD has been performing maintenance and overhaul work on H-53 helicopters for the US Armed Forces since 1989. For the Korean Navy, KAL-ASD performed overhauls on the Alouette III and Lynx helicopter.

One of the KO-1/ KA-1 prototypes, XKO-1-05, still soldiers on with the Korean Aerospace Research Institute. (Hwangbo Joonwoo)

Korea Aerospace Industries

This Korean aviation giant was established in 1999 through a joint venture of Daewoo Heavy Industries & Machinery, Hyundai Space and Aircraft, and Samsung Aerospace Industries. The KAI company should not be confused with the KAIA association

The first prototype KTX-1 was written off in 1995. The second prototype survived and, after it had been retired from flight testing, was put on display in the War Memorial Museum in downtown Seoul. (Robin Polderman)

The air force of Indonesia has taken delivery of 20 KT-1B trainers, some of which were used to equip the Jupiter aerobatic team. The contract marked the first time the Korean aerospace industry exported an indigenously designed aircraft. (Robin Polderman)

mentioned earlier, these are two different entities. The headquarters of the Hankook Hangkongwoojoosanup Jushikhoesa, as the company is named in the Korean language, is located just to the south of Sacheon Air Base, and it shares the runways with the 3rd FTW of the ROKAF. The company even has its own museum there, which is open to the public.

The company is involved in maintenance, repair and overhaul (MRO) work, as well as modifications and upgrades. KAI performed an upgrade on the ROK Navy P-3CK

The Peruvian Air Force operates the KT-1P in two different colour schemes, but it is the same aircraft in an identical configuration. (Katsuhiko Tokunaga/DACT)

fleet, extending their lifespan and installing advanced mission equipment, and is responsible for depot maintenance for the type. Additional depot maintenance is carried out on both PACAF and ROKAF F-16s as well as US Navy and US Marines Corps MH-53/CH-53 helicopters.

To advance into the MRO business of large civilian airliners, KAI established Korea Aviation Service (KAEMS) in July 2018. It managed to obtain a maintenance certification from the US Federal Aviation Administration in 2019 and has been undertaking overhauls of large civil aircraft since then. Although primarily civil in nature, the expertise gained could be used to overhaul the larger aircraft in ROKAF service, like the E-737 or KC-330, or win contracts from foreign air forces to provide overhaul for their large transports.

First indigenous design: KTX-1

During the second half of the 1980s, in a time of swift industrial growth and with the local economy rapidly developing, the desire to expand its aviation industry coincided with the need for new indigenous training aircraft to replace the T-37C and T-41B.

In 1988, Daewoo (which would merge into KAI later) and the ADD started work on the design of the KTX-1, later to be renamed KT-1.

After flying the first two prototypes with the 550hp Pratt & Whitney Canada PT6A-25A engine, the company decided it needed an engine in the 1,000hp class to make the KTX-1 a better performer. The Koreans eventually settled for the PT-6A-62 engine from the same manufacturer, flat-rated at 950hp. This was fitted to the third prototype, which first took to the air on 10 August 1995. The US test pilot Sean Roberts reported severe stability problems, and the engineers had to go back to the drawing-board to redesign certain areas of the aircraft. Following a change in design the fourth and fifth prototypes flew uneventfully and the company was able to complete the test programme in autumn 1998. Eventually, on 9 August 1999, a contract for 85 KT-1s was signed with the ROKAF, and production got underway.

Out of the five KTX-1 prototypes, two were modified to XKO prototypes, after the ROKAF indicated it would like a domestic aircraft to replace the O-2A Skymaster. To accentuate the light attack role of the type, both aircraft were resprayed in a green and brown camouflage scheme. At least one of them, serial number XKO-1-05, is still in service as a chase plane with the Korea Aerospace Research Institute based at Goheung, although it is rarely noted. Out of the XKO-project the KA-1 was born, and 20 examples were obtained by the ROKAF.

The KT-1 abroad

For the Korean aerospace industry, a historic moment took place in April 2003 when it exported its first domestically produced aircraft, a KT-1B basic trainer, destined for Indonesia. In a contract signed on 22 February 2001, the Indonesian Air Force ordered 17 examples of the KT-1B.

In November 2018, Indonesia ordered three additional aircraft as attrition replacements.

Turkey ordered 40 KT-1T aircraft in a USD 350 million deal signed during August 2007. The move was intended as a stopgap measure following the retirement of the T-37C and pending further development of the indigenous Hurkus trainer aircraft. The first five were produced in Korea, with the remaining aircraft built in Turkey by TAI

(Turkish Aerospace Industries). The last of these was handed over during a ceremony on 8 October 2012.

During 2015, a follow-on order for 15 aircraft was discussed, but a deal never materialised possibly due to the fall-out of the failed coup attempt by elements of Turkish Air Force, in summer 2016.

On 7 November 2012, Peru ordered 20 examples of the KAI Wongbee, with the order evenly split between the KT-1P trainer version and KA-1P light attack aircraft. The first four KT-1P aircraft were constructed by KAI in Korea, but six trainers and all KA-1Ps were assembled locally by SEMAN (Servicio de Mantenimiento), the overhaul and modification centre of the Peruvian Air Force (FAP) at Las Palmas air base.

Senegal took delivery of its first pair of KA-1S light attack aircraft on 3 April 2020, as part of a contract signed on 15 April 2016. A second pair was delivered to Dakar in March 2021.

To sustain the fleet of ROKAF KA-1 and KT-1 aircraft, KAI signed five-year contracts with the ROKAF for a Performance Based Logistics (PLB) package. The contract shifts traditional ROKAF spare parts inventory, supply chain, asset sustainment and technical support functions to Korea Aerospace Industries for a guaranteed level of performance at a similar or reduced cost.

Due to the COVID-pandemic and ensuing budget cuts in 2020, negotiations for the sale of KT-1 trainers to the Philippines were indefinitely delayed.

KTX-2

The T-50, an advanced trainer aircraft capable of reaching Mach 1.5, was developed jointly with Lockheed Martin. The project started out as KTX-2 at the beginning of the 1990s, but really got underway after the Koreans joined up with the American manufacturer. A full-scale development contract was signed in October 1997.

Since performing its maiden flight in August 2002, the T-50 has come a long way. Using the design, KAI developed a specified armed training and light attack aircraft, the TA-50, as well as a light fighter, the FA-50. The latter was developed from the A-50, a proposed light fighter-bomber, by adding an AESA radar and tactical datalink.

A dedicated aerobatics version, the T-50B, was built for the Black Eagles aerobatics team, with a dozen rolling off the production line. So far KAI has built a total of 212 T-50/TA-50/FA-50 aircraft for the ROKAF and various international customers, including four prototypes.

The T-50 production line at Sacheon is designed for a production capability of 1.5 aircraft per month while operated by a single shift. The assembly process could be accelerated to produce up to 2.5 aircraft per month by simply adding another shift.

Golden Eagle and Fighting Eagle export success

From the beginning of the programme, KAI envisioned the T-50 to be exported to other countries. In May 2011, the Indonesian government signed a USD 400 million contract with KAI stipulating the delivery of 16 examples of the T-50i Golden Eagle, a version of the T-50 which is able to carry ordnance on underwing pylons. The aircraft, used to replace the Indonesian Air Force's fleet of BAE Hawk aircraft, were delivered between September 2013 and January of the following year. The delivery made South Korea the sixth country on the globe to export a domestically produced supersonic jet after China, France, Russia, the United Kingdom and the USA.

The Indonesian Air Force opted to have the 15 remaining jets upgraded with the M61 20mm gun as well as the licence-produced KM2032 radar in a contract signed with KAI on 9 November 2018.

When Iraq started to rebuild its air force following years of conflict and ensuing attrition, it looked towards KAI to fulfill its need for an advanced trainer and light attack aircraft. In December 2013, a contract was signed detailing the aquisition of 24 T-50IQ aircraft, which is a version of the FA-50 Fighting Eagle, along with an extensive support package including spare parts, ground equipment and training. With KAI announcing it would provide support for a duration of 20 years, the contract could be worth in excess of USD 2 billion, although exact numbers were not disclosed.

The first T-50IQ aircraft were delivered to Iraq by ship in March 2017, with the last two arriving there in early December 2019.

The Philippine Department of National Defense signed a USD 420 million deal with KAI for the delivery of a dozen FA-50PH aircraft on 28 March 2014. The last aircraft of this contract was delivered three months ahead of schedule, on 4 July 2017. Following the delivery of the last FA-50PH, the Philippine Air Force stated it would like to order another dozen of the FA-50 aircraft but to date, no order has been placed.

The Thai Air Force signed an initial USD 110 million contract for four armed T-50TH trainers on 17 September 2015, with a commissioning ceremony taking place at Takhli Air Base on 4 April 2018. The T-50TH was chosen over the Chinese built L15 jet. A USD 260 million follow-on contract for eight additional T-50s was signed during July 2017. On 23 April 2021, KAI managed to secure another Thai order for two examples of the T-50TH.

In May 2019, KAI secured a USD 52 million contract to upgrade the 12-strong Thai fleet with radar warning receivers and a chaff/flare countermeasures system. The

The first prototype T-50 took to the air on 20 August 2002. This aircraft was used to showcase the type to several international customers, and even travelled to Dubai to be put through its paces at the international trade exhibition and airshow there. (Robin Polderman)

A pair of T-50B aircraft from the Black Eagles break high over the Korean peninsula.
(Katsuhiko Tokunaga/DACT)

aircraft should receive a fire control radar, most likely the tested IAI Elta EL/M2032, effectively changing the T-50 trainer aircraft into a FA-50 light attack aircraft.

In November 2020, the International Test Pilots School (ITPS) Canada signed a memorandum of understanding with KAI to acquire a fleet of FA-50 light combat aircraft.

The ITPS launched its International Tactical Training Center to provide advanced training for fighter pilots of air arms that cannot afford to set up and run Fighter Weapons Schools on their own. Since the ITPS has trained Indonesian as well as ROKAF test pilots, its attention was drawn to the FA-50. The company has not specified a timeline for the acquisition of the new aircraft, which are intended to replace the ageing fleet of L-39 Albatross currently in use.

Following its purchase of the KA-1S, and apparent satisfaction with the aircraft, Senegal entered negotiations over the purchase of the FA-50 on 3 March 2021. How many aircraft the Senegalese would like to purchase has not been disclosed.

Another potential customer for the FA-50 is Botswana, where the intention to buy a new combat aircraft to replace the F-5s in current service, gained momentum early in 2021. KAI has been actively promoting the FA-50 in Botswana since 2013.

Strangely, both Botswana and Senegal were not mentioned by the director of KAI during a webinar organised for investors. According to the CEO, contracts with Columbia and Malaysia, are near with additional countries in KAI's sights regarding T-50 sales being Peru as well as the Philippines again.

The ROKAF uses the FA-50 mainly in the Close Air Support role, with a secondary role as Quick Reaction Alert (QRA) aircraft. Some of its export customers however, use the FA-50 variants primarily for air defence, putting its El/M2032 radar to good use. But in order to increase the attractiveness of the aircraft to potential customers, its performance should be enhanced by adding a Beyond Visible Range capability. Following requests from both Indonesia and Thailand, along with an undisclosed number of interested parties, KAI has set out to investigate how to incorporate the aircraft with BVR missiles. This coincides with the planned capabilities upgrade offered for the ROKAF fleet of FA-50s.

Losing out with the T-50

The stiff competition on the advanced trainer market has seen KAI losing out on a few bids. The air forces of Israel, Poland and Singapore, all opted to buy the Leonardo M346 instead of a T-50 family aircraft.

Initially, it seemed to have better luck in South America. A delegation from Argentina visited Yecheon Air Base on 7 September 2016, in order for one of its pilots to flight test the TA-50.

In summer 2019, following consideration of the Aero L-159 ALCA, CAC/PAC JF-17 Thunder, Chengdu J-10, Leonardo M346 and second-hand aquisitions of upgraded Mirage F1 or IAI Kfir aircraft, the Argentinians announced selection of the KAI FA-50

A FA-50PH Fighting Eagle of the Philippine Air Force's 5th Fighter Wing during the 2020 Bilateral Air Contingent Exchange – Philippines (BACE-P) at Lt Cesar Basa Air Force Base, Pampanga, Philippines.
(Mark Codeno)

to fulfill its need for an interim fighter aircraft. The announcement stipulated the wish to purchase 10 examples of the FA-50.

However, in a letter dated 28 October 2020, a high ranking KAI official informed the Argentinian ambassador in Korea of the challenges concerning a potential sale of the jet to the South American country. The FA-50 contains six major components of British manufacture, including the Martin-Baker ejection seats, and consequently falls under the British weapon embargo concerning Argentina. The letter implies KAI is working to resolve the issue with UK exporting licences, but it is questionable whether the UK government would grant an exception.

USAF T-X programme

In the early 2000s the United States Air Force started to look for a replacement for its aging fleet of T-38 advanced trainers. The new trainer was required to close the gap that exists between the T-38 fleet and the 5th generation fighter aircraft that were soon to become operational.

To select the new trainer, the Advanced Pilot Training competition, more commonly known as the T-X programme, was initiated.

The USAF released the T-X programme requirements on 20 March 2015 and issued an official Request For Proposals (RFP) on 30 December 2016. The RFP specified the need for 350 aircraft (with options for 125 more) and required the new trainer to reach Initial Operational Capability (IOC) by 2024.

KAI teamed up with Lockheed Martin and offered the T-50A, a version of the FA-50 with minor changes to meet the requirements set out in the RFP. The aircraft has some changes in its avionics package and the cockpit features a single large area display, as seen in the office of the F-35. It can also be equipped with an aerial refuelling receptacle in a removable dorsal fairing.

On 2 June 2016, the first T-50A, serial number TX-1, made its maiden test flight from Sacheon, followed by the second prototype, appropriately numbered TX-2. Both aircraft were transported to the United States for further test and evaluation flights.

In anticipation of winning the competition, Lockheed Martin executed its plan to stand up a T-50A Final Assembly and Checkout (FACO) site in Greenville, South Carolina, the same factory that currently still builds the F-16 Fighting Falcon.

A dedicated Ground-Based Training System was offered alongside the T-50A aircraft. Featuring the latest technologies in flight simulation, the system was designed to prepare student pilots for a wide variety of different situations they might come across when airborne. Use of the training system would save valuable flight hours on the T-50A fleet.

The T-50A team believed that by offering a tried and tested concept already in service, it would have the edge over the clean sheet designs offered by some of its competitors, as these always seem to suffer delays and associated cost overruns. Furthermore, Lockheed Martin claimed the T-50A was the only offering that met all T-X programme requirements.

The KAI and Lockheed Martin T-50A team was dealt a blow on 27 September 2018, when Boeing and its T-7A Red Hawk emerged as the winner of the T-X programme.

Interestingly enough, during March 2020, news transpired that the USAF planned to lease between four and eight T-50 aircraft through the civilian company Hillwood Aviation. As a result of delays in the development and fielding of the T-7A, the lease of

Both the T-50A prototypes, TX-1 and TX-2, in flight over the United States. Much to KAI's disappointment, the USAF picked a clean-sheet design, Boeing's T-7A Redhawk, as winner of the T-X programme. (Lockheed Martin)

the T-50 would provide a limited number of student pilots the chance to fly a modern trainer. An official announcement of the plan has been delayed however, as the USAF seems to struggle to secure a budget for the lease as the country is diverting funds to its healthcare budget in order to battle the COVID-19 outbreak.

KF-X, pinnacle of Korean ambitions

On 20 March 2001, then President Kim Dae-jung announced the KF-X programme, an indigenously designed state-of-the-art fighter jet, at a speech held during the graduation ceremony for the 49th class of the Korean Military Academy. The following year saw the first requirements for the new fighter jet drawn up, and research into the feasibility of the project commenced. Initially Korea expressed its ambition by announcing it would develop a 5th generation stealth fighter, but that seemed rather unrealistic at the time. The Institute of Defense Science started research on the design technology for a modern fighter in 2004, conducting digital mock-up and reduced-scale windtunnel tests on models, in order to accumulate data.

Two different designs were proposed and tested, with both evolving into a large number of variants with only small differences compared to the original. The C100 design resembled the F-35, with twin, outward canted vertical tails, while the C200 design had canards and a large delta-shaped wing, resembling the Chinese Chengdu J-20. Both variants had dual engines, and following careful evaluation, design variant C103 was chosen to become KF-X.

DAPA, along with several research institutes, set out to develop a 4.5 generation fighter that outclasses the KF-16, the jet that currently forms the backbone of ROKAF airpower. The KF-X would operate alongside the F-15K and F-35A, the most advanced fighter aircraft in the ROKAF fleet.

KF-X has been designed to allow indigenously developed performance improvements in the future, effectively elevating the jet into a fifth-generation fighter, to adapt to the increasingly diversified battlefields of tomorrow.

The initial version of KF-X, dubbed the Block I, will have an air-to-air capability only, with air-to-ground and anti-ship missions becoming available when the Block II version is introduced. Through evolutionary development, KAI wants to be able to offer KF-X as a fifth-generation stealth aircraft eventually, with an internal weapon bay, low-observable coating and an even better sensor suite, as well as a fully digital AESA radar. This so-called Block III version will have sensors, antennas and targeting pod internalised for optimum stealth capabilities.

Somewhere around 2010, the radar absorbing material (RAM) under development for the KF-X was applied to an F-4D Phantom II, and allegedly also flown for testing. Needless to say, the outcome of the test was not publicly announced by ADD.

The KF-X project faced serious problems in early 2013 after Park Geun-hye became president of the Republic of Korea. Shortly after her election, Park began to reconsider the KF-X project, especially considering the amount of funds Korea would have to invest. Newly chosen members of parliament also refused to prioritise the KF-X project, and the decision was made to postpone development for 18 months. Following lenghty political debates, ultimately the decision was made to continue the project.

Both KAI and Korean Air made a bid for the KF-X contract, but given KAI's experience with developing and building the KT-1 and T-50, it came as no surprise the company was chosen for the project in early 2015.

The technology accumulated during the development of the FA-50, as well as the technology transfer that came with the acquisition of the F-35A, allowed KAI to develop a medium-class fighter used initially for air-to-air, and eventually also for air-to-ground and anti-shipping missions.

A KF-X development contract was signed between DAPA and KAI on 28 December 2015, and a development kick-off meeting was held the following month. A Basic Design Review Conference was successfully completed in June 2018, and the programme went ahead full steam. The Critical Design Review Conference was held in September 2019, and during this meeting KAI set a planned roll out of the prototype for the first half of 2021.

Although it was reported KF-X would be painted in the same dark colour as the F-15K, the roll-out revealed a lighter grey colour had been used.

According to its designers, KF-X was designed to fly at a maximum speed of Mach 1.8, and should have a range of 1,566nm (2,900km). With a length of 16.9m (55ft 3in), a width of 11.2m (36ft 9in), and a height of 4.7m (15ft 5in), the KF-X is slightly larger than an F-16 and similar in size to the F/A-18A/C Hornet.

A full-size mock-up of the KF-X was exhibited at the 2019 ADEX trade- and airshow at Seoul's Seongnam Air Base. During this event, KAI announced it plans to roll out the first prototype in June of 2021, with a first flight anticipated to take place from Sacheon in July 2022. In September 2020 final assembly of the first protoype commenced using the Fuselage Automated Splice System (FASS), which helps assemble 381 individual assemblies with a tolerance of less than 1/1000th of an inch (0.0254mm).

As the project apparently progressed smoother than excepted, the first prototype was already revealed during a ceremony on 9 April 2021.

The roll-out ceremony in Sacheon was attended by Korean President Moon Jae-In as well as the Indonesian Defense Minister, Prabowo Subianto. The KF-X received the designation KF-21 and was named 'Boramae', which translate as a young hawk used for the hunt. The general public was encouraged to come up with suggestions for an appropriate name, after which an internal vote decided in favour of 'Boramae'.

During his speech, Moon Jae-in reiterated the Korean ambition to be amongst the top seven nations in the global aviation industry by the 2030s . He praised the effect on the Korean economy by saying that '*more than 10,000 jobs will be created between 2021 and 2026 due to KF-21, with this number likely increasing to a total of 100,000 when full-scale production of the aircraft will be initiated*'.

KF-21 test programme

The test programme will be conducted using four single seat and two dual seat KF-21 prototypes. The company intended to complete assembly of the second and third prototype during 2021 also, with the remaining three aircraft rolling out by the first half of 2022. The fourth and sixth prototypes are expected to be dual seat variants, while the fifth prototype was planned to be constructed in Indonesia. Additionally, two static test airframes are to be built for ground testing only.

System development is expected to be completed during 2026, following a rigorous programme of ground and flight tests. From the Korean side, seven ROKAF test pilots

During the construction of the first prototype KF-X, KAI released several images of the aft fuselage being mated to the forward section.
(KAI)

and flight test engineers of the 52nd TEG as well as seven KAI test pilots will be involved.

Using its Systems Integration Laboratory (SIL), KAI is able to conduct a significant portion of testing by pre-verifying the functionality of various components, including integration tests of radar and navigation systems.

The company has also developed a Handling Qualities Simulator (HQS) to check flight characteristics and flight stability, and to increase reliability by proactively discovering possible defects, before flight tests actually take place. HQS is effectively a flight simulator run on experimental flight control software. Utilising these simulators provides engineers with feedback in the form of computerdata, as well as lowering cost by reducing the number of required test flights and the risks associated with these.

The development and production of the KF-21 prototypes is truly a joint effort, in which 11 research institutes, 16 universities and 553 Korean suppliers participated.

KF-21 weapons
During May 2020, the ROKAF announced the list of air-to-ground weapons it initially plans to integrate with the KF-21 Block II. The list includes the CBU-105 WCMD, GBU-12 Paveway II LGB, GBU-31/38 JDAM, GBU-54/56 LJDAM and GBU-39/B SDB. The ROKAF decided to pick air-to-ground weapons already in its inventory for integration with the new jet.

In November 2019, a contract was signed for the integration of MBDA Missile System's Meteor BVRAAM. For short range engagements the IRIS-T missile made by Diehl Systems is the weapon of choice, although to date no contract has been announced. The choice for European weapons signals a notable departure from the US route that is normally taken for air-to-air weapons, the ROKAF being a long standing user of the AIM-9, AIM-7 and AIM-120, all made in the United States. Since the Meteor and IRIS-T are not directly available, the AIM-9 and AIM-120 will be integrated with KF-21 nevertheless.

When Korea obtained the TAURUS KEPD-350K for its fleet of F-15K Slam Eagles, the contract included technology transfer. Various Korean defence companies acquired technologies aiding them in the development of an indigenous stand-off cruise missile, including information regarding the penetrator warhead.

The 'Long-Range Air-Launched Cruise Missile II' is currently being developed by LIG Nex1, in close cooperation with the ADD. Its expected range is currently unknown but an earlier requirement set by the ROKAF stipulated a minimum range of 155 miles (250km) at a speed of Mach 2.5. Defence experts anticipate the actual range of the 3,000lb (1,361kg) weapon should be closer to the 310 miles (500km) of the TAURUS KEPD-350K missile.

During a meeting by the South Korean Joint Chiefs of Staff in July 2020, it was confirmed KF-21 will be equipped with an anti-ship missile of indigenous development. This supersonic missile is among Korea's closely guarded secrets, and little to no information about its capabilities had been made public. A ship-launched version of this new missile should have become operational during 2020.

The KF-21 will be equipped with three hardpoints under each wing for the carriage of armament and external fuel tanks (on the innermost hardpoints). Additionally, four Meteor air-to-air missiles will be carried under the central fuselage with provision for

An artist rendering of a
fully armed KF-21, carrying
GPS-guided bombs, an
indigenous targeting pod as well
as IRIS-T and Meteor air-to-air
missiles.
(KAI via Robin Polderman)

a targeting pod on a hardpoint under the starboard intake as well. The fighter aircraft should be capable of carrying 15,432lb (7,700kg) of ordnance.

The air-to-ground weapon integration process for the Block II version is expected to run from 2026 to 2028.

KF-21 systems

When Korea signed a contract for the F-35A, it partially did so because the documented transfer of technology was too good of an opportunity to miss. In the USD 7 billion contract Lockheed Martin offered 25 technologies, used on the F-35A, for use in KF-X development. The US Congress however, refused technology transfer concerning the integration of four key technologies, which included the AESA radar, the infrared search and track (IRST) system, the electro-optical targeting system and the radio frequency (RF) jammer. Some of these systems, for example the radar, had been under development in Korea for a considerable time. The US refusal forced Seoul to reserve funds and assets for the integration of these seperate components in the overall system, known as sensor fusion. Additionally, it needed to accelerate work on these projects in order to be able to devote more time to integration testing.

Korean company LIG Nex1 designed the electronic warfare self-protection suite for integration on the KF-21 prototype. The system uses radio-frequency jamming, utilising the AESA radar installed in the radome, after signal analysis and threat identification. The built-in ECM system was developed based on the ALQ-200 pod (see page 125).

The countermeasures dispensing system (CMDS) directs the use of countermeasures in the form of chaff and/or flares. If the KF-21 fighter will also be equipped with a towed decoy countermeasures system has not been disclosed.

The Israeli firm Elbit Systems announced on 6 February 2020 it had been awarded a contract for the development of a Terrain Following/Terrain Avoidance System, as part of the avionics package for the KF-21.

The AESA radar that the Agency for Defense Development (ADD) has developed in cooperation with Hanwha Systems was revealed on 7 August 2020. Various research institutes and companies in Korea have been involved in the development of radar technology since 2006. The new radar passed Critical Design Review on 26 September 2019 and has been undergoing aerial testing since, assisted by ELTA Systems from Israel.

The system is capable of simultaneously detecting and tracking more than 1,000 targets. Reportedly, the prototype radar was very favourably received by Israeli personnel involved in the air tests. Once the KF-21 prototype takes to the air, the radar will undergo further integration and testing. The performance of the radar, including the electronic warfare capabilities and the SAR resolution, will be improved through software upgrades in the future.

Hanwha Systems is also responsible for the Electro-Optical Targeting Pod (EO TGP), which bears a striking resemblance to the Sniper XR pod. The pod is capable of generating target coordinates, search and track, and laser weapons guidance. The pod is also equipped with a datalink in order to send and receive data.

In late February 2021, the localisation rates of the aircraft's four key technologies were reported as 89 per cent for the radar, 82 per cent for the EO targeting pod, 77 per cent for the electronic warfare suite and 37 per cent for the IRST.

The low localisation rate for the IRST is due to the fact it is based on a foreign system, rumoured to be the Leonardo Skyward, also in use on the Saab Gripen. The system is being produced by Hanwha Systems, which teamed up with Leonardo during 2017.

Software for the system will be developed in Korea, while later production blocks of the KF-21 will see an IRST with a higher localisation rate as more domestic hardware becomes available.

The KF-21's cockpit features a Large Area Display in the shape of a 20×8 inch (50×20 cm) low-light resistant touch screen with a 2560×1024 resolution. At the pilot's discretion, it can display the flight data, aircraft system health data, mission specific data, threat data as well as targeting pod and IRST imagery. The direct voice input technology allows the pilot to activate and control some of the systems by voice command.

During March 2018, the Martin-Baker company was awarded a contract to provide the escape system for the KF-21. The selection of the Mk 18 ejection seat by KAI follows an earlier partnership cemented after the company choose Martin Baker seats for the F-5, KT-1 and T-50 family.

The Mk 18 seat was initially designed for the USAF's T-X programme, and Martin-Baker completed development and testing during 2018. The British company claims the Mk 18 is the most advanced ejection seat on the market today.

KF-21 propulsion

On 26 May 2016, DAPA selected GE Aviation (formerly General Electric) as the preferred bidder to supply F414 engines for the KF-X programme.

In a statement, DAPA said GE Aviation scored highest in all four main criteria for the contract: technology, costs, localisation and management. The US company is no

An anonymous-looking KC-100
on a test flight over the
southern part of Korea.
(KAI)

KC-100 Naraon

The KC-100 Naraon, a four-seater small aircraft made of the latest composite materials, is the first civilian aircraft to be completely designed and built in Korea. The airplane passed the requirements for certification by both the Korean Ministery of Land, Infrastructure and Transport, as well as that of the Federal Aviation Administration (FAA) in the United States.

The aircraft was built using composite materials which make it lighter and increases fuel economy, which was enhanced by being equipped with a state-of-the-art electronic engine control system.

In 2016, following an order from the ROKAF, KAI delivered 23 examples of the military version, the KT-100, to train cadets at the Air Force Academy.

Korean Utility Helicopter Surion

Development of the Korean Utility Helicopter (KUH) started in 2006, and the helicopter was specifically designed for local requirements, by a joint venture consisting of KAI, Eurocopter (now Airbus), DAPA and the Korean Aerospace Research Institute.

The first prototype of the Surion was rolled out of the KAI factory at Sacheon during a special ceremony, attended by Korean president Lee Myung-bak, on 31 July 2009. The first flight of the KUH prototype took place on 10 March 2010, and subsequently three additional prototypes joined the testflight programme that same year. The Surion became Korea's first domestically designed and produced helicopter.

The ROK Army ordered the KUH-1 Surion to replace its fleet of UH-1H Huey helicopters used in the troop assault, search and rescue, airlift and liaison role, with the first Surions entering service during late 2012. A dedicated medevac version of the Surion, the KUH-1M, was developed for the ROK Army by adding dedicated medical equipment, a nose-mounted Rockwell-Collins weather radar as well as an external

The KUH-1 Surion. This unusual colour scheme will give way to an overall olive drab colour as the helicopters rotate through depot maintenance. (SangYeon Kim)

winch to the helicopter. Auxiliary fuel tanks provide the KUH-1M with extended range when compared to the standard KUH-1.

More than 60 per cent of the Surion's parts have been sourced through local companies, and these components include the rotor blades. Eurocopter (now Airbus), which assisted KAI by dispatching expert engineers to Korea, provided the gearboxes, rotor mast and autopilot system.

The MUH-1 Marineon is fitted out with flotation devices, folding main rotorblades and a better anti-corrosion treatment. It has the ability to carry auxiliary fuel tanks for enhanced range, and its avionics package includes TACAN and a long-range UHF radio.

Besides the KUH-1CG variant for the Korean Coast Guard, further civil versions were delivered, specifically the KUH-1EM for the ROK Fire Safety HQ, the KUH-1FS for the ROK Forest Service, and KUH-1P for the Police.

Close to 220 KUHs were ordered and deliveries are ongoing to replace existing utility helicopters in the ROKA inventory, including veteran UH-1Hs and MD500s, and to build up a ROK Marine Corps aviation element.

Over the next 15 to 20 years, KAI aims to replace some 400 helicopters currently in South Korean service with new Surion helicopters, and hopes to export 600 examples to about 20 overseas markets, including South America, Southeast Asia and the Middle East. In particular, KAI has stepped up efforts to sell the Surion to Indonesia. The country became the first export customer for both the KT-1 as well as the T-50, and KAI believes there is a market for the helicopter there. Cambodia is the second country where KAI is close to signing a contract for the delivery of the KUH.

During 2020, DAPA pitched the Surion as the logical replacement for South Korea's 100+ UH-60 Black Hawk fleet in use with the ROKAF, ROKA and ROKN. But in October

The ROK Army hopes to introduce the LAH during 2022, to replace the AH-1S Cobra and MD500 helicopters. KAI hopes to sell the LAH to a number of countries, one of them being Vietnam.
(KAI)

2020 a lawmaker raised concerns that DAPA's preference to produce an additional 100+ KUH-1 helicopters would cost considerably more than upgrading the Black Hawk fleet.

On top of that, the ROK Armed Forces would receive a helicopter with inferior payload capacity and range, when compared to the Black Hawk.

LAH/LCH programme

The ambition to simultaneously develop a 10,000lb (4,536kg) civilian and light attack helicopter became known as the LAH (Light Attack Helicopter) and LCH (Light Civil Helicopter) development programmes. KAI hopes to produce a helicopter that is competitive on both the civil and military global market.

Through the synergy of maximising commonality in subsystems and parts with the LCH (Light Civil Helicopter), KAI will reduce the development, production, and sustainment cost.

In July 2014, DAPA and the Korean Ministry of Trade, Industry and Energy (MOTIE) selected KAI as the preferred bidder for the LAH/LCH programme. The MOTIE is a Ministry which is, among others, tasked with attracting foreign investment in Korean businesses.

As was the case with the earlier KUH Surion programme, KAI once again teamed up with Airbus Helicopters (previously known as Eurocopter) in a partnership to develop the LAH/LCH. In the competition for the contract, Airbus emerged as the victorious bidder, with AgustaWestland, which offered the AW169 helicopter, ending up empty handed.

The LAH/LHC is essentially an improved version of the Airbus Helicopters H155B1 helicopter (formerly know as the Eurocopter EC155) which in itself is a modernised version of the AS365 Dauphin. Compared to the H155B1, the LAH/LCH offers an improved gearbox and an upgraded cockpit.

The LAH is scheduled to replace both the MD500MD and AH-1S Cobra fleet of the ROK Army, with targeted service introduction during 2022. KAI hopes to deliver at least 214 LAH helicopters to the army. The civil variant will be marketed towards various civil government agencies and both variants will be up for export. By equipping the helicopter with optional or mission related equipment, the aircraft could be used for a variety of tasks.

The LAH prototype made its maiden flight from Sacheon on 4 July 2019, followed by the LCH prototype on 5 December 2019. A French-built LCH had already flown from the Marignane airfield, home of Airbus Helicopters, during 2018, and the type obtained civil certification in 2020.

The Korean company views Vietnam as a potential export customer, and hopes to sell the helicopter there, with first deliveries possible in 2026.

First armament to be integrated on the LAH will be a guided anti-tank missile, a 20 mm cannon mounted below the nose, and tube-launched unguided 70mm rockets.

Work on a new type of high-speed helicopter, most likely featuring a co-axial rotor, will begin towards the end of the decade. In April 2021, KAI announced this project as the 'Next-Generation Helicopter'.

UAVs

The Night Intruder 300, also dubbed RQ-101, is Korea's first indigenously produced tactical unmanned aerial vehicle for day and night surveillance and reconnaissance, providing battle field commanders with near real time imagery. Development of the UAV had started during the early 1990s, reaching IOC with the ROK Army during 2001 and deliveries complete by 2005.

Both the UAV as well as its ground control equipment have been upgraded over the years to improve its monitoring capabilities. The system has a range of 120km (75 miles) when using using Line-of-Sight datalink, or 200km (124 miles) when using a relay system.

The LCH bears a striking resemblance to the AS365 Dauphin, due to the partnership between KAI and its European partner Airbus Helicopters. (KAI)

The Next Corps Surveillance UAV, also known as CUAV-II, is currently under development and expected to be delivered to the ROKAF in the second half of the 2020s. The CUAV-II, with a wingspan of 17m (57ft) and a length of 9m (30ft), is able to carry an EO/IR and SLAR system simultaneously, and features an automated start and landing system. The range and endurance of the Next Corps UAV have not been disclosed. A prototype of the CUAV-II was shown to President Moon Jae-in during his visit to the KAI facilities on 9 April 2021.

Earlier, in March 2021, KAI signed an MoU with Elbit Systems regarding collaboration in the field of unmanned ISTAR platforms.

On 24 September 2019, KAI completed the first test flight of a prototype unmanned helicopter at the Korea Aerospace Research Institute at Goheung. The Night Intruder-600 Vertical Take-Off and Landing (NI-600 VT) requires no airstrip and can be used for surveillance, reconnaissance, cargo transport and assisting search and rescue. The helicopter has a maximum take-off weight of 600kg (1,323lb), but this could be increased as the development programme continues. KAI has invested heavily in the development of unmanned systems following a global trend and because it has identified a market for the technology, both domestic as well as international.

KAI is intends to offer the NI-600 VT to meet a forthcoming ROKA unmanned helicopter requirement, as the ROK Armed Forces shift to new tactics focused on the use of remote controlled systems.

Between 2021 and 2025 KAI would like to engage in a strategic alliance with a foreign UAV manufacturer to develop a MUM-T (Manned-Unmanned Teaming) system for its LAH/KUH helicopters. The MUM-T system allows control over the UAV's sensors from onboard the helicopter. Over a highly-contested battlefield, utilising a drone imposes less risk for the controlling helicopter and its crew, while still being able to absorb real-time tactical information and increase situational awareness, thanks to data fed by the UAV. A data-link will allow target information to be shared with ground stations and allied attack aircraft.

The company hopes to develop an idigenous UAV for this purpose before 2030.

Future portfolio
In April 2021 KAI presented its roadmap for the future. Through technology convergence, it would like to expand its portfolio and develop new or expand existing company branches. It will devote resources to the development of an electrically powered Vertical Take-Off and Landing aircraft (eVTOL), produce an advanced UAV capable of Manned-Unmanned Teaming (MUM-T), and will expand development of advanced avionics for air force and navy as well as the development of simulation and training systems, including the so-called synthetic battlefield.

The eVTOL will be an aircraft developed according to the Urban Air Mobility/ Personal Air Vehicle concept. Securing core technology for electrical propulsion, by expanding the cooperation with Korean universities and institutions, should be completed by 2025 and a prototype should be ready by 2029. KAI has stated the ambition to adapt the eVTOL for military use, including weapons integration.

Additionally, the company has the ambition to develop and export more satellites for both civil and military purposes. KAI has been involved in space programmes since 1994, when it became the leading participant in the development of the series of multipurpose utility satellites, designated KOMPSAT and named Arirang. Most of these satellites were equipped with either infrared equipment, high resolution optical equipment or a SLAR, and seem to have been brought into orbit primarily to allow observation of its northern neighbour.

Based on accumulated technology and experience, KAI has gradually expanded its space sector by assisting in the development of a 3-ton geostationary orbit satellite named GEO-KOMPSAT, a 500kg (1,102lb) next-generation medium-sized satellite named CAS-500-2 as well as various military reconnaissance satellites.

The Compact Advanced Satelllite CAS-500-2, an earth observation satellite, was developed in close cooperation with KARI and is slated to be sent into orbit during the first half of 2022 on a Russian Soyuz-2 launch vehicle. The CAS 500-3 and CAS 500-4 are planned for 2023, with CAS 500-5, a weather observation satellite, to be launched in 2025.

Hanwha Group

Hanwha Aerospace is the leading engine manufacturer for Korea's fighter jets and helicopters. The company forms part of the Hanwha Group, which was founded in 1952 as Samsung.

After it started collaboration with General Electric during 1980, it initiated work on the GE J85 engine used in the F-5A/B and (K)F-5E/F aircraft of the ROKAF.

In 1986, the company landed the contract for final engine assembly of the Pratt & Whitney F100 engine for the F-16C/D aircraft ordered by the Korean Air Force.

The aerospace division of Samsung Aerospace Industries merged into KAI during 1999, and the engine manufacturing division continued under the name Samsung Techwin.

During 2004 the company assembled a total of 78 GE F110 engines for use in the newly acquired ROKAF fleet of F-15K Slam Eagles, while it also took care of the GE F404-102 engine for the T-50 family.

The company has not only assembled the engines for fighter jets in use with the ROKAF, but it has also actively worked on the KUH programme to produce the T700-701K engines that power the Surion.

In 2015, after takeover by the Hanwha Group, it changed its name to Hanwha Techwin. In 2018, yet another change of identity occured, when the engine manufacturing division of Hanwha Techwin was renamed Hanwha Aerospace.

Hanwha Systems is the branch responsible for various specialised defence systems including radar, avionics and Command and Control.

The company started building Night-Vision Goggles for the ROK Armed Forces during 1978.

Over the past three decades, Hanwha Systems has been responsible for developing or sourcing a number of crucial technologies for various Korean defence projects. These include the EO/IR system for the KUS-FS UAV, as well as the targeting pod, mission computer and AESA radar for the KF-21 Boramae. The company has also provided avionics components for the KF-16, KUH-1, T-50 family and the LAH helicopter.

A TROUBLED PENINSULA IN A VOLATILE REGION

The Korean peninsula is home to arguably the most militarised border in the world. After the Korean War left much of the peninsula in ruins, the armistice signed in 1953 resulted in an uneasy status-quo that has been ongoing for almost 70 years.

During those seven decades, the cold war between both Koreas has been agonisingly close to hot more often than not.

With the unpredictability of its northern neighbour in mind, the Republic of Korea Armed Forces find themselves in a state of constant vigilance, and its deterrence lays in its ability to defend its territorial integrity.

The ROKAF has an indispensable role as it protects the nation against DPRK provocations, reflected in manpower levels, around 65,000, will remain identical or grow throughout the coming years, while the ROKA on the other hand, suffers a reduction in personnel.

The ROKAF easily outclasses the North Korean air arm due to superior hardware and training, but that does not automatically translate into regional air superiority.

The skies over North Korea are well protected by a dense air defence network, while nearby China is rapidly developing new technologies and Japan will soon field no fewer than 147 F-35s.

Two eventful years

Since North Korean leader Kim Jong-un's rise to power in December 2011, military observers have seen an increase in the development of short-range ballistic missile (SRBM) and inter-continental ballistic missile (ICBM) systems, able to strike not only the whole of South Korea but also targets in Japan and the continental United States. These provide a challenge, given the fact that most missiles are propelled towards their intended target using mobile launch vehicles, making their detection and destruction on the ground by the ROKAF and allied forces not an easy task in case of war.

The events in both 2017 and 2018 proved crucial for inter-Korean relations. Due to the rising tensions in 2017, eruption of conflict on the Korean peninsula was closer than ever and the world was holding its breath. In contrast, the year that followed was full of summits and the prospect for lasting peace had never been more real.

Following the inauguration of President Trump, in January 2017, the North Koreans picked up the pace on ballistic missile tests. The year saw more than 20 tests, ranging from short-range missiles all the way up to the launch of several intercontinental ballistic missiles (ICBMs). These tests included the launch of a Hwasong-15, an ICBM

A North Korean Hwasong-15 ICBM launcher. (KCNA)

capable of reaching any part of the continental United States. Pyongyang announced it had created a miniaturised nuclear warhead for use in its ballistic missiles, much to the dissatisfaction of both the South Korean government and the Trump administration.

As the icing on the cake, the North conducted an underground nuclear test on 3 September.

That same month saw the UN Security Council vote unanimously in favour of stricter sanctions. The new restrictions limited the amount of oil North Korea could import, and banned the export of textiles. The authorised technology transfers as well as foreign investments were trimmed back even further.

When the US President lashed out at North Korea verbally, the leadership in Pyongyang used the rhetoric to validate their own propaganda and innate paranoia among its population. On top of that, it merely stepped up its weapon development efforts in order to be ready for a potential American attack. The situation escalated quickly, and South Korea found itself in the middle, caught up in a stand off between its neighbour and its closest ally that could have dire consequences for the entire nation if not defused. Despite the rapidly changing security environment, the South Korean government continued its efforts to improve relations with North Korea and, finally, Pyongyang responded.

A North Korean Hwasong-14 intercontinental ballistic missile (ICBM) launched from an undisclosed location in North Korea on 29 July 2017. (AFP Photo KCNA via KNS)

On 9 January 2018, the first talks in two years between the South and the North took place in Panmunjom. The two countries agreed to compete in the upcoming PyeongChang Winter Olympics under a unified flag, a remarkable step given the tensions of 2017. The opening ceremony of the Winter Games was attended by Kim Yo-jong, the sister of the North Korean leader, and marked the first time a direct family member of the Great Leader set foot in South Korea since the 1953 Armistice.

The Olympics caused a further thawing in relations, as North Korea announced its willingness to enter talks with the United States.

On 1 April 2018, CIA director Mike Pompeo travelled to Pyongyang to meet Kim Jong-un, and three weeks later North Korea announced it would suspend further missile tests, and would shut down its nuclear test site at Punggye-ri.

The 27 April saw a historic meeting between the leaders of both Koreas, which resulted in the Panmunjon Declaration. The agreement details a number of steps for lasting peace between the Koreas, which includes working towards an official peace agreement to replace the 1953 Armistice, along with a phased disarmament programme. Additionally, both nations pledged to seek the support and cooperation of the international community for the denuclearisation of the peninsula.

In the month of May relations went through a rough patch again, as North Korea cancelled a high level meeting with South Korea and threatened to withdraw from the planned US-North Korea summit. As a result, President Trump cancelled the summit, citing 'tremendous anger and open hostily' from the side of North Korea. Trump reinstated the summit early June, following a surprise meeting between Moon Jae-in and Kim Jong-un a few days before.

The much anticipated meeting between Kim Jong-un and Donald Trump took place in Singapore on 12 June. It was the first time a sitting US president came face-to-face with a North Korean leader. The resulting joint-statement reaffirmed North Korea's commitment to work towards complete denuclearisation.

However, when dissatisfied with the progress concerning denuclearisation, Trump cancelled Pompeo's fourth visit to Pyongyang in late August.

A third inter-Korean summit

The Inter-Korean Comprehensive Military Agreement (CMA) was the product of a meeting between South Korean President Moon Jae-in and North Korean leader Kim Jong Un in Pyongyang during September 2018, their third meeting during that year.

The CMA details how to control and mitigate risks associated with the huge concentration of military fire power in the areas north and south of the DMZ, where misunderstandings and unintended encounters have led to small scale conflicts in the past. Therefore it was agreed to demilitarise the Joint Security Area in Panmunjeon and turn the DMZ into a peace zone.

Compared to the Armistice Agreement of 27 July 1953, which regulates arms control mechanisms in the DMZ, this agreement goes one step further. The document includes provisions relating to the air, with one of the key points being the establishment of a no-fly zone near the DMZ.

The zone is divided into several sub-areas for different types of aircraft. Fixed wing aircraft should observe a 20 (12.4 mile) to 40km (24.8 mile) no-fly area on each side of the Military Demarcation Line (MDL), while helicopters and UAVs should stay clear by at least 10km (6.2nm). Yet, how the no-fly zone will be monitored and controlled is something not specified in the CMA.

In the remaining months of 2018, no further progress was reported regarding nuclear disarmament.

A second summit between Kim Jong-un and Donald Trump took place in Hanoi in January 2019, but negotiations were broken off after only one day. Trump later revealed Pyongyang had demanded all sanctions to be lifted immediately, or any talks about denuclearisation would prove fruitless. Both leaders met once again in June, during a get-together with the South Korean president at the DMZ, apparently instigated by a tweet from Donald Trump, inviting Kim Jong-un to 'shake his hand and say hello.'

Back to square one

While 2018 offered an unprecedented opportunity for peace, it was not to be, and the status quo in place since the signing of the Armistice returned. Further negotiations during the course of 2019 yielded no results.

Relations between the two Koreas progressively deteriorated once again, and culminated in the demolition of the Inter-Korean Joint Liaison Office in the Kaesong industrial park, just over the border in North Korea, on 16 June 2020.

During a military parade in Pyongyang on 10 October 2020, marking the 75th anniversary of the DPRK Worker's Party, a new 22-wheeled TEL was shown carrying the massive Hwasong-16 ICBM. This missile, along with other developments on show, once again highlighted how the DPRK has continued to expand its military capabilities during a stalemate in nuclear negotiations with the United States.

In late March 2021, the DPRK performed its first ballistic launches since President Joe Biden took office. The test of two SRBMs caused the White House to react, call-

A North Korean Hwasong-16 ICBM shown to the world for the first time during a night parade on 10 October 2020. (KCNA)

ing the launches a violation of UN sanctions against the North, and could trigger 'responses' if test launches continue. President Biden made it clear that he is prepared for diplomacy, as long as complete denuclearisation is the focal point.

Kim Jong-un views his nuclear arsenal as the ultimate bargaining chip, and the question remains if he is willing to give it up if the survival of his regime is guaranteed in one way or the other. The Great Leader knows very well the North's nuclear programme serves as a credible deterrent.

In early March 2021, the USFK announced its traditional spring exercises, named Foal Eagle and Key Resolve, with the ROK Armed Forces would be toned down due to the Corona virus. These joint US-South Korean drills have always been closely monitored by Pyongyang, and consistently labeled as a prelude to military intervention. Kim Jong-un has stated that these shows of force merely confirm the right decision was made concerning the continued development of his country's nuclear arsenal, and ways of delivering them.

The current South Korean President, Moon Jae-in, has always been remarkably lenient in dealing with North Korea. Following the election of a new president, during March 2022, Seoul's attitude towards Pyongyang might be completely different.

Nuclear weapons on the peninsula

There are currently nine states on the globe, including China, France, United Kingdom, India, Israel, Pakistan, Russia, the United States and North Korea, that are in the possession of nuclear weapons. North Korea currently maintains an active, but highly opaque nuclear weapons programme and have at their disposal an estimated 30–40 nuclear warheads.

The country has been actively pursuing the development of a nuclear weapon since the early 1960s. Being a nuclear state would bring international recognition, national security and would deter the United States from using its nuclear arsenal against the North. During 1963, the Soviet Union refused to aid Pyongyang with their quest for assistance on developing a nuclear weapon, with China making the exact same decision the following year.

The Soviet Union did assist the North Koreans with the construction of a nuclear energy reactor for civil purposes nevertheless. When the International Atomic Energy Agency (IAEA) discovered discrepancies in North Korea's declarations on its nuclear programme during 1993, and subsequently demanded an inspection, the North Koreans refused and threatened to abandon the international Nuclear Proliferation Treaty (NPT) which the country had signed on 12 December 1985.

The North Koreans knew very well that the core United States foreign policy in the post-Cold War era was the prevention of the spread of weapons of mass destruction. As the assistance from both China and Russia dwindled, the North used their nuclear weapons programme as a bargaining chip in order to lure Washington in providing economic aid. On 21 October 1994, an agreement was reached with the United States to shutdown the nuclear reactor at Yongbyon and halt construction of two new reactors at Taechon and Yongbyon. In return, the US would provide a couple of proliferation-proof reactors and would provide 500,000 tons of heavy fuel oil to North Korea annually, for as long as these reactors were under construction.

Internal political struggles in the United States eventually blocked the construction of the reactors, while at the same time it transpired North Korea had continued development of its nuclear technology in violation of the agreement.

The ensuing distrust between the two countries became an impossible hurdle and on 10 January 2003 North Korea announced its withdrawal from the NPT and restarted its nuclear reactor the following month.

Between October 2006 and September 2017, North Korea conducted six underground nuclear tests at its Punggye-ri test site, in the north-eastern part of the country.

The summits held in Singapore and Panmunjom, where Donald Trump and Kim Jong-un met, did not yield any results when it came to nuclear proliferation.

More often than not, North Korean diplomats have referred to the fate of Libyan leader Muammar Ghadaffi, who voluntarily gave up his nuclear progam in 2003, only to be ousted and killed by NATO-backed rebels a mere eight years later.

The survival of the regime in Pyongyang depends on the nuclear weapons it possesses and it continues to prioritise its nuclear weapon programme as a central element of national security.

During 2019, North Korea tested three types of SRBM weapons, the KN-23, KN-24 and KN-25, each capable of reaching every corner of South Korean territory. These missiles are said to be dual-capable, implying they can carry either a conventional high-explosive warhead or a nuclear weapon. This creates a challenge as there is no way of knowing if the rapidly approaching SRBM will be nuclear armed, meaning the decision makers in the South might respond with disproportional retaliation.

In case of war, the ROKAF would be tasked with quickly and effectively neutralising the North's nuclear threat, including these SRBMs and their launchers. It would need to immobilise the stockpile of nuclear warheads which, most likely, will be dispersed and stored underground. Additional targets would be the reactor in Yongbyon, the uranium enrichment facility near Chollima, and the Pyongsan uranium mine and concentration plant, to terminate further production of nuclear weapons. In doing so, great care should be taken not to hit nuclear facilities directly, as a nuclear winter might ensue, which would have dire consequences for the whole region. A likely scenario would see air power take out the air and ground defence element surrounding the facilities, with ROK special forces then sweeping in to secure the plants.

Left:
The launch of a North Korean KN-24 short-range ballistic missile (SRBM).
(KCNA)

Right:
North Korea calls the KN-25 SRMB a 'super-large' multiple launch rocket system.
(KCNA)

A USAF F-15E Strike Eagle drops
an inert B61 nuclear bomb
during a test. The parachute is
intended to slow the weapon
down and give the delivering
aircraft a chance to escape.
(USAF)

Coalition nukes

In the early 1970s then president Park Chon-hee launched an indigenous programme
for the development of a South Korean nuclear weapon. The Republic of Korea gained
all knowledge required to construct a nuclear weapon but due to international pres-
sure, in particular that of its closest ally the United States, the programme never
matured beyond the research stage.

President Park signed the nuclear proliferation treaty during 1975, effectively kill-
ing off the South's nuclear ambitions. However, some sources indicate parts of the
research programme might have continued in secret and, with the right materials in
place, South Korea would be able to field a nuclear weapon within 18 to 24 months.
Following Pyongyang's nuclear tests, public support for a restart of the South's nuclear
weapon development programme has considerably increased.

The earlier mentioned US resistance against a potential South Korean nuclear
weapon would force the South, if an air dropped version is developed, to adopt an
indigenous aircraft for the nuclear mission as Washington would strongly object to
nuclear weapons on the F-15K, (K)F-16 or F-35A. In the unlikely case South Korea
would need a fighter jet to take on the nuclear strike role, the KF-21 will most likely be
its aircraft of choice.

The US Armed Forces moved the first nukes into Korea during January 1958. The
deployment of nuclear warheads reached its peak in the second half of the 1960s,
when nearly 950 weapons, in the shape of missiles, artillery shells and bombs, were
stored at various depots and air bases in South Korea.

The nuclear weapons storage site at Osan Air Base was deactivated in late 1977.
Further reductions in the stockpile of nuclear warheads followed, mainly brought
about by the retirement of older weapon systems and improvement of conventional
capabilities.

On 27 September 1991, when the Presidential Nuclear Initiative, a unilateral-recip-
rocal measure to reduce the amount of US nuclear weapons was announced by George
W. H. Bush, around 100 warheads remained in South Korea. Of these, 40 were in the
shape of the B61 nuclear bomb, to be carried to their target by the F-16 aircraft of the
8th TFW at Gunsan Air Base.

The last of these bombs were withdrawn from South Korean soil in December of 1991.

The United States still has the ability to protect its interests in the region by means of nuclear-capable bombers flying direct from the US, from the Pacific island of Guam or through SLBM equipped submarines.

The obsolete North Korean Air Force

Contrary to his grandfather Kim Il-sung and father Kim Jong-il, the current leader of the DPRK regularly tours KPAAF units and has these visits well documented by state media. The Supreme Leader seems to have a genuine interest in the daily business of his air force. Being it female pilots training in MiG-15 aircraft, a night-flying MiG-21bis squadron or the annual Combat Flight Contest at Wonsan airport; Kim Jong-un is there and so are the cameras. For military observers, researchers and aviation enthusiasts alike, the exposure of these visits provides a rare glimpse of the secretive air arm. Unfortunately a glimpse is just a glimpse and much that has been written on the KPAAF is based upon pure speculation instead of hard facts. Even today, the true capacity of the air arm remains largely in the proverbial shadows.

A capacity the KPAAF does have is quantity. It can field a large number of first generation jet fighter aircraft in the shape of the MiG-15 (ASCC Fagot) and the MiG-17 (ASCC Fresco). It is unclear if the Shenyang F-5 (a Chinese-built copy of the MiG-17) was delivered, although the KPAAF does seem to have the FT-5 two seater.

Since the MiG-15 was never produced by China, it seems likely the aircraft in KPAAF use today are the exact same aircraft that fought USAF F-86s and Royal Australian Air Force Meteors in the skies over the Yalu river, almost 70 years ago. That is fascinating, to say the least.

To bolster the fleet of MiG-15 and MiG-17 aircraft, the Chinese supplied the KPAAF with 174 examples of the Shenyang F-6 (a reverse engineered MiG-19S) between 1972 and 1978.

Although obsolete by today's (and even yesterday's) standards, the fleet could be used as a carrier for the DRPK's extensive stocks of biological and chemical weapons. The KPAAF has modified the outdated fleet with weapon pylons mounted on the fuselage allowing carriage of various, likely indigenously designed, bombs. The KPAAF F-6 aircraft defecting to South Korea both in the mid-1980s as well as in 1996 were devoid of these pylons, making it likely the modification programme started somewhere after that time. To fire the K-13 air-to-air missile, or its Chinese built variant, launch rails were retrofitted to many of the MiG-17 and F-6 aircraft in use.

In the mid-1950s, North Korea took delivery of the Ilyushin Il-28 (ASCC Beagle) bomber, with examples of the Harbin H-5, a Chinese built variant, entering KPAAF service during the 1970s.

In the mid-1980s, intelligence rapports suggested the KPAAF was trying to adapt the IL-28 fleet for the anti-ship role, by means of integrating existing guided missiles with the airframe.

Trials of an air-launched variant of the Soviet P-15 Termit (ASCC SS-N-2 Styx) anti-ship missile from an Il-28/H-5 bomber were reportedly carried out in both October 2008 and November 2011. This would have required considerable modification to the

aircraft, given the fact that the weight of the Termit exceeds the maximum payload of the Il-28. Its weight would restrict it to carriage on the Il-28's centreline, but there does not seem to be enough ground clearance for such a bulky missile.

It is more than likely a different missile was involved, and reports pointing to the Kh-35 (ASCC AS-20 Kayak), designated KN-05 in KPAAF service, have recently surfaced. Compared to the P-15, this missile is one-fourth of the weight and has a smaller diameter making carriage under the wing a possibility. The Kh-35 has four times the range of the Termit.

The KPAAF fleet of around 62 Il-28/H-5 bombers is split between the air bases of Changjin and Uiji, with all Il-28R reconnaissance aircraft, recognisable by their wingtip fuel tanks, concentrated at the latter base. Uiji Air Base is located very close to China, making it possible to observe North Korean Il-28 operations from across the border.

North Korean MiG-21s

The KPAAF operates a variety of MiG-21 (ASCC Fishbed) models of Soviet- and Chinese manufacture. According to CIA reports, a single squadron operating the MiG-21F-13 out of Pukchang air base was active in 1962. Another CIA report claims that in 1970, the KPAAF had little over 85 MiG-21s at its disposal. It is likely these consisted of the 14 MiG-21F-13s delivered during 1962, along with around 60 examples of the MiG-21PFM and MiG-21U/US, deliveries of which started in late 1967.

It is very likely that this KPAAF MiG-21bis, coded 42, was used to train Soviet pilots at the end of the 1980s. Its construction number, 75014205, reveals it was produced early in 1974. (Wim Verkerk)

The last batch of new-build single seat MiG-21 aircraft to be delivered to the KPAAF arrived in 1971-72, when a total of 20 (some sources say 22) MiG-21MF aircraft produced by the GAZ-30 factory in Moscow were received. Compared to the MiG-21F-13 and MiG-21PFM, the MF version has four underwing pylons instead of two. The pylons allow the carriage of two PTB-490 fuel tanks, which significantly boosts the range of the MiG-21MF when compared to its older stablemates.

In 1981, China and North Korea renewed the Sino-North Korean Mutual Aid and Cooperation Friendship Treaty, which was initially signed in Beijing on 11 July 1961. The treaty stipulated Chinese aid to North Korea in case the latter would come under attack. Therefore it might not be a coincidence that in May of 1982, a total of 40 examples of the Chengdu J-7I, second-hand from surplus PLAAF stocks, were delivered to the KPAAF as a security measure.

Compared to the MiG-21F-13, from which it was derived, the J-7I sacrifices 220lb (100 litres) of internal fuel in favour of an additional 30mm gun on the portside of the fuselage.

Based on the few known manufacturer serial numbers, some of the aircraft delivered belong to the 10th batch of J-7I to come off the production line in Chengdu.

North Korea's efforts to buy the withdrawn Mongolian Air Force fleet of MiG-21PFM and MiG-21US aircraft during 2011 went wrong and resulted in an inquiry being launched into the dealings of the former Mongolian Air Force commander. Apparently, the North Koreans had paid the officer and two of his associates the sum of USD 1.5 million for a package consisting of close to 15 MiG-21 aircraft, engines and spare parts.

The deal surfaced in November 2012 when a North Korean envoy complained to Mongolian officials that Pyongyang had paid but never received the MiGs. Apparently the shipment did move out of Mongolia but never reached North Korea.

The North Koreans had more luck dealing with Kazakhstan. Following the dissolution of the Soviet Union in the early 1990s, Kazakhstan gained independence and inherited a large number of former Soviet Air Force aircraft. Due to the economic problems that followed, the oldest and least capable machines were quickly grounded. Based at the airfield of Usharal, the 27th Guards Fighter Aviation Regiment, which trained fighter pilots before they were assigned to an operational unit, flew a large number of MiG-21bis aircraft, along with MiG-21UM two-seaters. The regiment was disbanded in June 1992 and this fleet ended up in storage. Efforts to buy a large number of these MiG-21s through diplomatic channels yielded no results and the North Koreans contacted local arms brokers to try the unofficial route. An alleged 40 MiG-21 aircraft were singled out as suitable for KPAAF use and were to be flown to North Korea on civil Russian freighter aircraft. It appears 30 aircraft were received before a shipment of six MiG-21s inside an An-124 freighter was intercepted by customs officials at Baku airport in Azerbaijan. The subsequent backlash alerted Kazakhstan authorities, halting further deliveries.

The bis variant is the most modern version of the MiG-21 currently in KPA use, but still outdated according to today's standards. Besides the 30 from Kazakhstan, it can not be ruled out more MiG-21bis aircraft have been received through Cuba.

The Cuban connection

In July 2013, the North Korean freighter *Chong Chon Gang* was stopped and inspected on the Atlantic side of the Panama Canal. Hidden beneath its cargo of 200,000 bags of

were shipped to North Korea in subassemblies between 1980 and 1984, and it seems unlikely any were built from scratch.

In 1985, North Korea managed to circumvent US export-control barriers and acquired 87 Hughes 369 helicopters through an export firm based in West Germany. A number of these aircraft have been modified to serve as light-attack helicopters.

Further deliveries of the Mi-8 and Mi-17 (ASCC Hip) took place, although detailed information regarding these deliveries is unavailable. It seems a number of newbuilt Mi-17s were delivered around 1989, with second-hand Mi-8MTVs following between 2010 and 2014. At least 24 Mi-8s remain in use during 2021.

North Korea intially ordered seven Mil Mi-26 (ASCC Halo) heavy lift helicopters for the KPAAF. These were built during 1994 but alledgedly never delivered due to sanctions imposed following the country's non-compliance with IAEA regulations concerning nuclear facility inspections.

Even so, the country managed to get its hands on four second-hand Mi-26 helicopters on the Russian market in the years that followed and took delivery of these somewhere in the early 2000s.

Not taking into account any attrition, a total of around 275 helicopters are in the inventory of the KPAAF. How many of these are serviceable at any given time is very difficult to determine.

Friction with the Empire

Making the region an even greater potential hotspot is South Korea's constant friction with Japan over a number of issues. Historical concerns stem from the times when Imperial Japan annexed Korea during 1910, and the 35 years of Japanese occupation that followed. Only in 1965, official diplomatic relations were established again with the signing of the so-called Basic Treaty. This did not end the issue however; as

To commemorate the 60th anniversary of 8 Hikotai in April 2021, the squadron performed an elephant walk at Tsuiki Air Base with 20 examples of the F-2.
(Katsuhiko Tokunaga/DACT)

recently as 2018, a trade conflict arose when South Korea's Supreme High Court ruled that certain Japanese companies should pay compensation for forced labour during World War II.

The recent COVID-19 pandemic saw both countries butting heads again, when instead of working together they launched mutual travel restrictions. The World Health Organisation claims the scale of these measures are unnecessary and will only worsen the growing economic impact.

Additionally, a feud over the Dokdo Islands (named Takeshima in Japanese language) has kept diplomats on both sides extremely busy. The islets are only slightly bigger than the Pentagon and therefore mere lumps of rock. Yet, the Liancourt Rocks, as they are known internationally, are at the centre of a territorial dispute between the two countries that goes back more than 300 years. The Dokdo Islands were annexed by the Japanese Empire at the beginning of the 20th century and only returned to South Korean rule at the end of the Second World War. However, the Treaty of San Francisco signed by Japan and the Allied Powers in September of 1951, makes no mention of the islets and therefore Japan still believes they form part of its territory.

The waters around the islets are considered rich fishing grounds while conflicting economic interests in terms of gas and oil deposits in the same area fuel the rivalry even more. Further to this, even the nomenclature of the sea in which the islets rest is a scene of a dispute. Located inbetween Korea and Japan, the South Korean side claims the area of water should not be called Sea of Japan, but rather East Sea.

To complicate the matter even further, North Korea has also raised its voice for the simple reason it views these islets as part of a greater Korea.

Rise of the Red Dragon

The People's Republic of China has manifested itself on the regional podium more firmly in the past few decades. The earlier mentioned Sino-North Korean Mutual Aid and Cooperation Friendship Treaty, signed in 1961 by Kim Il-sung and Chinese premier Zhou Enlai, details many fields of cooperation that fall outside the scope of this book.

However, the second article of the treaty states both nations shall undertake all necessary measures to counter any country, or coalition of countries, that might attack either of them. This means any action South Korea undertakes towards its northern neighbour could be met by a response from the Chinese. The prospect of South Korean and US armed forces reaching the communist Chinese border is Beijing's worst nightmare. The treaty between China and North Korea is up for renewal during 2021.

The People's Liberation Army Air Force (PLAAF) has embarked on a process of modernisation since the late 1970s and its journey has currently resulted in a capability edge over most Asian air forces.

Long gone are the days when the PLAAF just had quantity in the form of hordes of locally produced, but hopelessly outdated J-5 (MiG-17), J-6 (MiG-19) and J-7 (early MiG-21) aircraft.

The past few decades have seen the introduction of modern fighters like the indigenous J-10 and J-20 stealth fighter alongside either Russian-built or licence produced (or copied, depending who is asked) versions of the Su-27, Su-30, Su-33 and Su-35 (ASCC Flanker). To direct and support this fleet of fighter aircraft in a potential war,

A rare image of an armed H–6K carrying two KD–63B LACMs. This particular aircraft is assigned to the 28th Air Regiment, 10th Bomber Division based at Anqing North within the Eastern Theater Command. (via ROCAF)

the PLAAF has built up an impressive fleet of indigenously developed AEW&C aircraft along with many electronic warfare platforms. The Chinese Armed Forces have also invested heavily in the development and fielding of various indigenously designed and produced UAVs. No wonder many countries, including South Korea, observe these developments with a wary eye.

In early 2017 the US Army deployed its Terminal High-Altitude Aerial Defense (THAAD) system to South Korea. The THAAD, developed by Lockheed Martin, is a defence system that detects incoming missiles by ground-based radar stations as well as space-based satellites with infrared sensors. Able to intercept incoming missiles both inside and outside the atmosphere, the deployment to South Korea was announced by the US as a countermeasure against potential North Korean attacks, particularly after the country had engaged in multiple missile tests. Beijing vehemently protested the deployment of the system, claiming its advanced sensor systems could be used for surveillance of Chinese movements and therefore classified THAAD a threat against Chinese national interests.

The deployment triggered an unofficial trade boycott by the Chinese, which caused substantial damage to the South Korean economy, as the export plummeted and the stream of Chinese tourists dried up. It took more than a year for relations to normalise somewhat, following a statement by President Moon Jae-in to confirm no further THAAD systems would be deployed to South Korea.

The times when Japan and the United States were South Korea's premier trade partners have long gone. During the early 1980s, the vast majority of South Korean trade deals were done with both countries but since then, the People's Republic of China has established itself as the main trading partner of the Koreans, accounting for 26 per cent of all South Korean trade during 2018. Because of Sino-US rivalry, Seoul often finds itself walking on a tightrope, trying to find a balance between its strong historical ties to the United States and its strong economic ties with China.

A Tu-95MS like this example was involved in the joint Chinese-Russian air patrol in late December 2020. (Fydor Borisov)

Mother Russia enters the fray

In a much-publicised incident on 23 July 2019 a number of PLAAF and Russian Aerospace Forces (VKS) aircraft, apparently engaged in a mutual exercise, entered the KADIZ surrounding the disputed Dokdo islands without permission. The group, consisting of two PLAAF Xian H-6K bombers and two Russian Tu-95 bombers accompanied by a Russian A-50 AEW&C aircraft, was intercepted by ROKAF F-15K and KF-16 aircraft. The bombers left the area on their own accord, but warning shots had to be fired to expel the A-50 from the KADIZ on both occassions it entered. The JASDF also scrambled a pair of its F-15J fighters but these did not interfere with the interception of the Chinese-Russian formation.

Following the incident, on 1 October 2019 – which marked the 71st anniversary of the ROKAF, two F-15K Slam Eagles of the 11th FW performed a patrol mission over the disputed territory in a show of force. This provoked a reaction from the Japanese government claiming the islets are Japanese territory and therefore the overflight of the pair of ROKAF aircraft was in violation of international laws.

On 22 December 2020 the PLAAF and VKS conducted a second joint air patrol with long-range aircraft in the Asia-Pacific region. The air group consisting of two strategic Tu-95MS bombers of the Russian VKS and four H-6K strategic bombers of the PLAAF conducted aerial patrols over the waters of the Sea of Japan and East China. The Russian bombers were accompanied by at least 13 other VKS aircraft, including several Su-35s, according to a statement from the Korean Minsitry of Defense.

The Department of Information and Mass Communication of the Ministry of Defense of the Russian Federation stated: '*In the course of carrying out the tasks, the aircraft of both countries acted strictly in accordance with the provisions of international law. There were no violations of foreign airspace and the event was not directed against third countries*'.

Apparently the joint patrol flights were carried out; '*with the aim of deepening and developing the Russian-Chinese relations of a comprehensive partnership, further enhancing the level of cooperation between the armed forces of the two countries, improving their ability to conduct joint actions, and strengthening global strategic stability.*'

In reaction to the joint patrol flights entering the KADIZ, the ROKAF scrambled fighters to intercept and shadow the intruding aircraft. Before the formation penetrated the KADIZ, the Chinese defence ministry had informed South Korea that its planes were involved in routine training.

The joint exercise was the result of the implementation of provisions layed out in the Chinese-Russian military cooperation plan for 2020.

ROK-US partnership

The Korean phrase '같이 갑시다', pronounced as 'Katchi Kapshida' and best translated as 'We Go Together' is the motto of the partnership between South Korean and the United States, forged in blood during the Korean War of the early 1950s.

During these trying times, South Korea and Japan emerged as the only non-communist countries in the region, making them geopolitical priorities for the United States. South Korea is viewed by Washington as a critical ally and a linchpin of prosperity and stability in East Asia. To find itself under the umbrella of one of the world's leading powers, ensured stability and security for South Korea, and allowed it to become a global economic powerhouse.

Defence spending in the ROK comprises 2.7 per cent of its GDP, the largest percentage among the allies of the United States in the region. In 2019, more than 12 per cent of South Korean government expenses went to the Armed Forces.

Between 2013 and 2017, the South Koreans spent USD 13 billion on defence procurements via Foreign Military Sales (FMS), along with USD 2.8 billion in direct commercial sales of licenced defence articles and services from US manufacturers. Indeed, a quick glance at the inventory of the ROKAF confirms that, besides the increasing amount of indigenous products often developed with US assistance, little remains that was built outside of the United States.

Despite the promising numbers, trouble was brewing. After Donald Trump took office in January 2017, the longstanding relationship between South Korea and the

United States soon found itself at the lowest point ever. In his quest to level the trade balance, he imposed higher import tariffs for Korean produced goods.

Additionally, President Trump insisted South Korea would take a larger share of the cost associated with the deployment of US Forces to Korea. Instead of the USD 850 million that was wired from Seoul to Washington annually, Trump demanded this figure should climb to a staggering USD 5 billion per year, an increase of 588 per cent. When South Korea protested, Trump initially threatened to withdraw all US troops from the peninsula, but soon backed down and eventually lowered his demand to USD 1.3 billion. An agreement on the matter was not reached during the Trump administration however. It would take until 7 March 2021 before the US State Department announced the accord would be extended through 2025 and would include a meaningful increase in costs incurred by South Korea without providing any further details.

President Joe Biden's mission to get the US-ROK partnership on the right track again, by regaining credibility with its historical ally, is beginning to bear fruit.

USAF presence in Korea: a short history

Following the Korean War the USAF mostly vacated its wartime air bases, increasingly so when the conflict with Vietnam went live. The air base of Suwon was the first American air base to be handed over to the ROKAF on 28 November 1954.

In the 1960s the USAF maintained a nuclear quick reaction alert, consisting of four nuclear armed aircraft plus two spares at both Gunsan and Osan air bases. These assets were drawn from the 347th TFW and 475th TFW, both based in Japan and operating the F-4D Phantom II and rotated in and out of Korea on a monthly basis.

Gunsan Air Base had been constructed by occupying Japanese Imperial forces during 1938, while a US Engineer Batallion started construction of Osan Air Base in 1951. Both airfields were heavily utilised during the Korean War.

On 23 January 1968, the US Navy spyship USS *Pueblo* was captured by the North Korean Navy, tensions rose to an unprecedented level. The USAF put various fighter-wings on high alert and within a matter of only two weeks a number of deployments took place under the code name Combat Fox:

Table 4: Operation Combat Fox

Wing (Squadron)	Base	Number and type	Home base
51st FIW (64th FIS)	Gimpo (USAF)	24 F-102A	Naha, Japan
51st FIW (82nd FIS)	Suwon (ROKAF)	22 F-102A	Naha, Japan
325th FIW (318th FIS)	Osan (USAF)	24 F-106A	McChord, Washington
4525th FWW (4537th FWS)	Osan (USAF)	6 F-105G	Nellis, Nevada
4th TFW (334th TFS)	Gwangju (ROKAF)	24 F-4D	Seymour Johnson, North Carolina
4th TFW (335th TFS, 336th TFS)	Gunsan (USAF)	48 F-4D	Seymour Johnson, North Carolina
12th TFW (558th TFS)	Gunsan (USAF)	14 F-4C	Cam Rahn, Vietnam
18th TFW (12th TFS)	Osan (USAF)	12 F-105D	Kadena, Japan
18th TFW (15th TRS)	Gunsan (USAF)	14 RF-4C	Kadena, Japan
475th TFW (356th TFS)	Gunsan (USAF)	14 F-4C	Misawa, Japan
363rd TRW (19th TEWS)	Daegu (USAF)	6 EB-66	Shaw AFB, South Carolina

A Lockheed SR-71 over mountainous terrain. For many years, SR-71s on reconnaissance missions used South Korean airspace to fly to their area of interest.
(Lockheed Martin)

Tensions remained high and it took a few months for the dust to settle. Many deployments ended or turned into rotating detachments. Eventually, Operation Combat Fox gave birth to the basing of the first USAF Fighter Wing in Korea since the draw down of the Korean War. The 3th TFW moved to Gunsan Air Base permanently on 15 March 1971 and its three squadrons started operations with the F-4D Phantom II.

To keep tabs on military movements of the KPA, a flight of RF-4C reconnaissance Phantoms from Kadena deployed to Osan to fly Peacetime Aerial Reconnaissance Program (PARPRO) missions along the DMZ every two weeks. The aircraft carried the G139 LOROP long range photopod that hung so low under the fuselage it could snag arresting cables at the end of the runway. The PARPRO programme was code named 'Big Safari' and took place between 1972 and early 1990.

Besides the Phantom, the USAF used bigger birds to keep tabs on the region. On 8 March 1968, the first Lockheed SR-71A Blackbird deployed to Kadena Air Base on the southern Japanese island of Okinawa, to replace the A-12 in service there. A mere two weeks later, a first mission over Vietnam was flown. When the SR-71 aircraft were tasked with missions over China, Southern Russia and/or North Korea, they would occasionally cross South Korean airspace. In the night of 22 November 1969, one of the mighty Blackbirds ran into trouble when, on the way back to Kadena and still in South Korean airspace, a generator failure occurred with the aircraft low on fuel. As the aircraft was unable to make it to its primary divert location at Gunsan, it tried to radio Daegu Air Base before landing, claiming to be an RF-4C Phantom with an engine out. It was not until after landing the shocked ROKAF personnel on base realised it was not quite an F-4 that had descended out of the darkness.

The Minnesota ANG's 179th FS deployed to Osan in early 2016 as part of a Theater Security Package. F-16C serial number 96-0081 is carrying a pair of captive AMRAAMs, a CATM-9X, ACMI pod, LAU-118 launch rails for the AGM-88, as well as an ALQ-119 ECM pod. A Sniper pod and HTS on the intake complete the load-out.
(Hywell Evans)

In spring of 1981, the 8th TFW became the first overseas USAF unit to be equipped with the Fighting Falcon after receiving examples of the F-16A/B to equip its squadrons.

Following the economic turmoil of the late 1980s, coupled to improving relations with China, the USAF decided to downscale its presence in Korea and concentrate its forces at Gunsan and Osan. On 24 January 1989 the 497th TFS at Daegu, flying the F-4E, was disbanded and some of its aircraft were turned over to the ROKAF. The air base of Gwangju, which was used by the USAF's Military Airlift Command, was largely vacated by US troops. The 25th FS and its A/OA-10As moved from Suwon Air Base to nearby Osan and joined the 51st TFW. During 1992 the USAF vacated Daegu, Gwangju and Suwon, and turned these airfields, along with Busan-Gimhae and Cheongju, into Collocated Operating Bases (COB), keeping only a small detachment in place. These airfields function as wartime deployment bases for US Forces, operating alongside ROKAF units already based there.

An Osan-based A-10C of the 25th FS heads out for a training mission carrying a pair of AGM-65 Maverick training missiles, ALQ-119 ECM and Litening targeting pods, as well as a captive AIM-9. (Robin Polderman)

Currently, almost 9,000 USAF airmen comprise the airpower component of the USFK at the two main operating bases and five COBs. The elements of the USAF deployed to South Korea operate on a wartime alert footing against a clearly perceived threat, reflected in their motto 'Fight Tonight'.

Warthogs and Vipers

The 25th Fighter Squadron, nicknamed 'Assam Draggins', has been stationed in the Pacific almost continuously since the United States was drawn into World War II. On 1 October 1993, the 25th FS and its A-10A aircraft became attached to the 51st TFW at Osan Air Base.

The A-10 aircraft has had a bumpy ride since the end of the 1991 Gulf War, and its retirement has been announced more than once, as the USAF dealt with tight budgets and tried to allocate funds to multirole aircraft including the F-35 Lightning II. But the pugnacious aircraft's fearsome firepower and its continuous success in various con-

flicts the United States has engaged in since, effectively postponed its retirement time and again.

The 25th FS took delivery of upgraded A/OA-10C aircraft during 2012. The integration of a datalink and improved HOTAS (Hand On Throttle And Stick) capabilities are some of the major differences with the A/OA-10A. The upgraded Warthogs have two large MFDs in the cockpit, a new digital stores management system and a tactical awareness display, which incorporates the datalink as well as having a 'moving map' display. The upgraded aircraft can carry both the Litening AT and Sniper XR targeting pods as well as almost every air-to-ground weapon in the USAF inventory.

The squadron's task in times of conflict would be to provide combat ready pilots in serviceable A/OA-10 aircraft for forward air control, combat search and rescue, close air support and air interdiction in the defence of the Republic of Korea.

Following on from its successes over the battlefield, a re-winging programme that started in 2011 will allow the Warthog to continue in service until the late 2030s. The upgraded wings should last for up to 10,000 flight hours without requiring a depot inspection. The re-winging programme is carried out by the Korean aerospace industry, circumventing the need to ferry the aircraft back to a modification facility in the continental United States.

Co-located at Osan Air Base is the 36th FS 'Flying Fiends' which operates F-16C single-seat and F-16D dual-seat aircraft. The unit started trading in its fleet of F-4E Phantom II aircraft for the F-16 on 10 August 1988, when the first Block 30 Fighting Falcons arrived. After a short stint, the Block 30 aircraft were replaced by Block 42 aircraft. Subsequently, the 36th FS became the first unit to receive the LANTIRN pod during 1992, severely boosting the squadron's capabilities day and night. As other PACAF units were flying General Electric F110 powered Block 30 and Block 50 F-16s, the Block 42 and its Pratt & Whitney F100 engine provided some logistical challenges. These were solved during 1994, when the unit once more swapped airframes and converted to the Block 40 F-16, also powered by the GE engine, and the 36th FS continues to fly this version of the Viper today.

In the spring 2012 the Flying Fiends acquired the AN/ASQ-213, which is carried on the port or starboard intake station of the F-16 and serves as the targeting system for the AGM-88 HARM anti-radar missile. In January 2021, the first F-16 in the darker Have Glass V colour scheme appeared at Osan.

Co-located at Osan are the four U-2S Dragon Ladies of the 5th Reconnaissance Squadron, providing US intelligence agencies with accurate imagery of designated areas of interest. The 5th RS conducts day-and-night, all-weather reconnaissance and surveillance missions. It carries out missions for USFK, US Pacific Command, Air Combat Command, and other national authorities through the Joint Chiefs of Staff.

A detachment of the 33rd Resque Squadron from Kadena Air Base is in place to provide the USFK with a search and rescue capability.

Wolf Pack legacy
During the Vietnam War, the Thailand-based 8th Tactical Fighter Wing (TFW) was referred to as the 'Wolf Pack' by its commanding officer, the legendary Colonel Robin Olds. The name stuck and the 8th FW, having moved to Gunsan Air Base in September 1974, currently has two F-16 squadrons at its disposal.

A U-2S, carrying the badge of the 5th RS on the tail, comes in to land. The type is used to keep tabs on South Korea's neighbours, and the 5th RS is the only U-2 squadron permanently based outside of the continental United States. (Robin Polderman)

Some of Gunsan's Block 30 F-16s were painted in aggressor colours shortly before being transferred to Eielson in Alaska to join the newly established 18th AGRS. (Robin Polderman)

225

Both the 35th FS 'Pantons' and 80th FS 'Juvats' received the F-16A/B during 1981 and changed to the more capable Block 30 variant of the F-16C/D in autumn 1987.

The F-16 squadrons at Gunsan were tasked for the nuclear strike role, and as such, were qualified for operations with the B61 nuclear weapon. After the Presidential Nuclear Initiative of 1991 the bombs were transported back to the United States and the 8th TFW gave up its nuclear role.

In November 2000, the first Block 40 F-16s for the 35th FS arrived at Gunsan. The 80th FS had to wait eight more years before receiving their complement of LANTIRN-capable Vipers.

When the 18th FS at Eielson in Alaska changed to the aggressor role to support the Red Flag – Alaska exercises and in doing so became the 18th AGRS (Aggressor Squadron), it exchanged its 20 F-16s Block 40 with the Block 30 aircraft of the 80th FS. Before relocating to Alaska, the 80th FS F-16s received a respray in aggressor colours at the Korean Air Lines overhaul facility in Busan. As they were not immediately flown to Alaska but returned to Gunsan after painting had been completed, F-16s wearing either a blue/grey or black/white/grey colour scheme could be observed flying around Korean skies for a few months during late 2007 and early 2008.

All F-16s belonging to the squadrons at both Osan and Gunsan underwent modification to CCIP (Common Configuration Improvement Program) standard in the early 2010s.

The programme encompasses the most extensive retrofit of the aircraft and involved major changes to the avionics and cockpit of close to 650 USAF Block 40/42/50/52 F-16C/D Fighting Falcons.

The modifications brought commonality to the USAF fleet while at the same time the improvements established a large degree of hardware and software commonality with other F-16 upgrades. Structural improvements prolonged the useful life of the CCIP F-16s from 6,000 to 8,000 flight hours.

To upgrade PACAF's fleet of F-16 aircraft to CCIP standard, the US Government signed a contract with the Aerospace Division of Korean Air to perform the work in South Korea.

A USAF F-117A, trailing its drag chute, rolls out at Gunsan during a deployment in 2007.
(USAF/SrA Darnell Cannady)

The initial target set for full OPCON transfer, April 2012, was not met due to budget limitations and security concerns and a new deadline failed due to concerns over North Korean nuclear tests.

In the talks that followed, the US and South Korea agreed to delay the transfer indefinitely, and adopt a conditions-based OPCON transfer plan, identifying five critical capabilities required:

- Sufficient intelligence, surveillance, and reconnaissance (ISR) assets for round-the-clock monitoring
- Command, control, communication, computers, and intelligence (C4I)
- Ballistic missile defence
- Countering WMD (warning, protection and decontamination capabilities)
- Critical munitions (increased conventional munition stocks)

Furthermore, both parties have agreed to transfer OPCON only if the security environment on the peninsula is stable, but without clearly defining what exactly this means. If the situation with North Korea keeps deteriorating, it might push OPCON transfer back even further.

Due to the COVID-19 pandemic, several planned US-South Korea drills were cancelled or scaled down, taking away the chance to assess South Korea's readiness to take over OPCON, the transfer of which has been highly coveted by President Moon Jae-in before his term ends in 2022. Unfortunately, there are rumours suggesting the US is not keen on delegating wartime OPCON to South Korea due to the US-Sino hegemonic rivalry.

The perils of a Taiwanese declaration of independence

Is there a link between the sovereignty of Taiwan and peace in South Korea? The People's Republic of China regards the island of Taiwan as part of its territory, under the so-called 'One-China' policy. The self-governing which Taiwan has undertaken over the past decades has always been viewed by the Chinese with a wary eye. Beijing has openly threatened with war should the breakaway republic continue on the path of pursuing independence, and diplomatic ties were cut after the election of a pro-independence Taiwanese government during 2016. For many Taiwanese, the way Beijing handled the Hong Kong protests during 2019 vapourised any chance for a peaceful resolution of the simmering conflict.

Under the Trump administration, the US policy on Taiwan has slightly changed with the White House taking a tougher stance against Chinese rhetoric.

This had led to a more open collaboration between the Taiwanese and United States armed forces, with the latter's special forces training on the island alongside their Taiwanese counterparts. It also resulted in a number of weapon contracts between the Taiwanese government and US defence companies, with one of these contracts detailing the sale of 66 Lockheed Martin F-16V fighter jets, much to the disapproval of Beijing.

Although the Taiwan Relations Act, signed in 1979, guarantees US support for the island, and asserts the United States will aid Taiwan by providing defence articles, it does not state it is obliged to go to war alongside the Taiwanese military.

A conflict in the Taiwan Strait, and the period leading up to it, would be highly destabilising for the Asia-Pacific region, particularly the Korean penisula. As part of its modernisation efforts to counter the threat, Taiwan is re-embarking on its indigenous defence efforts, which in the past produced the F-CK-1 Ching-kuo fighter. (ChunYang)

Following frequent incursions into Taiwanese airspace by Chinese bomber, early warning, and fighter aircraft, the United States rerouted the USS *Roosevelt* carrier strike group to sail near Chinese-claimed waters in the South Chinese Sea during early 2021.

On 23 January 2021, in a show of force, the PLAAF launched a number of its Xian H-6K bombers to simulate an attack on the carrier strike group. These simulated raids continued for two days and contained more than a dozen aircraft. Over the years, the Chinese have devoted considerable resources to the development of a hypersonic anti-ship missile to be fired from the H-6K and specifically aimed at neutralising US Navy carriers and their escort group.

The Chinese exercise sent a strong message to the Biden administration, which seems to continue in the same direction on matters concerning Taiwan as the previous government led by Donald Trump.

China and Taiwan have been bracing for conflict for decades, and recent developments make it no longer a question of 'if', but more 'when' China will reclaim the island it regards as part of its territory. In March 2021, top US military official Admiral Davidson said he believes China could invade Taiwan by 2027, as with each year that passes the military balance grows in favour of China. If Beijing would revert to force to stop

Taiwan's drift toward independence, multiple scenarios could unfold, most severely effecting South Korea, and the whole region for that matter.

In case the United States sits idly by as Chinese forces launch an attack towards Taiwan, due to either being pre-occupied with domestic issues or not willing to bear the cost in human lives and material, the government of South Korea, as well as other allies of the United States in the region, will seriously reevaluate its strategic alliance with Washington. The ensuing distrust will likely increase Seoul's efforts to become an independent power considering its defence, which will have a severe effect on US presence and influence in the region.

Should the United States be drawn into an all-out war with China over the sovereignty of Taiwan, the consequences for East Asia in general and South Korea in particular would be considerable. Given the close proximity of South Korea to China, the distance from Seoul to Beijing measuring only 600 miles (1,000km), it is likely the air bases of the USAF in Korea would be actively used to launch attacks against targets in China. Before that happens, the Chinese might launch pre-emptive strikes aimed at US Forces in Korea, effectively drawing South Korea into the conflict. This in turn could provoke a reaction from North Korea, and an international conflict ensues which could easily snowball into a third world war. The precarious balance South Korea tries to maintain between its historical ally, the United States, and its economic ally, China, would come to an end, and Seoul would be obliged to pick a side.

Walking a fine line

Should a massive conflict between the two divided countries erupt, their interlocking relationships with surrounding nations could draw many more into combat. Simply put, events on the Korean peninsula have the potential to disrupt not only the region, but the whole world. When comparing players in the East-Asian arena, significant differences between numbers of troops as well as budgets come to light.

Table 6: A comparison between the major players around the Korean peninsula

	North Korea	South Korea	USA	USFK	China	Japan	Russia
Population (million)	25.7	51.2	331	not applicable	1,439	126.4	145.9
Troops	1,280,000	600,000	1,301,000	28,500	2,035,000	347,000	900,000
Air Force personnel	110,000	65,000	330,000*	9,000	395,000	47,000	165,000
Fighter aircraft	800	400	2,100**	100	1,600+	330	875
AEW&C aircraft	0	4	31	4***	22+	19	28
Defence budget****	3.9	45.7	778.2	4.5	252.3	49.1	61.7

* excluding 173,000 civilians and 107,000 Air National Guard
** excluding 1,200+ US Navy and US Marines Corps aircraft
*** stationed in Japan
**** 2020 data, in USD billions

North Korea has a severe technological disadvantage although it has, at least on paper, more combat aircraft available. The numerical advantage is short lived, knowing the modern fleet of ROKAF fighter aircraft is capable of tracking and attacking multi-

A twoship of F-35A aircraft comes in to land at Cheongju during sunset. A possible acquisition of a further 20 examples of the Lightning II would see a reactivation of the 156th FS, although the squadron is also rumoured to be reestablished upon delivery of the new batch of TA-50s to Yecheon.
(SangYeon Kim)

ple aerial targets at the same time. Gaining air superiority in a potential conflict should therefore pose no substantial challenge for the ROKAF. Additionally, the air force in the South is far better equipped for network-centric operations, with the sharing of data between air assets and ground control stations creating increased situational awareness, a substantial advantage in Seoul's favour. The North Koreans have heavily invested in asymmetric warfare in an attempt to challenge this ROKAF superiority. The development of long-range air defence systems, as well as a ballistic missiles aimed at neutralising ROKAF air bases in the opening stages of a conflict, all testify to this.

Conclusions

Although rivalry with Japan exists, the fact that both Seoul and Tokyo have the same principal ally, the United States, means armed conflict between the two nations is highly unlikely. With tensions between both Koreas sustained, Russia seeking to re-establish itself as a global power, and China's ceaseless efforts to wrestle the Republic of Korea from the claws of the USROK partnership, it will be interesting to see how the balance of power evolves over the coming decade. The ongoing tensions in East Asia

A two-ship of F-15K Slam Eagle fighters release flares while overflying the disputed Dokdo islets.
(ROKAF)

are proof that the area is a hotbed of confrontation and diplomatic crisis, and the deep scars that continue to hamper regional relations are very much visible today, which begs the question, what nation will be first to spin the wheel of escalation?

Should a second chapter of the Korean War begin, the ROKAF is ready to perform the full spectrum of tasks bestowed upon it. Whether it be intelligence gathering, surpression of enemy air defences, the extraction of a downed pilot, or decapitation strikes against North Korean leadership, the ROKAF has the capability to do it.

Additionally, the acquisition of force-multipliers like the KC-330 aerial refuelling tanker and E-737 AEW&C aircraft, as well as ISR assets like the Falcon 2000S (RC-2000) and Global Hawk, have transferred the ROKAF from a local fighting force into a regional player. The ongoing modernisation of its fleet of fighter aircraft underlines the ROKAF's determination to defend its homeland and territorial waters. At the start of the next decade, the Koreans will have at their disposal a powerful fleet of F-35 and KF-21 aircraft, backed up by modernised F-15K, KF-16 and FA-50 fighters. The fleet of low-observable fighter aircraft can use their capabilities to penetrate North Korean airspace and neutralise air defences, most likely aided by an arsenal of stand-off munitions fired over the border from other aircraft. If destruction of the North's air defences allows non-stealthy aircraft to more safely operate over North Korea, in a so-called permissive environment, the ROKAF's fleet of fighter aircraft would need to destroy the North Korean Army from the air, to prevent it from crossing the 38th parallel and advancing south. It would also be tasked with eliminating KPAAF assets before they can leave the ground.

This would be enormous task, given the KPA's size in both manpower and equipment. Parallel with its modernisation efforts, the ROKAF strives to become more independent by developing and fielding indigenous equipment, while being very close to taking over operational wartime control of its armed forces in order to reduce the level of interdependence between the United States and South Korean military headquarters in case of a war on the peninsula. At the heart of East Asia and therefore in the midst of this extremely dynamic and complex security environment, South Korea has long since realised that a lasting peace on the peninsula can only be secured by preparing for war. In that preparation, the Republic of Korea Air Force takes centre stage.

APPENDIX I:
PATCHES OF THE ROKAF

Operations Command

Logistics Command

Education and Training
Command

Air Combat
Command

Air Mobility and
Reconnaissance
Command

Air Defence
Missile Command

Air Defence
Control Command

Air Combat Command (ACC)

1st FW

189th FTS
'Charging
Archer'
T-50

206th FS
'none'
F-5E/F

216th FTS
'none'
T-50

8th FW

103rd FS
'none'
FA-50

203rd FS
'none'
FA-50

237th FS
'none'
KA-1

288th EWS
'none'
Harpy

10th FW

101st FS
'none'
KF-5E/F

153rd FS
'none'
F-4E

201st FS
'none'
KF-5E/F

11th FW

102nd FS
'Blue Dragon'
F-15K

110th FS
'none'
F-15K

122nd FS
'Roaring
Jaguars'
F-15K

16th FW

115th FS
'none'
TA-50

202nd FS
'none'
FA-50

17th FW

151st FS
'none'
F-35A

152nd FS
'none'
F-35A

18th FW

105th FS
'Flying Archers'
(K)F-5E/F

112th FS
'none'
(K)F-5E/F

19th FW

155th FS
'Rhino'
KF-16
Block 52

161st FS
'Boramae'
F-16
Block 32

162nd FS
'Black Eagle'
F-16
Block 32

20th FW

120th FS
'none'
KF–16
Block 52

121st FS
'none'
KF–16
Block 52

123rd FS
'none'
KF–16
Block 52

157th FS
'none'
KF–16
Block 52

29th TFWG
'none'

191st TTS
'none'
as required

192nd TDS
'none'
as required

Adversary Flt
'none'
(K)F–16

38th FG
'Eagle Group'

111th FS
'none'
KF–16
Block 52

Air Mobility and Reconnaissance Command (AMRC)

3rd FTW

213th FTS
'Dragon Flight'
KT-1

215th FTS
'none'
KT-1

217th FTS
'White Eagle'
KT-1

236th FTS
'none'
KT-1

5th AMW

251st AS
'none'
C-130H/J

258th AS
'none'
CN235

261st ARS
'none'
KC-330

15th SMW

255th SOS
'none'
C-130

256th AS
'none'
CN235-100
HS.748

39th RW

131st RS
'none'
RQ-4B

159th TRS
'none'
KF-16D Block 52
RF-16C Block 52

296th RS
'Black Bat'
RC-800
Falcon 2000

**6th SAR
Group**

231st SAR Sqn
'none'
CH–47NE,
HH–47D

233rd SAR Sqn
'none'
V/HH–60P

235th SAR Sqn
'none'
misc.

28th FG

208th Sqn
'none'
An–2

35th FG
'none'

257th AS
'none'
VIP aircraft

51st ACG
'none'

271st ACS
'none'
E–737

Direct Reporting Units

52nd TEG

281st TFS
'none'
FA/T-50

53rd SFG

239th SS
'Black Eagles'
T-50B

AFA

55th FTG

212th FTS
'none'
KT-100

APPENDIX II:
PATCHES OF THE USAF IN KOREA AND JAPAN

**Pacific Air Forces
(PACAF)**

5th Air Force

35th FW

13th FS
'The Panther
Pack'
F–16CM/DM
Block 50

14th FS
'Fighting
Samurai'
F–16CM/DM
Block 50

**374th Airlift
Wing**

36th AS
'Eagle Airlifters'
C-130J

459th AS
'none'
C-12J, UH-1N

7th Air Force

8th FW

35th FS
'Pantons'
F-16C/D
Block 40

80th FS
'Juvats'
F-16C/D
Block 40

9th RW

5th RS
'Black Cats'
U-2S

18th Wing

33rd Rescue Sqn
'none'
HH–60G

44th FS
'Vampires'
F–15C/D

67th FS
'Fighting Cocks'
F–15C/D

909th ARS
'Shoguns'
KC–135R

961st AACS
'Eyes Over the Pacific'
E–3

51st FW

25th FS
'Assam
Draggins'
A–10C

36th FS
'The Flying
Fiends'
F–16C/D
Block 40

AFSOC

353rd SOG

1st SOS
'Batcats'
MC–130J

421st SOS
'Dust Devils'
CV–22B

BIBLIOGRAPHY

ARMS CONTROL ASSOCIATION, '*The U.S.-North Korean Agreed Framework at a Glance*', July 2018 https://www.armscontrol.org/factsheets/agreedframework

DONALD, D., 'KAI KT-1 Woongbee', *International Air Power Review*, Volume 5 (Summer 2002): 18-19

HENSEL, H.M., '*Air Power in the Indian Ocean and the Western Pacific*' (Abingdon: Routledge, 2020) ISBN 978-0-367496-93-7

HEWSON, R., 'Airtech CN.235', *World Air Power Journal*, Volume 25: 26-37

JOHNSON, C. A. and Wood, S. G., '*The Transformation of Air Forces on the Korean Peninsula*', Air & Space Power Journal, Fall 2008 https://www.airuniversity.af.edu/Portals/10/ASPJ/journals/Volume-22_Issue-1-4/2008_Vol22_No3.pdf

KRISTENSEN, H. M. and Norris, R. S., 'A history of US nuclear weapons in South Korea', *Bulletin of the Atomic Scientists*, Volume 73, 26 October 2017: 349-357 https://www.tandfonline.com/doi/full/10.1080/00963402.2017.1388656

LAKE, J., '*McDonnell F-4 Phantom, Spirit in the Skies*' (London: Aerospace Publishing Ltd., 1992) ISBN 1-874023-28-X

MITZER, S. and OLIEMANS, J, '*The Armed Forces of North Korea, on the path of Songun*' (Warwick: Helion & Company Ltd., 2020) ISBN 978-1-910777-14-5

NORDIN, J., '*Taking Back Control: South Korea and the Politics of OPCON Transfer*' (Stockholm: Institute for Security and Development Policy, 2020) https://isdp.eu/content/uploads/2020/01/South-Korea-and-the-Politics-of-OPCON-Transfer-30.01.20.pdf

POLDERMAN, R., 'ROKAF at a crossroads', *Air Forces Monthly*, Issue 364 (July 2018): 56-61

STOCKHOLM INTERNATIONAL PEACE RESEARCH INSTITUTE, '*SIPRI Yearbook 2020*' (Oxford: Oxford University Press, 2020) ISBN 978-0-198869-20-7

Further reading

Central Intelligence Agency, '*North Korea's Air Force; impact of Soviet deliveries*', December 1985 https://www.cia.gov/readingroom/docs/CIA-RDP86T00590R000400600002-4.pdf

Korea Institute for Defense Analysis https://kida.re.kr/index.do

Ministry of National Defense of the Republic of Korea, '*2018 White Paper*', Seoul, 31 December 2018 https://www.mnd.go.kr/mnd_book/DefenseWhitePaper/2018/final(eng)/index.html

ROKAF '*AFzine*' monthly magazine https://afzine.co.kr/home/list.php

So Chin Tae, '*Recasting the Viability of a Small Ally's Airpower: South Korea in Focus*', USAF Air University, 2000 https://www.airuniversity.af.edu/Portals/10/ASPJ/journals/Chronicles/tae.pdf

UN Command, Combined Forces Command & USFK, '*2018; The Year On Pen*', Strategic Digest, 2019 https://www.usfk.mil

UNGEGN Working Group, '*Report on the current status of United Nations romanisation systems for geographical names*', September 2013 https://digitallibrary.un.org/record/469456

INDEX

RC-2000 34, 36, 38, 43, 61, 62, 158, 235
RF-4C 19, 20, 29, 30, 78, 85, 220, 221
RF-16C 43, 78, 121, 241
RQ-4 38, 39, 43, 83, 85, 158, 241
Su-25 212
Su-27 55, 216
Su-30 55, 216
Su-35 55, 216, 219,
T-50 20, 21, 25, 26, 30, 35, 41, 44, 66, 68–70, 126, 136, 137, 139,
      153, 155, 169, 180, 182–186, 190, 191, 196, 200, 238, 243
T-50A 184
T-50B 25, 26, 35, 44, 66, 69, 180, 243
T50i 180
T-50IQ 181
T-50TH 181
TA-50 21, 30, 32, 35, 36, 41, 70, 71, 94, 99, 116, 139, 153, 180,
      183, 191, 239
T-103 22, 23
U-2 89, 225, 228, 246
VCN-235M 44, 60, 62
VH-60P 36, 43, 44, 47, 89–92
VH-92 36, 44, 91, 92

Armaments
Air-to-Air missiles
  AIM-7 93, 95, 188
  AIM-9 14, 31, 70, 78, 79, 87, 94, 95, 125, 126, 188
  AIM-120 31, 78, 79, 93, 95, 96, 188
  Meteor 97, 98, 188, 189
  IRIS-T 96, 97, 188

Air-to-surface missiles
  AGM-65 70, 87, 98, 99, 102, 212
  AGM-84 56, 99, 100, 116
  AGM-88 78, 79, 101, 225
  AGM-142 83, 102, 103, 116
  KEPD-350K 56, 103, 104, 154, 188

Air-to-ground bombs
  CBU-58 105, 106
  CBU-105 71, 106, 108, 188
  GBU-10 108, 109
  GBU-12 108, 109
  GBU-24 109
  GBU-28 109–111
  GBU-31 78, 111, 188
  GBU-38 71, 111, 112
  GBU-39 112, 154, 163, 188
  GBU-54 112, 113, 188
  GBU-56 112, 113
  Guided Graphite Bomb 114
  KGGB 87, 113
  Mk 82 104, 108, 111–113
  Mk 84 104, 105, 108, 111, 113
  Spice 2000 113, 114

Miscellaneous systems
  A/A37U-15 122
  AGTS-36 122, 123
  AIS pod 123, 125, 148
  ALQ-200K 125, 189
  AN/ALQ-88K 125
  HMP-250 126
  SUU-20 125

Rockets
  Hydra 70 87, 114, 116, 172

SAM systems
  MIM-104 PAC-3 127, 128
  KM-SAM 129

Targeting and reconnaissance pods
  AN/AAQ-13 117–119
  AN/AAQ-14 112, 117–119
  AN/AAQ-33 112, 118, 119
  AN/AAS-42 119
  AN/AWW-13 100, 116
  AN/ASW-55 83, 102, 116
  AN/AVQ-23 116
  AN/AVQ-26 117
  ARD-300K 121
  Condor2 121
  TAC-EO/IR 121, 122

Locations
Busan 28, 48, 54, 62, 75, 87, 171, 175, 176, 222, 226
Cheongju 18, 22, 27, 28, 36, 38, 47, 50, 51, 55, 59, 72, 81–83, 91,
      123, 129, 131, 134, 136, 148, 149, 222, 230
Daegu 13, 14, 17–20, 23, 24, 29, 31, 37, 39, 56, 57, 76, 81, 82,
      119, 131, 145, 166, 167, 220–222
Gangneung 31, 87, 193, 214
Gimhae 30, 43, 48, 54, 60, 75, 143, 171, 175, 176, 222
Gunsan 30, 37, 76, 78, 79, 144, 207, 220–222, 225, 226, 228
Gwangju 15, 18, 19, 25, 26, 31, 69, 87, 136, 137, 139, 144, 167,
      220, 222, 228
Haemi 19, 23, 29, 79, 91, 101, 142, 146
Hoengseong 16, 21, 25, 26, 31, 38, 63, 64, 72, 126, 136
Jeju 26, 27, 134
Jinju 39, 131, 133
Jungwon 19, 38, 42, 43, 78, 79, 134, 159
Kadena 19, 52, 220, 221, 225, 228, 230
Misawa 220, 230
Osan 14, 24, 39, 82, 89, 145, 160, 207, 220–223, 225, 226
Pilseung Range 73, 230
Pyongyang 8, 23, 48, 52, 88, 159, 202-207, 210, 211, 213
Sacheon 16, 20, 21, 26, 38, 39, 54, 58, 65, 68, 69, 78, 85, 135,
      136, 147, 175, 178, 180, 184, 186, 187, 195, 198
Seongmu 22, 49, 50, 66, 132, 133
Seongnam 16, 27, 28, 30, 34, 38, 52, 60, 62, 64, 74, 89, 91, 92,
      142, 169, 186

Modern USMC Air Power | Aircraft and Units of the 'Flying Leathernecks'
Joe Copalman

256 pages, 28×21 cm, softcover

38.95 Euro, ISBN 978-1-9503940-2-9

As America's expeditionary force-in-readiness, the US Marine Corps operates an eclectic mix of fixed-wing, rotary-wing, tiltrotor and unmanned aircraft to support the marine rifleman on the ground. The first two decades of the 21st century have seen an almost complete transformation of the marine air wings, as Cold War-era legacy aircraft yield to digital-age replacements. In Harpia's first book dedicated to a North American air arm, Joe Copalman explains the significance of each aircraft transition in the Marine Corps over the previous 20 years – community by community – on the Marine Air-Ground Task Force and its ability to conduct amphibious and expeditionary warfare.

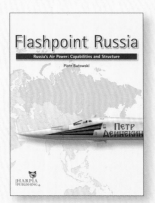

Flashpoint Russia | Russia's Air Power: Capabilities and Structure
Piotr Butowski

144 pages, 28×21 cm, softcover

24.95 Euro, ISBN 978-0-9973092-7-0

Russian military aviation has undergone several upheavals in the post-Soviet era. There have been two driving forces behind these changes. First, the Russian experience of air power in conflicts has led to an increasing integration of the various branches of the armed forces. Today's VKS was created as a result of the absorption of the Air Defence Troops (VPVO) by the Air Force (VVS) in 1998, and then a merger of the Air Force with the Aerospace Defence Troops (VVKO) in 2015.
The fourth title in Harpia Publishing's series on Russian military aviation details all fixed-wing aircraft, helicopters and other aerial vehicles operated by Russia's military air arms. Like the previous volumes, Flashpoint Russia is a comprehensive reference work, presenting organisational structure and the quantitative potential of Russian military aviation.

Modern Chinese Warplanes | Chinese Air Force – Aircraft and Units
Andreas Rupprecht

256 pages, 28×21 cm, softcover

38.95 Euro, ISBN 978-0-9973092-6-3

In 2012 the original *Modern Chinese Warplanes* set the standard as a uniquely compact yet comprehensive directory of modern Chinese air power, combining magnificent illustrations and in-depth analysis. Now almost six years later, much of the fascination that Chinese military aviation holds for the analyst and enthusiast still stems from the thick veil of secrecy that surrounds it. However, in the time that has passed since the first edition, a plethora of new types, systems and weapons has been revealed. What is more, the structure of the People's Liberation Army Air Force (PLAAF) has been completely revised by transforming the former Military Regions into Theater Commands.